D1475502

THE STEPHEN S. WEINSTEIN SERIES
in Post-Holocaust Studies

The Stephen S. Weinstein Series in Post-Holocaust Studies carries on the work and publications of the Pastora Goldner Series (2004–2007), exploring questions that continue to haunt humanity in the aftermath of Nazi Germany's attempt to destroy Jewish life and culture. Books in this series address the most current and pressing issues of our post-Holocaust world. They are grounded in scholarship undertaken by the Stephen S. Weinstein Holocaust Symposium, whose membership—international, interdisciplinary, interfaith, and intergenerational—is committed to dialogue as a fundamental form of inquiry and understanding. The symposium and the series are generously supported by Stephen S. Weinstein, who, with his wife, Nancy, is dedicated to the work of *tikkun olam,* the healing of the world, and whose commitment to combating present-day evils in our world has inspired the participants in the symposium who contribute to this series.

THE STEPHEN S. WEINSTEIN SERIES
in Post-Holocaust Studies

*After-Words: Post-Holocaust Struggles with Forgiveness,
Reconciliation, Justice* (2004)
Edited and Introduced by David Patterson and John K. Roth

Fire in the Ashes: God, Evil, and the Holocaust (2005)
Edited and Introduced by David Patterson and John K. Roth

Open Wounds: The Crisis of Jewish Thought in the Aftermath of the Holocaust (2006)
By David Patterson

Testimony, Tensions, and Tikkun: *Reflections on Teaching
the Holocaust in Colleges and Universities* (2007)
Edited and Introduced by Myrna Goldenberg and Rochelle L. Millen

Disappearing Traces: Holocaust Testimonies, Ethics, and Aesthetics (2012)
By Dorota Glowacka

Encountering the Stranger: A Jewish-Christian-Muslim Trialogue (2012)
Edited and Introduced by Leonard Grob and John K. Roth

Different Horrors, Same Hell: Gender and the Holocaust (2013)
Edited and Introduced by Myrna Goldenberg and Amy H. Shapiro

Losing Trust in the World: Holocaust Scholars Confront Torture (2017)
Edited and Introduced by Leonard Grob and John K. Roth

Facing Death: Confronting Mortality in the Holocaust and Ourselves (2017)
Edited and Introduced by Sarah K. Pinnock

Losing Trust in the World

Holocaust Scholars Confront Torture

Edited and Introduced by

LEONARD GROB and JOHN K. ROTH

A Samuel and Althea Stroum Book

UNIVERSITY OF WASHINGTON PRESS
Seattle and London

Losing Trust in the World is published with the assistance of a grant
from the Samuel and Althea Stroum Endowed Book Fund.

UNIVERSITY OF WASHINGTON PRESS
www.washington.edu/uwpress

LIBRARY OF CONGRESS CATALOGING-IN-PUBLICATION DATA
Names: Grob, Leonard, editor. | Grob, Leonard. Torture during the Holocaust: responsible
witnessing. Container of (work):
Title: Losing trust in the world : Holocaust scholars confront torture /
edited and Introduced by Leonard Grob and John K. Roth.
Description: Seattle ; London : University of Washington Press, [2017] | ?2017 |
Series: The Stephen S. Weinstein series in post-Holocaust studies |
Includes bibliographical references and index.
Identifiers: LCCN 2016008401 | ISBN 9780295998459 (hardcover : alk. paper) |
ISBN 9780295998466 (pbk. : alk. paper)
Subjects: LCSH: Torture—History—20th century. | Torture—History—21st century. |
Torture—Moral and ethical aspects. | Holocaust, Jewish (1939–1945)—Historiography.
Classification: LCC HV8593 .L67 2017 | DDC 364.6/7—dc23
LC record available at http://lccn.loc.gov/2016008401

Cover and part illustrations: *First Station: Auschwitz-Birkenau,* by Arie Galles (1998, 47½ ×
75 in., charcoal and white Conté on Arches with barbed wire–impressed wrought-iron frame),
from the suite of fifteen drawings *Fourteen Stations/Hey Yud Dalet (Hashem Yinkom Daman),*
the latter phrase meaning, "May God avenge their blood." The title of the suite refers both to
the Stations of the Cross and to the fact that the Nazi concentration camps and killing centers
were near railroad stations. Galles's drawings are based on Luftwaffe and Allied aerial
photographs of those sites. Within this drawing and all the others are invisibly embedded,
hand-lettered phrases from the Kaddish, the ancient Jewish prayer for the dead.

In Memoriam
Jean Améry (1912–1978)

Somewhere, someone is crying out under torture.
Perhaps in this hour, this second. . . . I dare to assert
that torture is the most horrible event a human being
can retain within himself. . . . Whoever has succumbed
to torture can no longer feel at home in the world.
    —Jean Améry, "Torture," in *At the Mind's Limits*

CONTENTS

Prologue: The Questions of Torture *xi*
Leonard Grob and John K. Roth

PART I. WHAT IS TORTURE?

1 Torture during the Holocaust: Responsible Witnessing *7*
Leonard Grob

2 Torture *23*
Björn Krondorfer

3 Speech under Torture: Bearing Witness to the Howl *42*
Dorota Glowacka

PART II. IS TORTURE JUSTIFIABLE?

4 Johann Baptist Neuhäusler and Torture in Dachau *67*
Suzanne Brown-Fleming

5 The Emerging Halachic Debate about Torture *83*
Peter J. Haas

6 Torture in Light of the Holocaust: An Impossible Possibility *99*
Didier Pollefeyt

7 The Justification of Suffering:
Holocaust Theodicy and Torture *114*
Sarah K. Pinnock

PART III. WHAT CAN BE DONE ABOUT TORTURE?

8 Assuaging Pain: Therapeutic Care for Torture Survivors *135*
   Margaret Brearley

9 Torture and the Totalitarian Appropriation of the Human Being:
   From National Socialism to Islamic Jihadism *153*
   David Patterson

10 Crying Out: Rape as Torture and the Responsibility to Protect *171*
    John K. Roth

Epilogue: Again, the Questions of Torture *189*
Leonard Grob and John K. Roth

Selected Bibliography *195*
Editors and Contributors *201*
Index *207*

Reality is reasonable only so long as it is moral.
—Jean Améry, *Radical Humanism*

Prologue

The Questions of Torture

LEONARD GROB AND JOHN K. ROTH

> What happened, happened. But *that* it happened cannot be so
> easily accepted.
>
> —Jean Améry, *At the Mind's Limits*

As this book's governing epigraph indicates, the Jewish philosopher Jean
Améry—torture victim and Holocaust survivor—believed that "reality is
reasonable only so long as it is moral."[1] Little, if anything, in his experience
made him think that reality was or ever would be that way. Torture did
much to account for his loss of trust in world, and yet Améry's statement
stands: reality is reasonable only so long as it is moral.

Losing Trust in the World takes its title from a persistent theme in Améry's
thought. Its authors stand in solidarity with him, and in doing so we all
intend this book to oppose power that condemns anyone to torture. Resisting torture may not be enough to restore lost trust, but this book keeps that
goal in mind. Its project—to reflect on losing trust in the world in ways
that could help to make reality more moral and thus more reasonable—
begins with key questions about torture.

What is torture? Is torture justifiable? What can be done about torture?
To introduce how this book grapples with those issues, note that the United
Nations consists of more than 190 member states. As of June 2016, 159 of

them have become parties—officially signaled basic agreement—to the UN Convention against Torture and Other Cruel, Inhuman or Degrading Treatment or Punishment, which was adopted by the General Assembly on December 10, 1984, and entered into force on June 26, 1987. The UN Convention defines *torture* as follows:

> Any act by which severe pain or suffering, whether physical or mental, is intentionally inflicted on a person for such purposes as obtaining from him or a third person information or a confession, punishing him for an act he or a third person has committed or is suspected of having committed, or intimidating or coercing him or a third person, or for any reason based on discrimination of any kind, when such pain or suffering is inflicted by or at the instigation of or with the consent or acquiescence of a public official or other person acting in an official capacity.[2]

This statement might seem to be a definitive answer to the question "What is torture?" and in significant ways it is. But rarely, if ever, are the questions of torture put to rest by definitions. Whenever torture is involved, the issues are more complex and contested than that. They reflect and produce collisions—not only national and international, political and economic, but also legal and ethical, cultural and religious.

What is torture? Is torture justifiable? What can be done about torture? Such questions can never be adequately answered by words alone, because the actions that inflict torture are as numerous as they are abusive, as "imaginative" as they are unimaginable, including, to mention only a few of the methods: beatings (sometimes with iron pipes and baseball bats), electric shock, stress positions, prolonged isolation and abysmal detention conditions, hooding and blindfolding, mock executions, waterboarding, whipping, electric drill attacks, fear-inducing exposure to dogs and rats, being forced to drink one's own urine, asphyxiation, starvation, and rape. The intention of the UN Convention is to reject such acts totally. "In legal terms," as Amnesty International (AI) puts the point, "the absolute prohibition on torture and other ill-treatment is 'non-derogable,' that is, it cannot be relaxed even in times of emergency."[3] Essential though they are, such intentions and statements would not be so urgently necessary—and also, sad to say, so minimal in their impact—if the actions that inflict torture were few and far between. In the twenty-first century, unfortunately, those latter circumstances do not prevail.

Emphasizing that "a comprehensive and categorical statistical assessment of the global scale of torture is impossible [because] torture takes place in the shadows," Amnesty International has stated that between January 2009 and May 2013, it "received reports of torture and other ill-treatment committed by state officials in 141 countries, and from every world region." While noting that "solid country-by-country statistics are not available," which makes it "impossible to say how many people were tortured in the last century, the last decade or the last year," AI nevertheless stresses that torture is "under-reported." Indeed, reliable evidence shows that "torture is flourishing," but why is that the case?[4] Two reasons loom large. First, despite their public postures and pronouncements that deplore torture and deny that it is being inflicted, "governments believe that they benefit from torture."[5] Second, "the persistence of a culture of impunity" aids and abets the perpetrators, who prescribe and administer pain—often with the assistance of psychologists and physicians—without fearing that they will be held responsible for "serious violations of human rights and international humanitarian law."[6]

Such factors have been in play in the United States, where issues about torture reached a momentary crescendo on December 9, 2014, when the Senate Select Intelligence Committee released its report on torture, which concentrated on the Central Intelligence Agency's "detention and interrogation program."[7] Senator Dianne Feinstein, who chaired the committee, summed up its finding by saying that "the bottom line is, torture occurred."[8] The report emphasized that the agency's euphemistic "enhanced interrogation techniques" were both brutal and ineffective. Waterboarding, beatings, sleep deprivation, rectal hydration, threats of death and sexual abuse—these inflictions of "severe pain or suffering, whether physical or mental," to use the words of the UN Convention against Torture, produced little, if any, "actionable intelligence" but definitely violated international law.

The report had critics as well as defenders. Among the most vociferous detractors was former vice president Dick Cheney, a key architect and advocate of "enhanced interrogation," who denounced the report as "full of crap," rejected the claim that "enhanced interrogation" was torture, and affirmed his continuing support for such tactics.[9] American opinion about torture reflected the mixed reception of the Senate report. Conducted in mid-December 2014, a *Washington Post*–ABC News poll disclosed that "by a margin of almost 2 to 1—59 percent to 31 percent—those interviewed said that they support the CIA's brutal methods, with the vast majority of supporters saying that they produced valuable intelligence. In general, 58 percent say the torture of suspected terrorists can be justified 'often' or 'sometimes.'"[10]

Meanwhile, it is worth noting that on May 29, 2007, the political commentator Andrew Sullivan published an article called "Verschärfte Vernehmung."[11] He explained that the German phrase—*verschärfte Vernehmung*—is translatable as "enhanced interrogation." Alternatives would be "intensified" or "sharpened" interrogation. His research suggests that the term probably became current in Nazi police and security circles around 1937. Also, Sullivan's article reproduces, in translation, a directive from Heinrich Müller, chief of the Gestapo, Nazi Germany's secret state police. Dated June 12, 1942, it outlines procedures to be followed when, "on the strength of the preliminary interrogation, it has been ascertained that the prisoner can give information about important facts, connections or plans hostile to the state or the legal system, but does not want to reveal his knowledge, and the latter cannot be obtained by way of inquiries." The directive seems rather restrained and appears to restrict excesses, but those qualities scarcely characterized Müller and his underlings, who played key parts in a vast Nazi network of torture that arguably reached its zenith in the Holocaust, the Third Reich's genocide against the Jews.[12]

Likely aware of the Müller memo about *verschärfte Vernehmung*, some of his men were at work in Nazi-occupied Belgium when they arrested an obscure member of the resistance movement in July 1943. The prisoner did not know the answers to the Gestapo's questions, but when the "preliminary interrogation" did not give the agents what they wanted, he was sent to Breendonk, the Nazi detention camp established in a former Belgian fortress that stood between Brussels and Antwerp. There, SS personnel, one of them named Praust, another Wajs, tortured Jean Améry—as he eventually called himself.[13] Améry denied that he was heroic. Even though what he said could scarcely qualify as "actionable intelligence" because he had little, if anything, to give his captors in that regard, Améry says, "I talked. I accused myself of invented absurd political crimes, and even now I don't know at all how they could have occurred to me, dangling bundle that I was."[14] When his torture-inflicting interrogators determined that he was of no use to them and, in addition, learned that he was a Jew, Améry was deported to Auschwitz in January 1944. Liberated from Bergen-Belsen in 1945, he went on to write a remarkable series of essays about his Holocaust experiences. One of them is not-so-simply titled "Torture."[15] For two primary reasons, that essay grounds and governs this book.

First, arguably no writing about torture is more concise, insightful, and compelling than Améry's. Given that torture still abounds, his essay contains warnings and imperatives that we overlook at our peril and ignore with disastrous consequences. When Améry wrote that "what happened, happened. But *that* it happened cannot be so easily accepted," the entire Holocaust was on his mind, but he took that catastrophe to be inseparable from torture, a point that the following chapters will help to make clear.[16] In both—the Holocaust and torture—one must acknowledge and emphasize that what happens, happens, a disposition that should lead to finding out and never forgetting *how* and *why* what happened, happened. But even more crucial—and here the warnings and imperatives intensify—that such things do happen must never be acceptable or accepted. This book aims to support and encourage Améry's protest against torture, his *resentment* of it—the term he liked to use.[17]

Second, the contributors to this volume are Holocaust scholars who work together in the Stephen S. Weinstein Holocaust Symposium, which meets biennially in Oxfordshire, England, at the Wroxton College campus of Fairleigh Dickinson University. The thirty-six members of the symposium share a concern to use their base in Holocaust studies as a means to work toward *tikkun olam*, "the repair of the world." That commitment can scarcely be authentic unless torture is confronted and, as much as possible, curbed as well. Never before, to our knowledge, has a group of Holocaust scholars *writing as such* collaborated on a volume dedicated to that aim, but, inspired by Jean Améry, the contributors to this book are convinced that those who possess expertise in Holocaust studies have a distinctive responsibility to resist torture as best they can.

Words alone will never be sufficient to stop torture, but, as the impact of Améry's essay testifies, they can focus attention on that atrocity and help to change the culture of impunity that aids and abets it. Améry's essay has had that effect on the authors of the chapters that follow. If their reflections reproduce even a small fraction of Améry's impact, this volume will be worthwhile. If that outcome does take place, the book's dialogical format may contribute to it. Each chapter has a three-part organization. The author's main essay is followed by questions from other contributors and then by a response. This structure reflects the fact that the writers do not speak in unison about the questions of torture. In these pages, differences of opinion reverberate, arguments conflict, and disagreements remain unresolved. But the spirit in which dialogue takes place about the questions of torture goes beyond the tensions contained in the discussion.

All of the contributors stand in solidarity with Améry in agreeing on the following points: (1) Euphemistic language about torture must be exposed, and denials of torture by those who perpetrate it must be challenged and refuted. (2) Torture is never good. (3) Whether it is ever a necessary evil, a proposition that must be questioned long and hard, torture remains evil. (4) Every legitimation of torture, especially the claim that it "works" to ensure security or to serve some noble cause or "higher good," should be greeted with resounding suspicion and resistance, if not rejected altogether. (5) The less torture in the world, the better off persons everywhere are likely to be. (6) Much more can and should be done to assist torture victims and to hold perpetrators accountable. No one can do everything that needs to be done in these areas, but everyone can do something of significance and has the responsibility to do so.

Jean Améry declared that the victim of torture loses trust in the world at the torturer's "very first blow."[18] Such blows continue to be struck, again and again. Thus, the most important question of torture is whether trust in the world will be restored, at least to some extent. No words alone can answer that question, but the actions of those who write and read books like this one undoubtedly have much to say and do about that hope.

NOTES

The contributors to this book are deeply grateful to the editorial team at the University of Washington Press, who did so much to support, encourage, and improve this project. That team especially includes director Nicole Mitchell, assistant editor Whitney Johnson, production editor Jacqueline Volin, copyeditor Elizabeth Berg, indexer Margie Towery, advancement and grants administrator Beth Fuget, and marketing director Rachael Levay. Their careful and caring work makes significant contributions to restoring trust in the world.

1   Jean Améry, *Radical Humanism: Selected Essays*, trans. Sidney Rosenfeld and Stella P. Rosenfeld (Bloomington: Indiana University Press, 1984), 65.

2   The text of the Convention is accessible at http://www.ohchr.org/EN/Profession alInterest/Pages/CAT.aspx. A highly significant supplement to the Convention is a 2011 document called *Interpretation of Torture in the Light of the Practice and Jurisprudence of International Bodies*. It guides the deliberations, policies, and practices of the United Nations Voluntary Fund for Victims of Torture (UNVFVT),

which the General Assembly of the United Nations established in 1981. The document is accessible at www.ohchr.org/Documents/Issues/Torture/UNVFVT/Inter pretation_torture_2011_EN.pdf. Debate continues to focus on issues about how the Convention and related provisions of international law apply to non-state actors—organizations that have significant political influence and control, often by means of violence, but are not officially allied to any particular country or state. Helpful insight can be found in "Torture by Non-State Actors: A Primer," an analysis by the Redress Trust as part of the Prevention through Documentation Project, an initiative of the International Rehabilitation Council for Torture Victims (IRCT), the World Medical Association (WMA), the Human Rights Foundation of Turkey (HRFT), and Physicians for Human Rights USA (PHR USA). The document is accessible at www.irct.org/Files/Filer/IPIP/training/Torture_by_Non-State_Actors -Primer.pdf. The trend is to ensure that non-state actors are held accountable when they resort to torture.

3 Amnesty International, "Torture in 2014: 30 Years of Broken Promises," 8. This report is accessible at http://www.amnestyusa.org/sites/default/files/act400042014en .pdf. In addition to Amnesty International, other significant organizations that protest against torture include the American Civil Liberties Union, the Association for the Prevention of Torture, the Center for Victims of Torture, the Committee against Torture, the Danish Institute against Torture, Human Rights Watch, the International Crisis Group, the International Rehabilitation Council for Torture Victims, the International Rescue Committee, the United Nations Voluntary Fund for Victims of Torture, Women under Siege, and the World Organisation against Torture. All of these organizations maintain Internet sites that provide current information and identify steps that concerned people can take to advocate against torture and to assist torture victims. A few Internet sites defend the legitimacy of torture in special circumstances, but for the most part, organizations dealing with torture stand in strong opposition to it.

4 Ibid., 10.

5 Ibid., 12. Evidence against the argument that torture "works" includes findings in the field of neuroscience. See, for example, Shane O'Mara, *Why Torture Doesn't Work: The Neuroscience of Interrogation* (Cambridge, MA: Harvard University Press, 2015). Documenting what neuroscientists know about the brain's reactions to fear, starvation, thirst, sleep deprivation, and other tools in the torturer's kit, O'Mara shows why the "information" produced by torture is highly unreliable.

6 Amnesty International, "Torture in 2014," 12. In 2015, issues about psychologists' complicity in torture received notable attention in the *New York Times*. Articles by James Risen and Andrew Rosenthal revealed that some American psychologists and even the American Psychological Association (APA) helped the George W. Bush administration to promote the use of torture in "enhanced interrogation." See, for example, James Risen, "American Psychological Association Bolstered C.I.A. Torture Program, Report Says," *New York Times*, April 30, 2015, http://www.nytimes .com/2015/05/01/us/report-says-american-psychological-association-collabo rated-on-torture-justification.html; and Andrew Rosenthal, "Did Psychologists

Help the Government Torture?" *New York Times*, April 30, 2015, http://takingnote .blogs.nytimes.com/2015/04/30/did-psychologists-help-the-government-torture/. Risen's article includes a link to the identified report, which was produced, in the words of the *New York Times*, by "a group of dissident health professionals and human rights activists." The APA contested the report's findings and implications, but subsequently an independent investigation, led by attorney David H. Hoffman, found that APA officials had aided and abetted the American military's often brutal interrogations during George W. Bush's presidency. Resignations of top APA officials followed. On these matters, see James Risen, "Outside Psychologists Shielded U.S. Torture Program, Report Finds," *New York Times*, July 10, 2015, accessible at http://www.nytimes.com/2015/07/11/us/psychologists-shielded-us-torture-pro gram-report-finds.html; and James Risen, "3 Leave Jobs Over Psychologists' Involvement in Terrorism Interrogations," *New York Times*, July 14, 2014, accessible at http://www.nytimes.com/2015/07/15/us/politics/3-leave-jobs-over-psychologists-involvement-in-bush-era-interrogations.html. The July 10 article includes a link to the 542-page report. On August 7, 2015, the APA overwhelmingly approved a resolution barring its members from taking part in national security interrogations. It stated that "psychologists shall not conduct, supervise, be in the presence of, or otherwise assist any national security interrogations for any military or intelligence entities, including private contractors working on their behalf, nor advise on conditions of confinement insofar as these might facilitate such an interrogation." See Ian Wilhelm, "American Psychological Association Bans Members from Military Interrogations," *Chronicle of Higher Education*, August 7, 2015. The article, which includes a link to the APA resolution document, is accessible at http://chron icle.com/article/American-Psychological/232255/?cid=at&utm_source=at&utm _medium=en.

7   For the report and helpful information about it, see "The Senate Committee's Report on the C.I.A.'s Use of Torture," *New York Times*, December 9, 2014, which is accessible at http://www.nytimes.com/interactive/2014/12/09/world/cia-torture-report-document.html. Although the report is more than 500 pages long, it is an executive summary of the full document, which exceeds 6,000 pages and remains classified.

8   See Feinstein's *Los Angeles Times* editorial, December 9, 2014, http://www.latimes .com/opinion/op-ed/la-oe-feinstein-torture-report-20141209-story.html#page=1. Several months earlier, on August 1, 2014, President Barack Obama acknowledged that "we tortured some folks" after the attacks of September 11, 2001. See Kathleen Hennessey, "Obama: 'We Tortured Some Folks,'" *Los Angeles Times*, August 1, 2014, http://www.latimes.com/nation/politics/politicsnow/la-pn-obama-torture-2014 0801-story.html.

9   On these points, see, for example, the National Public Radio (NPR) account, "Dick Cheney on Senate Torture Investigation: 'The Report Is Full of Crap,'" which is accessible at http://www.npr.org/sections/thetwo-way/2014/12/11/370055472/dick -cheney-on-senate-torture-investigation-the-report-is-full-of-crap.

10 See Adam Goldhill and Peyton Craighill, "New Poll Finds Majority of Americans

Think Torture Was Justified after 9/11 Attacks," *Washington Post*, December 16, 2014, http://www.washingtonpost.com/world/national-security/new-poll-finds-major ity-of-americans-believe-torture-justified-after-911-attacks/2014/12/16/f6ee1208 -847c-11e4-9534-f79a23c40e6c_story.html.

11 Appearing in *The Dish*, the article is accessible at http://dish.andrewsullivan.com /2007/05/29/verschfte_verne/.

12 For historical perspective on these matters, see, for example, Darius Rejali, *Torture and Democracy* (Princeton, NJ: Princeton University Press, 2007); and two studies by Nikolaus Wachsmann, *Hitler's Prisons: Legal Terror in Nazi Germany* (New Haven, CT: Yale University Press, 2004) and *KL: A History of the Nazi Concentration Camps* (New York: Farrar, Straus and Giroux, 2015). One of the questions of torture—it is discussed in this volume, especially in part 1—is the extent to which the term *torture* is rightly applicable to the abuse, violence, suffering, and murder inflicted on the Jews by Nazi Germany. For example, what about "excremental assault"—the term coined by Terrence Des Pres to designate systematic subjection to filth during the Holocaust? Was it torture, or should *torture* be more restricted in its meaning? Or what about "sonic torture," coercive and abusive uses of music with regard to prisoners during the Holocaust and more recently? Is the meaning of the term *torture* stretched too far by its application in those cases, or is *torture* the apt and accurate term? On the latter issue, see Melissa Kagen, "Controlling Sound: Musical Torture from the Shoah to Guantánamo," *Appendix*, August 20, 2013, http://theappendix.net/issues/2013/7/controlling-sound-musical-torture-from -the-shoah-to-guantanamo.

13 For further information about Breendonk, including photographs, consult the Internet sites provided by the United States Holocaust Memorial Museum and the Belgian National Memorial Fort Breendonk. These sites are accessible at http://www .ushmm.org/wlc/search/?langcode=en&query=Breendonk&group= and http://www .breendonk.be/EN/index.asp?ID=Home. Améry was born Hans Maier in Vienna on October 31, 1912. He adopted the pen name Jean Améry in the 1950s. He took his own life on October 17, 1978, in a Salzburg hotel.

14 Jean Améry, *At the Mind's Limits: Contemplations by a Survivor on Auschwitz and Its Realities*, trans. Sidney Rosenfeld and Stella P. Rosenfeld (Bloomington: Indiana University Press, 1980), 36. Améry suggests that most victims of torture-interrogation behave in this way.

15 The essay is the second in *At the Mind's Limits*, 21–40.

16 Ibid., xi.

17 See Améry's essay "Resentments," in ibid., 62–81.

18 Améry, *At the Mind's Limits*, 28.

LOSING TRUST IN THE WORLD

PART ONE

WHAT IS TORTURE?

*T*orture is a word but devastatingly much more than that. The contributors to part 1 underscore the importance of that fact, but at the start it is important to consider some aspects of the word. Noun or verb, *torture* has clear meanings. The *Oxford English Dictionary*, for example, defines torture as "the infliction of severe bodily pain, as punishment or a means of persuasion," adding that torture includes "severe or excruciating pain or suffering (of body and mind); anguish, agony, torment; the infliction of such."[1]

The clarity in such definitions is significant for multiple reasons, but among the most important are the following: (1) Torture refers to specific conditions and actions. Only some conditions and actions are instances of torture, but many conditions and actions are just that. (2) Torture is a human condition and action. Absent specific perpetrators and victims, actual torture does not exist. (3) Definitional clarity makes a strong case that torture is never good. Nobody, moreover, wants to be tortured, a fact that complicates, if it does not falsify, every claim that torture is justifiable. (4) Definitional clarity invites, indeed requires, further clarification because even the best definitions cannot answer every question that lurks within them. They are insufficient, for instance, to name who inflicts torture or who is ravaged by it. Nor can definitional clarity adequately grasp the pain, suffering, anguish, agony, and torment unleashed by torture. (5) The shortfalls of definitional clarity give ambiguity, evasion, and denial a foothold to compound and even escalate the damage done by torture. Those gaps give the defenders and practitioners of torture room to say, "Such things didn't happen on our watch." "Of course, torture is deplorable, but the actions we took on behalf of national security were not torture." "Unpleasant though it is, torture is still a justifiable option, even a necessary one, because it works."[2]

The fact that *torture* is a word lets other words obscure and even justify torture's carnage. Further words, no matter their clarity or their potential to arouse protest and encourage resistance, are not likely to be enough to keep that atrocity at bay. But without attempts to address the question "What is torture?"—efforts that include but do not rely entirely on definitional clarity—that goal will be a forlorn cause. Jean Améry, who noted that *torture* is derived "from Latin *torquere*, to twist," understood as much, including the likelihood that those who inflict torture would twist language itself to cover their tracks and to silence their foes.[3] In opposition, Leonard Grob, Björn Krondorfer, and Dorota Glowacka use their words to keep language untwisted and to say what torture is in ways that improve the chances that it will be at least less prevalent in the twenty-first century than has been the case thus far.

Focusing explicitly on Améry's essay "Torture" and developing an outlook about the widespread presence of torture during the Holocaust, Grob clarifies what it means to bear "*responsible* witness" to testimony about suffering under torture. This approach means that Grob's response to "What is torture?" emphasizes what torture victims have to say about that question. They are the ones who should be heard and heeded when it comes to "defining" torture, telling when and where it has happened, and depicting its effects and consequences, including the losing of trust in the world emphasized by Améry. Bearing *responsible* witness to such testimony requires painstaking reading and empathetic listening, but even more than that too. It entails action in response, doing what one can to resist torture and its aftereffects. Grob's chapter helpfully illustrates what action of that kind could include, answering the question "What is torture?" by showing that no answer will be acceptable unless it includes and acts upon the word *unacceptable*.

Krondorfer's approach differs from but also complements Grob's. Krondorfer's definition of torture is more restricted than Grob's, and arguably, its interpretation of torture is also narrower than that of the UN Convention against Torture. Arguing that "torture is a specific kind of violence" not to be "conflated with other forms of extreme violence," Krondorfer develops an outlook that sees torture not primarily as punishment or as an accompaniment to genocide but rather as a distinctive and "necessary" tool deployed in interrogations aimed to support and defend ideological "truth." Torture is typically used and defended by those who are ideologically "sincere," by those who claim to know with deep conviction what is right and good and are determined to vindicate their conviction by coercing, for example, "confessions" that corroborate what must be the case for their ideology to stand. Both Grob's wide-ranging perspective on torture and Krondorfer's more restrictive understanding of it have their place in the quest to comprehend the nature of torture. The explorations in these two chapters shed important light on the question "What is torture?" because Grob and Krondorfer are in solid agreement that torture is and always must be unacceptable.

Dorota Glowacka brings part 1 to a close by underscoring that every answer to the question "What is torture?" will be lacking unless it includes the screams of torture's victims. Amplifying Grob's emphasis on bearing responsible witness to testimony, Glowacka shows that torture robs its victim of language. Thus the *howl* of the tortured person, Glowacka suggests, may have more to say about torture than countless attempts to obtain definitional clarity. The howl helps to explain, for instance, why torturers typically do their work in secret and in places that make the screams of torture publicly inaudible. Such silence prevails at humanity's peril. No attempts to answer the question "What is torture?" are likely to make much difference unless they disrupt the torturers' attempts to prevent the screams of the tortured ones from being heard. But hearing and heeding the howl might make all the difference in the world.

What is torture? It is something worse than words can say and therefore something that not only words but also actions must resist. Jean Améry believed that "reality is reasonable only so long as it is moral."[4] The three chapters that follow go far to show why and how that judgment condemns torture, an atrocity that, in the words of Jamie Barnett, "removes moral authority and legitimacy from any cause, no matter how worthy otherwise."[5]

NOTES

1   In addition to directing our attention to these definitions, William Germano provides insightful commentary about them in "Words for Beginners," *Chronicle of Higher Education*, January 5, 2015, http://chronicle.com/blogs/linguafranca/2015 /01/05/words-for-beginners/.

2   Neuroscience increasingly debunks this problematic instrumental justification of torture. See, for example, Shane O'Mara, *Why Torture Doesn't Work: The Neuroscience of Interrogation* (Cambridge, MA: Harvard University Press, 2015).

3   Jean Améry, *At the Mind's Limits: Contemplations by a Survivor on Auschwitz and Its Realities*, trans. Sidney Rosenfeld and Stella P. Rosenfeld (Bloomington: Indiana University Press, 1980), 32.

4   Jean Améry, *Radical Humanism: Selected Essays*, trans. Sidney Rosenfeld and Stella P. Rosenfeld (Bloomington: Indiana University Press, 1984), 65.

5   See Jamie Barnett, "Americans Should Never Use Torture. In Any Circumstances," *Newsweek*, June 7, 2015. Barnett is a retired rear admiral in the United States Navy. His essay is accessible at http://www.newsweek.com/americans-should-never-use -torture-any-circumstances-340062.

1

Torture during the Holocaust

Responsible Witnessing

LEONARD GROB

In the preface to the 1977 reissue of *At the Mind's Limits: Contemplations by a Survivor on Auschwitz and Its Realities,* Jean Améry claims that just as he did not strive to explicate his experience of torture in the previous (1966) edition, "in the same way now too, *I can do no more than give testimony.*"[1] His suffering at the hands of Nazi torturers, Améry says, can neither be understood nor even imagined by others. An infinite gap exists between the ones tortured and those who attempt to *account for* their suffering. Suffering transcends classification, categorization, comparison, empathy. Try as we might to comprehend or even to exercise compassion in the face of depictions of such suffering, we remain in the world of the human, while, as Améry argues, the victim of torture lives a dehumanized existence forever.

In this chapter, I reflect on the possibility of bearing *responsible* witness to testimonies of suffering. In so doing, I fully acknowledge Améry's assertion that no *explication* of torture is possible: I respect Améry's claim, which speaks to the divide between those who, like himself, have experienced torture and those who compose the rest of humankind. Thus, I do not strive to attribute *meaning* to suffering that transcends any and all attempts to account for it. Rather, I pose and address the following questions: What would constitute a truly responsive reading of a text, like

Améry's, replete with firsthand testimony about torture that is "ineradicably burned" into its witness? Are we to resign ourselves to facing an unbridgeable gap between reader and that which is read? Will any attempt to come to terms with acts of torture be nothing but a betrayal of the witness to these acts? How do we respond authentically to the words of those who have suffered torture or other forms of violence at the hands of another? Is there a mode of bearing witness to a testimony of human suffering that—while remaining responsible to such suffering—might offer hope for a world where we are enjoined from being the agents of further affliction? In the face of irreparable suffering—in the face of that for which there can be no "restorative restitution"[2]—might "repair" *of another order* be possible? Might the reader-as-witness to Améry's testimony respond in a way that affirms our humanity by offering an *ethical* vision for the future? Might our witness-as-reader open an ethical horizon in response to suffering in general and, in particular, to Améry's suffering, what he terms "the most horrible event a human being can retain within himself"?[3]

Améry's essay on torture in *At the Mind's Limits* is not only a meditation on torture in general: He speaks of *torture during the Holocaust.* Arrested in 1943 by the Nazi SS as a member of a Belgian resistance movement, Jean Améry bears witness to torture that he argues "was not an accidental quality of this Third Reich, but its essence."[4] Although other regimes had embraced torture, he contends that the Nazis alone "had expressly established it as a principle."[5] Though the Nazis did not invent it, torture became nothing short of the "apotheosis"[6] of National Socialism. The Nazis did indeed place torture "in their service. But even more fervently they were its servants."[7]

Although Nazis tortured to extract information, to terrorize, to punish— some of the most common uses of torture—Améry claims that, ultimately, the Nazis tortured because they were drunk "with power, dominion over spirit and flesh."[8] The Jew, the source of a "virus" or "cancer" on the Aryan body politic, was the primary object of such mastery "over flesh and spirit, life and death."[9] As "absolute sovereign," the Nazi torturer, suffused with ideology, could undo the social contract by means of which "we can live only if we grant our fellow man life, ease his suffering, bridle the desire of our ego to expand."[10] The tortured individual loses trust in the world— forever.[11] Faith in humanity cannot return. One can no longer assume as the foundation of sociality that "the other person will spare me . . . that he will respect my physical, and with it also my metaphysical, being."[12] Améry exclaims that "a part of our life ends and it can never again be revived."[13] Améry's contemporary, the French Jewish philosopher Emmanuel Levinas, held that to obey the commandment "Thou Shalt Not Murder" is to hear and enact the injunction to help "defend the life of the other."[14] For Améry, however, there was no such help.

For the purposes of my focus in this chapter, torture is understood to include a range of actions that dehumanize *an entire community* through the designed infliction of physical or mental pain. Just as the murder of one individual may be contrasted with the genocide of a people, so the dehumanization of one person may be contrasted with the intended dehumanization of a community. In this sense, Jews qua Jews were "tortured" by the Nazi regime; they suffered indignity upon indignity until two-thirds of Europe's Jews were subjected to the ultimate dehumanizing act: murder. From daily humiliation in the public arena to roundup, ghettoization, and forced railway passage—all the way to either lethal enslavement or immediate gassing in *l'univers concentrationnaire*—millions of Jews were deemed mere objects, excess population. In eastern Europe, 1.5 million Jews were forced to dig their own graves, stripped naked, and finally shot at close range either by Nazi soldiers or by eager recruits from local populations. Yet other hundreds of thousands died slow, painful deaths from starvation and unsanitary conditions in the ghettos and camps throughout Europe. Whether or not they were subject to the particular mode of suffering in extremis experienced by Améry, Jews qua Jews were subject to a range of dehumanizing acts on a continuum whose end point was the degradation of the person to death.

Nazi torture of Jews was inflicted by those who considered themselves, in Ariel Dorfman's words, "custodians of the common good."[15] In his view, one with which Améry would agree, the Nazis tortured "in the name of salvation, some superior goal, some promise of paradise."[16] Paradise, for the Nazis, was a world in which Jews were progressively stripped of their humanity—a world finally to be rendered *judenrein*. The Nazis chose to torture and ultimately murder Jews not to further military aims, at least not in any conventional understanding of warfare. In an "orgy of unchecked self-expansion,"[17] they tortured and killed Jews in order, finally, to annihilate the injunction in the Hebrew Bible that forbids unbridled egoism: Thou Shalt Not Murder. For the Nazis, manifold modes of torture, followed by outright murder, were undertaken first to dehumanize and then to destroy every vestige of the humanity of the Jew. The Nazis aimed to murder Jews as a people whose central message consisted in the imperative to respect the personhood of the other.

In other words, torture *during the Holocaust* is a case of human suffering writ large, prompting us to ask how we might act responsibly in the face of depictions of such torment. Although the Holocaust is not the only instance in which suffering in extremis occurs—we should have no recourse to "comparative suffering"—the torment of Holocaust victims presents us with a case study in which the question of responsible witness to irremediable suffering comes to trouble us *with brutal clarity.* And so, we must return to a governing question of this chapter: What is our responsibility toward the witness of those who, like Améry, have suffered processes of dehumanization during the Holocaust, a time, James Hatley rightly says, "in which the extremity of violence undergone by the victim revealed only too clearly the transcendence of the victim's suffering, which is to say, its irremediableness"?[18]

My response recalls Primo Levi's memoir *Survival in Auschwitz* and, in particular, its poetic opening, which calls to mind Jewish scripture, tradition, and liturgy:

> *You who live safe*
> *In your warm houses, . . .*
> *Meditate that this came about:*
> *I commend these words to you.*
> *Carve them in your hearts*
> *At home, in the street,*
> *Going to bed, rising;*
> *Repeat them to your children,*
> *Or may your house fall apart, . . .*
> *May your children turn their faces from you.*[19]

A contemporary of both Améry and Levinas, Levi has taken the words immediately following the Shema, a key Hebrew prayer that resounds, "Hear O Israel, the Lord is our God, the Lord is One," and he has recast them in the shadows of Auschwitz. Referring to God's words, the original passage—reformed by Levi—says: "You shall teach them to your children, speaking of them when you sit in your house, when you walk along the way, when you lie down, when you rise up." In the liturgy, the words we are enjoined to teach are clearly those that constitute the Shema. The words to which Levi refers, however, are the words that follow in his memoir, words of testimony to his irreparable suffering in Auschwitz. We who live in our "warm houses" are charged to bear witness, responsibly, to such suffering or else face the curses that will accrue to those who fail to do so. The task is daunting; understanding fails us. Levi insists that teaching, learning, and remembering must take place. Jean Améry agrees, but he also complicates matters by arguing that even if Jews in the post-Holocaust world understandably take the Holocaust as their "existential reference point . . . only we, the sacrificed, are able to spiritually relive the catastrophic event as it was or fully picture it as it could be again."[20]

If we cannot understand the suffering, or even imagine it, how are we to escape the penalty of curses to be levied upon those who fail to carve in their hearts the witness of those who suffered at Auschwitz? We read the works of Améry and Levi, we encounter the testimonies of others who survived and of those who did not. How are we to respond? James Hatley, who has written well on Emmanuel Levinas, sums up the dilemma: "What exactly is commanded of the reader so that she or he might step *responsibly* through the portal of these texts, so that she or he might read them in attentiveness to those who have suffered?"[21] In any endeavor on our part to affirm the other's suffering, we come to realize how likely it is that we will fail to do justice to that other. We pale at the thought that we might "betray the extremity of that suffering."[22] If such suffering overflows any attempt on our part to address it, are we thus doomed, as Levi warns, to have our children turn their faces from us and to have our houses fall apart?

Perhaps unexpectedly, hope may be found in our *continuing to be troubled* at the very point when an authentic response to suffering seems impossible. As we have seen, such hope cannot rest upon any "taking account" of suffering, any attempt to grant it meaning. As Levinas holds, suffering is useless, nothing other than a "gratuitous non-sense of pain."[23] Although he offers a litany of sites of useless suffering during the twentieth century, Levinas, like Améry, argues that the Nazi preoccupation with obliterating the humanity of the other makes the pain of Nazism's victims paradigmatic of a suffering that is always "excessive," always disproportionate to the weight of our futile attempts to understand it. If we cannot conceptualize suffering, however, we can come to realize that it is possible— indeed, necessary—for us to offer a response of a different *order*, a response of a fundamentally different *kind* or *quality*.

What would constitute a response "of a different order"? Levinas urges us to begin by granting that "all" we can do in response to the other's suffering is to remain "true to him or her." In James Hatley's words, such recognition means "one is summoned to attentiveness, which is to say, to a heartfelt concern for and acknowledgment of the gravity of violence directed toward particular others. In this attentiveness, the wounding of the other is registered in the first place not as objective fact but as a subjective blow."[24] Such attentiveness can do little, in the ordinary sense of *do*, but, importantly, it can beget more attentiveness. In responding to the call of the other who suffers, "all" I can do is be wakeful. I must become an "insomniac," Levinas declares. My witness must be unremitting, untiring; I must respond with a perpetual "unease" that never permits resolution of what is ultimately irresolvable. In this sense, my response, like the pain it witnesses, is gratuitous. In responding to the suffering of the other, I must perpetually watch my words and deeds. I must be constantly aware that I may likely say or do too much or too little—or say something *about* the other, *accounting for* his or her suffering rather than being *attentive to* it.

One mode of saying "too much" is for me to fall back on the desire to empathize with the victim—an intention that can falsely presume my ability to conceptualize how his or her suffering might be comparable to my own. To protect myself from the temptation to empathize, I must arrive at an *existential* awareness of the infinite gap between us: I must come to realize that the root of an authentic suffering in the face of the suffering other lies precisely in my suffering, as Hatley puts it, the "*impossibility of suffering the other's suffering*."[25] In Levinas's words, I become "persecuted," obsessed with the other's suffering; I am traumatized by an inability to suffer that suffering which has now "infected" my life.

To be truly wakeful in the presence of the suffering other is not, however, to be passive. On the contrary, obsessed with the suffering of the other, I enter a realm fundamentally different from the ordinary world in which I act according to the laws of self-interest. I arrive at the existential understanding that an infinitely excessive suffering calls for an infinitely excessive response. For Levinas, if the suffering of others is always ultimately gratuitous, excessive, I am called upon to offer a response in excess of my own egoistic desires—desires that exist at the beginning of a continuum whose end point is the Nazi goal of the absolute sovereignty of that ego. I realize that I must rupture the realm of egoistic endeavors and enter the domain of the *interhuman.* In so doing, I enlarge a fundamentally ethical horizon by effecting a breach in a seemingly all-encompassing world of self-interest, a world ultimately prone to genocidal actions.[26] Reading and witnessing depictions of torture during the Holocaust, I am summoned to let go of "egoistic ambition," which serves as the ground of thoughts and actions that have led us—at the end of a continuum—to Auschwitz. As a result of such existential awareness, I acknowledge that the other's suffering is of greater concern to me than my own. In Levinas's words, I realize "that there is something more important than my life, and that is the life of the other."[27] I "invert" a fear of death—the essence of an ego-based, self-interested existence—into a fear of allowing or committing murder, thereby opening the realm of the ethical.[28]

How, more concretely, do I open this ethical horizon? Levinas is not sanguine, not hopeful about a "happy ending" to a century of genocide: "The meaning of Auschwitz," he asserts, "is a suffering, a faith completely without promise."[29] "But after Auschwitz," Levinas claims, "even though it doesn't 'pay' to be good" within a universe of self-interest, "one cannot deduce from that that one *should not be* good. Hence to stop preaching for the good would not suffice. Stop preaching, but accept the obligation to . . . do the good."[30] In responding to the other's suffering, I am called to assume responsibility for that other—and ultimately for all others. Borrowing terms from the Hebrew Bible, Levinas refers to the call of the suffering other as the appeal of the poor one, the widow, and the orphan, summoning me to responsibility.

With regard to enacting this responsibility, Levinas summons us to avoid any alleged dichotomy between matter and spirit: "The other concerns me in all his material misery. . . . As if with regard to the other I had responsibilities starting from eating and drinking."[31] In responding to the other's suffering, I must not abandon the everyday world to move into some alleged world of the spirit. As he underscores the need to respond to suffering in concrete and specific ways, Levinas also responds to the charge that his ethic is too abstract and unrealistic.[32] Levinas was often asked about the *practice* of an ethical relation: "I reply that its being utopian does not prevent it from investing our everyday actions of generosity, of goodwill towards the other: even the smallest and most commonplace gestures, such as saying 'after you' as we sit at the dinner table or walk through a door, bear witness to the ethical."[33] To be ethical is thus not to remove ourselves from the world, but rather to invest that world with ethical import. In sum, fully witnessing the suffering entails a radical break with the world of self-interest, a break that inaugurates ethical practice.

Even with this radical break, however, sobering realizations remain. In the face of the torture of Jean Améry during the Holocaust—in the face of the torture and murder of millions of Jews—I am powerless to engage in any *project* that could claim to overcome the evil of Nazi genocidal actions. In the face of such suffering, I am dis-abled from acting, at least in the ordinary, ego-oriented sense of *act*. As we have seen, "all" I can do is respond, gratuitously, with my witness to the irreparable suffering that yet summons me to rupture the world of self-interest in the name of ethical conduct. In Levinas's words, we know after Auschwitz that "evil surpasses human responsibility [in the egoistic realm]. . . . But perhaps this thesis is precisely a call to man's infinite responsibility."[34] Our response to the Holocaust, Levinas proclaims, is not to understand the suffering of the other but rather to assume, in concrete acts of justice, "my responsibility for the other person."[35] There is no "happy ending" after the torture and murder at Auschwitz; there is, however, the life of responsibility to others that we humans can and must enact.

The "life of responsibility to others" may take limitless forms. We can work toward *tikkun olam*—healing the world—through seemingly small individual deeds such as enacting the Levinasian "after you"; by soothing a child's tears; by coming to the aid of the widow, the orphan, the poor one. We can also take collective and political steps aimed at healing on a larger scale by helping to relieve the burden of loneliness, poverty, cruelty, and violence on a local, regional, national, or global scale.[36] We are thus faced with a multiplicity of demands to respond to the other. However, when called forth by our witness to depictions of torture, we are particularly enjoined to work to relieve and remove this suffering: to work for a world free of any and all acts of torture. Thus we are especially charged to support and join the work of organizations dedicated to healing victims of torture[37] and to ending torture and other human rights violations.[38]

As witnesses of acts of torture during the Holocaust, we return to Jean Améry. Again and again, Améry spoke about the fragility of the social world. At the first blow of the torturer, the trust that no one will violate me—the scaffolding upon which all sociality rests—is dispelled. In an instant, the social contract is voided. The Holocaust, perpetrated in the midst of high European culture, points vividly to the fragility of a social world that coheres-as-world only insofar as I can trust that my neighbor will do me no harm. When that trust is broken—as it so often has been and continues to be—the nature of our response to violations of human dignity becomes critical: whatever solidity the social world possesses is provided by living a life of responsibility toward those who have suffered. Heeding the Levinasian call to responsibility creates a balm that can begin to heal a troubled world.

CONTRIBUTORS' QUESTIONS FOR LEONARD GROB

1. Following Emmanuel Levinas, you say that all of us must "bear witness, responsibly," to torture. You continue by clarifying the point that such "infinite responsibility" must take concrete forms. Yet how are we to decide what action, in particular, to undertake? For once a person becomes attentive to torture and the suffering it inflicts, that attentiveness raises questions about priorities. For example, one can imagine Jean Améry saying that the most important thing to do about torture is to stop it. How does one decide exactly what to do in the face of such suffering, especially when torture works to dehumanize an entire community? Further, if the moral imperative is "living a life of responsibility toward those who suffer," can we exclude from recipients of responsible action those who inflict or remain indifferent to torture? Améry believed that *resentments* toward perpetrators and bystanders were fundamental to "moral truth." Do you agree with him, or are there better ways to live responsibly toward perpetrators and bystanders?

2. An absolute, categorical rejection of torture makes ethical sense as long as only one perpetrator and one victim are involved. But when Levinas emphasizes "acts of justice," he underscores that we live in a social world of many persons, "the Third" in his lexicon. In addition to my ethical relationship to what Levinas calls "the other," I must consider all others; I must take into account the political ramifications of my actions. Thus we cannot interpret Levinas's philosophy as if there were only two persons in the world, a tendency that seems to be present in your essay. Hence, with torture specifically in mind, might not a situation exist in which justice toward the Third calls for the torture of someone who knows but refuses to divulge the whereabouts of perpetrators who intend to do harm to many others? Might such a consideration undermine any absolute condemnation of torture?

RESPONSE BY LEONARD GROB

In the face of limitless ways to "bear witness, responsibly" to torture, I am asked how one would prioritize such acts of witness. Reflecting on the immensity of the task at hand, I am reminded initially of the rabbinic injunction: "Yours is not to complete the task, yet neither are you free to desist from it."[39] That is to say, I must not allow the enormity of the task to deter me from beginning to make what will inevitably be excruciatingly difficult choices.

I am asked, more concretely, how I would reply to an imagined call by Améry to work toward *stopping* torture. What action would be most efficacious in doing so? This question helps me to focus my initial realization: I am not alone in assuming the seemingly impossible task at hand. Although my response to the suffering other is always singular—I am the one "being faced" by that other—each of us inhabits the world as a *being-with-others*. I live within and among communities already engaged in the unending work of helping to prevent torture, communities whose work I may join.

One example is an American initiative called the National Religious Campaign against Torture (NRCAT). Established in 2006 in protest against the American military's use of torture on 9/11 detainees at Guantánamo Bay and during the war in Iraq—the latter atrocities depicted in infamous photographs from the Abu Ghraib prison—the NRCAT states its aims as follows:

MISSION STATEMENT

The National Religious Campaign Against Torture mobilizes people of faith to end torture in U.S. policy, practice and culture.

GOALS

1. Ensure that U.S.-sponsored torture of detainees never happens again.

2. End the use of torture in U.S. prisons and detention facilities, in particular the use of prolonged solitary confinement.

3. Promote U.S. policies that enable other countries to end their torture practices and advocate for an end of U.S. support (direct or indirect) of any country that engages in torture.

4. End the bigotry and hatred that promotes the practice and acceptance of torture against religiously, ethnically, and other targeted groups.[40]

In lending my hand to the work of such an association and others with similar goals to be realized globally, I help make a contribution—small though it may be—toward realizing Améry's goal of stopping torture.

What action in particular, I am asked, would resist torture that victimizes *whole peoples*? Here, activism would initially take the form of immersion in and dissemination of the findings of genocide scholars regarding the heeding of early warning signs of genocide. To contribute to the end of torture that dehumanizes whole populations, one can attend to the work of such organizations as Genocide Watch[41] and the International Association of Genocide Scholars,[42] both of which have articulated forms of genocide alerts. And when it is too late for warnings to be of help because genocide is already under way, an organization such as United to End Genocide acts not only to prevent genocide but also to curtail or end it once it has begun. United to End Genocide proclaims its aims as follows:

> United to End Genocide is dedicated to preventing and ending genocide and mass atrocities worldwide by building a powerful, lasting movement of community activists, faith leaders, students, artists, investors and genocide survivors, and all those who believe we must fulfill the promise the world made following the Holocaust: "Never Again!" . . . We believe the only way to prevent mass atrocities, and to end genocide once and for all, is to build a large and powerful activist movement that will sound the alarm, shine a spotlight on those who cause or enable genocide or mass atrocities, and demand action by our elected leaders and anyone who has the power to protect those who face the threat of genocide or mass atrocity, anywhere in the world.[43]

I am also asked by my co-contributors to this volume to respond to Améry's bold claim that a victim of torture—as well as any bystander to torture who considers him/herself a moral agent—must continue to harbor "resentments" toward those who torture. For "moral truth" to be established, according to Améry, we must guard against "problematic atonement," superficial forgiveness, spurious reconciliation. Améry is troubled by any facile overcoming of the past; he protests what he deems the "antimoral natural process of healing that time brings about."[44] The victim of torture and, indeed, all bystanders who wish to inhabit a moral universe must, according to Améry, remember-with-resentment.

In response to Améry, I contend that there are ways to remember, ways to live responsibly with perpetrators and bystanders, other than by remembering-with-resentment. To remember the pain inflicted by the individual torturer and by a society that turned a blind eye to torture is literally to re-member—that is, to re-collect, re-gather that which has been rent asunder. Such re-membering, in my view, does not deny the irremediable nature of the pain inflicted by the torturer or the averting of eyes by the larger society. What it does do is re-commit me to assume, in concrete acts of justice, my responsibility for the other person. To remember, in this sense, is to rededicate oneself to live in the world in such a way as to help prevent suffering or to help heal it wherever or whenever it manifests itself. Only thus can the world in which the tortured one has lost trust be made whole—literally, re-membered—and thus become a world worthy of a "cautious" trust.

I am asked, further, if the perpetrators of torture, or those who remain indifferent toward it, are in principle excluded from serving as recipients of the responsible actions detailed throughout this chapter. While working to stop torture—while working to protect potential victims and supporting judicial processes that punish those who torture—I argue that we must not, on principle, exclude bearing witness to a suffering of its own kind experienced by perpetrators. Although Améry would not have cared about such suffering—he was concerned that torturers be punished and their deeds be recalled with active resentment—I contend that any and all suffering, including that of those who have failed, heinously, to honor the face of the other either through inflicting torture or through engaging in bystander behavior, must be addressed responsibly. Acknowledging the possibility of past trauma on the part of many perpetrators, as well as an often societally sanctioned lack of moral agency in the case of both perpetrators and bystanders, one must lend active support both to rehabilitative therapeutic initiatives and to an approach to education and child-rearing that places the sanctity of human personhood at its center.[45]

A final challenge has been posed to me: I am asked to consider Levinas's quandary with regard to the fact that although we live in a world of many persons, the emphasis of his ethics, at least as far as torture is concerned, seems primarily to be on the relationship between one perpetrator and his or her victim. How am I to reconcile *ethical* concerns, which exist chiefly in the relationship of a singular face-to-face relationship, with *political* concerns that inevitably impact all others—whom Levinas calls the "Third"? More specifically, I am asked to rethink any absolutist prohibi-

tion of torture in the face of a hypothetical—but potentially realizable—
situation in which torture might be inflicted to prevent a yet greater evil:
the murder of many.

To avoid a misplaced criticism of Levinas, it must be underscored that
the Third is always present in the ethical encounter between two individuals: I am always aware "that the other is from the first the brother of all the
other men," and therefore that "I am another for the others."[46] Immediately troubling questions arise: What is the nature of my own relationship
to the Third? Which one is my *true* other? How does my other relate to the
Third? In the course of attempting to respond to these questions, I am
called upon to "calculate the incalculable."[47] Thus an uneasy but creative
tension exists between ethics—my relationship to one other—and politics,
the endeavor to bring about justice by formulating rules applicable, in
principle, to the totality of humankind. The uneasy relationship between
ethics and politics in Levinas's thought manifests itself in statements such
as "Justice is already the first violence,"[48] the claim that in regulating
human conduct on a societal level I am forced to see my other as merely
one among many in a universal order. "Violence" here means that I bow to
impersonal rule-making at the expense of hearing, exclusively, the summons of my other to become a responsible—and thus moral—being.

Although existing in this state of tension with one another, ethics and
politics complement one another; neither is subject to any simplistic reduction to the other.

Yet when all is said and done, Levinas does grant a measure of primacy
to the ethical relationship, thus giving weight to my claim that torturing
another is an absolute wrong. For Levinas, justice never supplants ethics;
rather, justice is grounded in an ethics that serves as paradigmatic for the
former: "I believe . . . that politics must be controlled by ethics: the other
concerns me."[49] I agree with Levinas: political theory does not begin with
the individual ego as a building block; rather, the ethical relationship of
the face-to-face undergirds all authentic politics. Citing Dostoevsky, Levinas makes a universal claim grounded in particularity: "All men are responsible for one another and I more than everybody."[50] Thus, when confronted
with the hypothetical situation in which justice would seemingly call for
torturing one other who has knowledge of the whereabouts of many potential perpetrators, I would join Levinas in remaining faithful to the absolute
prohibition on torturing my other, whose face embodies an infinite call to
responsibility.

NOTES

1   Jean Améry, "Torture," in *At the Mind's Limits: Contemplation by a Survivor on Auschwitz and Its Realities,* trans. Sidney Rosenfeld and Stella P. Rosenfeld (Bloomington: Indiana University Press, 1980), viii. Italics are mine.

2   James Hatley, *Suffering Witness: The Quandary of Responsibility after the Irreparable* (Albany: State University of New York Press, 2000), 1.

3   Améry, "Torture," 22.

4   Ibid., 24.

5   Ibid., 31.

6   Ibid., 30.

7   Ibid., 31.

8   Ibid., 36.

9   Ibid.

10   Ibid.

11   Ibid., 40.

12   Ibid., 28.

13   Ibid., 29.

14   Emmanuel Levinas, "In the Name of the Other," trans. Maureen V. Gedney, in *Is It Righteous to Be? Interviews with Emmanuel Levinas,* ed. Jill Robbins (Stanford, CA: Stanford University Press, 2001), 192.

15   Ariel Dorfman, "The Tyranny of Terror: Is Torture Inevitable in Our Century and Beyond?" in *Torture: A Collection,* ed. Sanford Levinson (Oxford: Oxford University Press, 2004), 16.

16   Ibid.

17   Améry, "Torture," 35.

18   Hatley, *Suffering Witness,* 2.

19   Primo Levi, *Survival in Auschwitz: The Nazi Assault on Humanity,* trans. Stuart Woolf (New York: Simon and Schuster, 1996), 11.

20   Jean Améry, "On the Necessity and Impossibility of Being a Jew," in *At the Mind's Limits,* 93.

21   Hatley, *Suffering Witness,* 4. Italics are the author's.

22   Ibid., 2.

23   Emmanuel Levinas, "Useless Suffering," trans. Richard A. Cohen, in *The Provocation of Levinas: Rethinking the* Other, ed. Robert Bernasconi and David Wood (New York: Routledge, 1988), 160.

24   Hatley, *Suffering Witness,* 3.

25   Ibid., 5. Italics are mine.

26   For a detailed argument regarding the role of egoistic behavior in the creation of a genocidal mind-set, see Leonard Grob, "Emmanuel Levinas and the Primacy of Ethics in Post-Holocaust Philosophy," in *Ethics after the Holocaust: Perspectives, Critiques, and Responses,* ed. John K. Roth (St. Paul, MN: Paragon House, 1999), 1–14.

27   Emmanuel Levinas, "The Paradox of Morality: An Interview with Emmanuel

Levinas," trans. Andrew Benjamin and Tamara Wright, in *The Provocation of Levinas*, 172.

28 Emmanuel Levinas, "The Other, Utopia, and Justice," trans. Michael B. Smith, in *Is It Righteous to Be?*, 204.

29 Emmanuel Levinas, "Judaism and Christianity after Rosenzweig," trans. Andrew Schmitz, in *Is It Righteous to Be?*, 260.

30 Emmanuel Levinas, "Being Toward Death and 'Thou Shalt Not Kill,'" trans. Andrew Schmitz, in *Is It Righteous to Be?*, 134. Italics are mine.

31 Emmanuel Levinas, "Interview with François Poirie," trans. Jill Robbins and Marcus Coelen, with Thomas Loebel, in *Is It Righteous to Be?*, 52.

32 Levinas's ethics can be termed a "metaethics" in the sense that, unlike most ethical thinkers, he is concerned neither with any list of moral obligations nor with the principles upon which they are based. "Ethics," for Levinas, is an "optics," a way of seeing that constitutes the fundamental structure of human existence.

33 Emmanuel Levinas and Richard Kearney, "Dialogue with Emmanuel Levinas," in *Face to Face with Levinas*, ed. Richard A. Cohen (Albany: State University of New York Press, 1986), 32.

34 Emmanuel Levinas, *Nine Talmudic Readings*, trans. Annette Aronowicz (Bloomington: Indiana University Press, 1990), 93.

35 Levinas, "Useless Suffering," 165.

36 In a similar vein, an older contemporary of Améry, Levi, and Levinas, German Jewish philosopher Martin Buber, argues that responsibility—literally, the ability-to-respond—moves along a continuum from a loving concern for one person to a loving concern for humankind as a whole. See Martin Buber, *I and Thou*, trans. Walter Kaufmann (New York: Simon and Schuster, 1970), 66–67. Buber proclaims that we stand in the presence of "the equality of all lovers, from the smallest to the greatest and from the blessedly protected man, whose life is circumscribed by the life of one beloved human being," all the way to the person who "is nailed his life-long to the cross of the world, capable of what is immense and bold enough to risk it: to love *man*."

37 For example, the Center for Victims of Torture, founded in 1985, has worked to rehabilitate more than 20,000 torture victims across the globe. For further information, see the center's web site: http://www.cvt.org/.

38 For example, the World Organisation against Torture is a coalition of nongovernmental organizations whose mission is "fighting against torture, summary executions, enforced disappearances, and all other cruel, inhuman or degrading treatment." The organization's mission statement is available at http://www.omct.org/about/.

39 *Ethics of the Fathers*, 2:20.

40 Available at http://www.nrcat.org/about-us/what-is-nrcat/mission-statement-and-goals. Further information about NRCAT is available at its Internet site: http://www.nrcat.org/.

41 See Genocide Watch's mission statement at http://www.genocidewatch.org/aboutus/missionstatement.html.

42 See a description of the activities of this organization at http://www.genocide scholars.org/.

43 Available at http://endgenocide.org/who-we-are/programs-and-campaigns/end -genocide-network/.

44 Jean Améry, "Resentments," in *At the Mind's Limits*, 72.

45 For a series of arguments supporting the latter claim, see Leonard Grob, "Higher Education in the Shadows of the Holocaust," in *The Uses and Abuses of Knowledge: Proceedings of the 23rd Annual Scholars' Conference on the Holocaust and the German Church Struggle*, ed. Henry F. Knight and Marcia Sachs Littell (Lanham, MD: University Press of America, 1997), 223–46.

46 Emmanuel Levinas, *Otherwise Than Being or Beyond Essence*, trans. Alphonso Lingis (The Hague: Martinus Nijhoff, 1981), 158.

47 Levinas, "Being-Toward-Death and 'Thou Shalt Not Kill,'" in *Is It Righteous to Be?*, 133.

48 Emmanuel Levinas and Florian Rötzer, "Emmanuel Levinas," in *Conversations with French Philosophers*, trans. Gary E. Aylesworth (Atlantic Highlands, NJ: Humanities Press, 1995), 44.

49 Emmanuel Levinas, "God and Philosophy," trans. Richard A. Cohen and Alphonso Lingis, in *The Levinas Reader*, ed. Sean Hand (Oxford: Basil Blackwell, 1989), 182.

50 Emmanuel Levinas, "Philosophy, Justice, and Love," trans. Michael B. Smith, in *Is It Righteous to Be?*, 169.

2

Torture

BJÖRN KRONDORFER

During genocidal reigns of terror, multiple forms of violence occur. This is true especially when genocides are embedded within large-scale wars and forced population transfers, as was the case in Europe during the 1930s and 1940s. Different genocides might be remembered for particularly iconic images of violence (the Nazi death chambers, the Cambodian killing fields, the machetes in Rwanda, the mass rapes in the Congo), but all genocides comprise a wide range of cruel and often lethal activities: labor exploitation, mass executions, juridical and extrajuridical killings, individual shootings, massacres, torture, mental cruelties, beatings, forced starvation, death marches, sexual violation, pogroms, rape, excremental assault. What must also be included in this litany of evils are the many daily humiliations and fear-inducing orders designed to assault body, mind, and soul.

This chapter argues that torture is a specific kind of violence. It should not be conflated with other forms of extreme violence. In particular, torture assaults the *individual* body, not the *communal* body. I emphasize this difference because, arguably, one can understand genocides, such as the Holocaust, as an assault on the body of a community. Understood that way, genocide's unfolding violence might be interpreted as torture inflicted on a communal body. I contend, however, that torture is first and foremost an assault on the individual body. In this narrower (and classic) sense, torture is coercive violence enacted on individuals by regimes. As such, torture is used in genocidal situations insofar as authoritarian regimes always need to quell political dissent; however, as a specific type of extreme violence, torture does not always or easily advance the goals of genocidal campaigns. As John Perry indicates, "Within an atrocity dynamic, the torturer's work is relatively slow and methodical."[1] Requiring laborious effort, torture would slow down the genocidal killing of declared enemies.

I draw attention to these diverse understandings because public debate about torture's moral permissibility is recurring in liberal democracies, a development that would have seemed almost unthinkable in the immediate aftermath of World War II and the Holocaust. But in the wake of 9/11, including the threat posed by the self-proclaimed Islamic State of Iraq and Syria (ISIS), issues surrounding the morality of torture loom large in Western democracies. Emphasizing that torture is a political act of coercive violence that should be differentiated from other forms of extreme violence, I offer an ethical response that undercuts the aura of legitimacy and ideological sincerity on which torture's defenders depend.

Torture and Other Forms of Extreme Violence

Misconceptions about torture include taking it to be gratuitous, sadistic, inefficient, and inflicted for base motives, perverted pleasure, or sheer hatred. This outlook sees torture as an unleashing of primitive and brute forces that produce and intend pure terror. Torture, however, rarely works that way, at least not when it is seen and justified as a necessary and even inevitable, though regrettable, tool of politics or warfare. Avoiding the misconceptions that a "pure terror" view of torture infliction might involve, this mind-set seeks ways to make torture morally permissible as a lesser evil.[2] It leads to claims like those made by the American lawyer Alan Dershowitz after 9/11: "If torture is going to be administered as a last resort . . . , it ought to be done openly, with accountability, with approval of the President of the United States."[3] Short of seeking official authorization to legitimate torture, one might send suspects to "less squeamish allies," as Jonathan Alter wrote in *Newsweek* in 2001, and let them do the work deemed necessary.[4]

Interpreting torture as gratuitous or characterizing it simply as a perversion of the exercise of brute force tends to depoliticize this violence. As Michel Foucault says, however, torture "is not an extreme expression of lawless rage" but "a technique" aiming at "a calculated gradation of pain."[5] As such, torture is deeply political in that it is a means of communicating "truth." It functions as a particular "language" of violence that, in the logic of the perpetrator, permits and legitimates the infliction of harm. At the same time, this "language" of violence trivializes the devastating scars that torture indelibly leaves on its victims.

Rejecting any justification for the use of torture, I consider torture a wrongful act that is morally and legally indefensible. It violates human dignity and religious precepts.[6] It is a profoundly problematic orientation toward the world, which most often operates in the mode of what I call *ideological sincerity*. Emblematic of this "sincerity" is the torturer—including the political culture that authorizes and requires his or her work—who becomes the agent revealing "truth" through the fear and suffering entailed by the threat or infliction of pain. A political act administered in "sincerity" and cloaked in "moral necessity," torture seeks communication through the infliction of pain but simultaneously denies the harm done to the victims.

Nazi Germany and its collaborators used multiple forms of violence to dominate, subjugate, punish, terrorize, and eventually annihilate targeted population groups. Torture was part of the arsenal of coercion used to create and enforce a regime driven by racial and antisemitic ideology. It would be mistaken, however, to designate as torture all of the cruelties the Nazis and their collaborators perpetrated on individuals and communities, although one shudders at accounts, such as the following, that document the extremity of the Third Reich's assaults on the Jews and other people deemed subhuman.

> Local hooligans armed themselves with axes, special clubs studded with nails, and other instruments of torture and destruction and chased all the Jews into the street. As the first victims of their devilish instincts they selected seventy-five of the youngest and healthiest Jews. (Jan Gross, *Neighbors*)[7]

> The fact is that the German personnel's beating of the prisoners was so routine that a survivor, when describing one of the more outstanding torturers in camp, can remark upon the camp's routine cruelty in passing, as if it had been an ordinary expectation. (Daniel Jonah Goldhagen, *Hitler's Willing Executioners*)[8]

> The peasants dragged me straight toward a large manure pit. . . . Its brown, wrinkled surface steamed with fetor like horrible skin on the surface of a cup of hot buckwheat soup. . . . I retched. The peasants swung me by the

hands and feet [and] I was hurled into the very center of the brown filth.
(Jerzy Kosiński, *The Painted Bird*)⁹

Through the point-blank shot that was thus required, the bullet struck
the head of the victim at such a trajectory that often the entire skull or at
least the entire rear skullcap was torn off, and blood, bone splinters, and
brains sprayed everywhere and besmirched the shooters. (Christopher
Browning, *Ordinary Men*)¹⁰

Such scenes of violence—horrific and nauseating to the point of being
unbearable, edging toward the de-creation of the imagination itself—do
not constitute torture as I understand it in this chapter. What Gross, Goldhagen, Kosiński, and Browning describe are atrocities that occurred in permissive environments of violence, the results of overlapping and multifarious
motivations: opportunities to enrich oneself, religious contempt, localized
hatreds, peer pressure, voracious greed, perverted pleasure, military discipline, revenge, and so forth. These acts were performed by local communities and neighbors as well as by the invading and occupying forces. In most
cases, acts of extreme violence of the kind described above, ranging from
sudden orgiastic spurts of carnage to systematic and frequently lethal humiliations, were enacted not in secret but in public or semipublic spaces.

For anthropologist Talal Asad, such open enactments of cruelty illustrate "public rituals of torture." Asad argues that in premodern times, often
under the auspices of religious and feudal authorities, public rituals of
torture were "deemed necessary to the maintenance of sovereign power,"
whereas in modern times, torture is performed in spaces "typically secret."¹¹
If we were to adopt Asad's distinction between torture performed publicly
in the past and that performed secretly in the present, then the public performance of torturous acts during the Holocaust was meant to enforce and
uphold the sovereignty of the Nazi regime. If this were the case, the Holocaust would have to be interpreted as a regression into premodern forms
of violence. Indeed, in Jan Gross's *Neighbors*, a study of the destruction of
the Jews in the village of Jedwabne by their Polish neighbors during World
War II, the author interprets that violence as an anachronism. "The murder of Jedwabne Jews," says Gross, "reveals yet another, deeper, more
archaic layer of this enterprise. I am referring not only to the motivations
of the murderers . . . but also to primitive, ancient methods and murder
weapons: stones, wooden clubs, iron bars, fire, and water."¹²

I contend, however, that these openly enacted cruelties are better understood as "performances of spectacular violence" rather than "public rituals of torture."[13] As the term *spectacular* suggests, this kind of violence needs to be witnessed and seen (or, in any event, the perpetrators do not mind that the violence is seen). Spectacles of violence take place in the open. When acted out by nonauthorized people, spectacles of violence openly demonstrate a permissive environment in which one can behave with impunity; when performed by authorized personnel, these spectacles constitute the execution of punishment. Torture, however, precedes trial and punishment, is enacted by authorized personnel, and requires an enclosed, secret, almost intimate space. Here are a few characteristics of what torture, in my understanding, is *not*:

- Torture is not punishment.
- Torture is not the same as terror or torment.
- Torture is not the same as torturous execution.
- Torture is not the sexual pathology of a sadistic individual.

Although elements of the above can be present in the actual torture process, they do not determine what torture is. For example, a torturing agent might have an individual inclination toward sadism, but the training manuals for torture and interrogation techniques spell out methodic procedures that build upon ideological indoctrination, peer cohesion, and the eradication of empathy.[14] Torture might be used to terrorize a population, but this is done only within the limits of half-knowledge; that is to say, torture is rumored but rarely officially acknowledged. Torture might carry elements of punishment but only insofar as the prisoner is already assumed to be a "radically negated other" whose basic human right to be free from maliciously inflicted pain has been taken away.[15] Finally, executions can carry elements of torture if they are prolonged through torturous means. Yet, as spectacles of violence, cruelly extended executions seek the death of the condemned, while torture itself involves keeping its target alive, albeit in extreme pain.[16]

If torture can contain these elements but is not defined by them, how does torture differ from other forms of cruelty? I regard the following characteristics as pivotal in that differentiation.

- Torture is a violent process that seeks to establish "truth" through verbal interrogation and infliction of pain. Securing "truth," in this context, must be understood as obtaining information or confession from a person undergoing torture, as well as impressing the torturer's ideological worldview upon the victim.

- Torture is conceived by authorized torturing agents as a means of obtaining information or evidence and determining the guilt of the prisoner.[17] It is not punishment itself. A confession (by which is meant the admitting of guilt or the surrendering of information) may lead to trial and punishment, but torture itself is primarily about evidence gathering, not punishment.
- Torture needs secrecy. For torture to achieve what its perpetrators intend, it needs enclosure, not openness to the public. Torture is not inflicted publicly, for, as Asad indicates, "the effectiveness of certain kinds of disciplinary knowledge is enhanced by its secrets."[18]
- Torture is a gradual process of destruction, both physical and mental.
- For the perpetrators, torture is a labor of moral necessity. Hence, its meaning may be metaphysical as well as political. Torture does not require that torturers be sadistic or pathological (though some individuals who torture may possess such characteristics), but torture does entail the torturer's ideological sincerity. Meanwhile, the tortured person endures senseless pain that destroys meaningful relations to the world.

Torture's Dynamics and Ideological Sincerity

From early on in the Western tradition, torture has been related to truth seeking.[19] It is only in modernity that secular humanism disconnected it from the search for truth and instead interpreted it as intentionally inflicted harm, authorized by state representatives but motivated by a number of possible reasons. Anti-torture views that emerged in Europe after the sixteenth century speak to the inviolability of human rights (based on the notion of human dignity) and also argue, more pragmatically, that torture is gratuitous and inefficient.[20] But claims about gratuity and inefficiency need to be further investigated so as to avoid a misreading of torture's dynamics.

Torture inflicts more than pain and suffering on its victim. It impresses on a victim's body and mind a particular "truth," and it does so with ideological sincerity.[21] When I speak of ideology, I refer to an overarching belief system that brings some cohesion to a polyphony of political, national, religious, and racial motivations and justifications for exercising power. Within such a system, perpetrators act not only with impunity but also with utmost sincerity. Within an ideology of coercive power, torture does not consist of acts of deranged individuals but rather is authorized and executed in the name of an (imagined) collective. Hence, the idea that people can torture others with a good conscience should not surprise us. "We were proud of what we did," a former Brazilian torturer testified. "[We were] ridding the country of a threat" and were "doing a patriotic job." He adds, for good measure, that "we were religious people, a Christian people."[22]

By "sincerity," a concept introduced by Adam Seligman and others, I refer to an orientation toward the world that tends to absolutize its convictions. As these authors argue, modernity is dominated by the mode of sincerity, which sees the world not as it could or might be but instead in terms of "an 'as is' vision" that becomes "a totalistic, unambiguous vision of reality."[23] With Hannah Arendt, we might say that this kind of sincerity reached its ideological zenith in the totalitarianisms of the twentieth century, but it continues to manifest itself in the developing world as well as in liberal democracies.[24]

Torture and the search for truth are intertwined in a system that operates within a totalizing mode of sincerity.[25] Such a system sees torture not as gratuitous or as penalizing violence, but as an efficient process by means of which "truth" can be established. Here "truth" is determined and defined by the reality envisioned and defended by the torturer, and by the ideology that authorizes his or her labor, dubious and false though the vision and the ideology may be.[26] Torture as truth seeking is a political act insofar as the violence inflicted is authorized, legitimated, and justified; it is almost always carried out with sincerity, employing the rationale that torture is necessary to avert a greater danger and that it is expedient because torture is the lesser evil. For the torture process to succeed (from the perspective of the torturing regime), it must rely on the interaction of both verbal interrogation and infliction of physical pain within an enclosed space, a process perceptively analyzed by Elaine Scarry.[27] As such, torture is a laborious process that moves forward gradually and methodically. "You may not realize," an anonymous torturer once testified, "but [torture] is very tiring."[28]

Through the exchange of verbal acts between victim and torturer (interrogation) and the one-sided infliction of intense harm on the victim's body, torture seeks information or confession (or both), and its acquisition is read as truth by the torturing regime. The need to acquire such truth not only justifies the bodily harm inflicted but also denies its severity. By employing a seemingly legal and objectified language of sincerity and necessity, Scarry argues, the torturing regime obscures the atrocious pain it inflicts. From the torturer's perspective, pain is defined not by the victim's subjective experience but as an objective means of obtaining and communicating truth. As a result, torturing regimes blind themselves to the severe harm they inflict on people. In the perception of the torturing agents, torture is not inefficient but effective; thus, they proceed with utmost care and precision, while regarding themselves as working within a morality of political and ideological necessity.

For the victim, the torturer's questions may initially be mistaken as relevant (insofar as providing an answer seems to promise cessation of pain), but during the unrelenting process of torture, questions become increasingly irrelevant, while pain becomes incontestably real. Tortured by Nazis, Jean Améry said that "the *how* of pain defies communication through language. . . . Whoever is overcome by pain through torture experiences his body as never before."[29] Because it is so overwhelming, pain destroys everything the victim has taken to be his or her world—with the result that victims even testify against themselves.

Torture comes to an end when the victim's confession is finally read by the torturer and his regime as truth. "To accept torture, even to approve of it and to impose it," an anonymous torturer testified, "is not ultimately difficult. It is sufficient to be convinced that the cause you espouse is just, that the action being undertaken is indispensable and that because of this the end justifies the means. One is not born a torturer."[30] The torturing agent is eventually convinced that he or she has found or identified yet another terrorist, communist, witch, jihadist, or antigovernment agent. Only then begins the legal trial, which eventually concludes with a judicial verdict and penalty.

Torture allows for no ambiguity, and that is why its victims are never seen as innocent. The torturing agents deny that they have created a fictional truth because they are blind to the fact that they convert a subjective experience of suffering into an objective confirmation of their own reality. Instead, they read torture as a sincere performance leading to the acquisition of truth. Successful torture rests on the creation of a persuasive, albeit largely fictional, truth: most people are tortured because they are *suspected* of having valuable information, not because they actually *possess* it. "It is as if they felt themselves to be masters of the force required to alter reality," writes Jacobo Timerman about his torturers in Argentinian prisons. "Every totalitarian interrogator . . . has a definite conception of the world he inhabits and of reality."[31] Leigh Gilmore echoes this thought in her analysis of confessions in the Abu Ghraib prison in 2003: "Confession, torture and truth exist in a triangular relation: torture names the implicit threat that elicits confession, truth names its goal, and the successful production of truth via confession sanitizes the threat that impels it."[32]

Sincerity rules in the enclosed world of torture. Because torture entails perceiving reality in absolutizing terms, it forces the victim into the world of the torturing regime; it makes the victim submit to the ideological sincerity that informs the torturing agents' perception of reality. "Torture is not merely an attack on, but the creation of, individuals," writes William Cavanaugh about the Chilean dictatorship. "[It] discipline[s] the citizenry into a complex performance scripted by the state."[33] The worldview of the perpetrator is impressed upon the bodies and minds of the victims.[34]

Jean Améry, Torture, and the Holocaust

When we analyze torture as specific acts of political power that operate in the mode of ideological sincerity, we can see why torture needs to be distinguished from other forms of extreme and spectacular violence that are part of the arsenal employed in genocidal campaigns. To advance that understanding, consider in more detail Jean Améry, the Holocaust, and "Torture," his widely quoted essay.

By 1942, the Nazi regime had officially adopted a policy of torture, when SS leader Heinrich Himmler issued an order that permitted "third degree" interrogations to be used on "communists, Marxists, Jehovah's Witnesses, saboteurs, terrorists, members of resistance movements, antisocial elements, refractory elements, or Polish or Soviet vagabonds."[35] Notably, Jews were absent from this list, because the directive targeted political dissenters and resistance fighters, not the populations selected for death (unless Jewish individuals were suspected of belonging to the resistance). A Jewish resistance fighter who had been arrested and tortured by the Gestapo in Belgium, Améry said that the torture he experienced had little to do with sadistic pathology. Instead, his torturers demonstrated an immense, unrestrained will to power, while he, as prisoner, experienced utter powerlessness.[36] This asymmetry destroyed his trust in the world. Although Améry was subsequently deported to Auschwitz because he was Jewish, he was tortured by the Gestapo not for that reason but because he was suspected of belonging to the resistance. In the Gestapo cell, Améry did not suffer the public humiliations, torments, and carnage that eastern European Jews endured at the hands of the German occupying forces, but instead was exposed to the methodical destruction of his being through interrogation by state officials, who went about their work with the ideological sincerity of dictatorial power.

From the point of view of victims, it makes little difference how we think about different types of extreme violence. For them, severe pain that is maliciously inflicted is so overwhelming that the circumstances hardly matter. For the tortured, the inflicted pain is utterly meaningless since it eludes all references to any kind of morality. As Jacobo Timerman put the point, "It is a pain without points of reference, revelatory symbols, or clues to serve as indicators."[37] But while the victim experiences torture as utterly gratuitous, the perpetrator perceives it as necessary and efficient. While neither may be fully right, the victim, if he or she survives, comes closer to understanding what has been inflicted. The victim understands the severity of harm inflicted, whereas the perpetrator justifies the inflicted harm as necessity in the name of ideological sincerity.

I thus contend that torture shows itself to be neither *efficient*, as the torturing regime claims, nor *gratuitous*, as the victim may claim. From the point of view of a torturing agent, torture may seem efficient, but from a critical-analytical perspective it is ultimately *inefficient* due to the fictional reality created in the torture chamber. In the end, little, if anything, is obtained in torture chambers that could not be revealed in other ways—except that the torture chamber plays a key part in confirming the torturer's worldview. Torture, however, is also not simply gratuitous if by that we mean sheer and random cruelty enacted by hateful and depraved individuals. It takes an ethical perspective—based on an analysis arrived at from *outside* the atrocity dynamic—to see the ultimate *gratuitousness* of the coercive violence in torture. Such violence is gratuitous not because it is an act of unrestrained, arbitrary cruelty but because it is an act of gradually inflicting extreme pain to uphold the ideological convictions of a torturing regime. As such, torture does not, of course, prove the truth of the regime's worldview, but merely demonstrates the regime's political will and ability to impose unrestrained power. In sum, the violence in torture as a political act is gratuitous not because it is exercised in sheer hatred but because it is based on the intrinsically delusional nature of the truth production that justifies it.

The search for links between torture (coercive political violence) and the Holocaust (genocidal violence) should not conflate them under the umbrella of extreme violence. Instead, what these two modes of violence have in common is that they are both invested in a legitimizing mode of sincerity: a totalizing and coercive ideological sincerity operates in both spheres of extreme violence. Similar to the atrocity dynamic in torture cells, as Hannah Arendt suggests, "the concentration and extermination camps of totalitarian regimes serve as the laboratories in which the fundamental belief of totalitarianism that everything is possible is being verified [and in which] the appalling spectacle of the camps themselves is supposed to furnish the 'theoretical' verification of its ideology."[38] The absolutizing sincerity of their perpetrators is what links torture and genocide, but it is not accurate or helpful to call every aspect of genocidal violence torture.

To delegitimize torture, we need to restore an orientation toward the world that counters any rationalization of extreme violence in the name of ideological sincerity and expediency. Rogue states continue to use torture, and disturbingly, liberal democracies have begun to soften their attitude toward its permissibility in the current war against terror. This state of affairs urges us to adopt an ethical stance that demands a disruption of the enclosed world of torture. Our voices must persistently resist the fictitious reality created by the absolutizing sincerity of torturers and the regimes they serve. The certitude with which core values are defended— by others and also ourselves—must always be questioned. Stepping into the realities of others, even our enemies, is a fundamental condition for questioning our own absolutes and for fostering empathy. While empathy has been methodically dislodged from the vocabulary of torturers, it must be strengthened among those who have the privilege of not being caught in the immediacy of the atrocity dynamic. Critical voices must call attention to the fact that the annunciated mode of sincerity perpetuates, and thus coercively maintains, its own ideological convictions. In turn, these convictions legitimize disciplinary techniques of coercive cruelty as morally permissible. Inflated political sincerity emboldened Nazi Germany and led to the Holocaust. An antidote to such inflated sincerity is a stance of radical empathy that questions the core values in whose name torture is legitimated.

Although they are different, versions of that sincerity drive contemporary political life, even in liberal democracies. The harm, including torture, made possible by such sincerity should not be underestimated. Empathy for those who are, or may become, targeted is crucial to keeping sincerity's absolutizing inclinations in check.

CONTRIBUTORS' QUESTIONS FOR BJÖRN KRONDORFER

1. You rightly argue against indiscriminate use of the word *torture*. Holding that the term should not be a moniker for almost any violence committed under extraordinary circumstances, you define *torture* as "a political act of coercive violence" that is "enacted on individuals by regimes" and, as such, must be recognized in its full political import. You also claim that for the perpetrator, "torture is a labor of moral necessity. Hence, its meaning may be metaphysical as well as political." But if we situate torture within the realm of the ethical, then torture has to be understood in terms that transcend political ideologies posing as moral imperatives to which the torturer appeals. Confining the notion of torture to political contexts alone, as you tend to do, runs the risk of rendering our response to it ethically bankrupt. Torture is not fundamentally an act inflicted on a cog in the political machine by some zealous agent of ideological "truth," but rather is inflicted by a human being on another person as a rending of the face-to-face relationship. Your readers will be helped if you clarify what you take the relationships to be between your strongly political definition of torture and your understanding of the place of torture within the realm of the ethical.

2. "Successful torture," you state, "rests on the creation of a persuasive, albeit largely fictional, truth." Established through power, "truth" for the torturer is willed as an absolute: truth does not lay claim to the torturer, but rather the torturer lays claim to truth through the totalizing embrace of an ideology. Does this description, which implies that the torturer's truth is ultimately a "delusion," lead to the insight that some other truth is at stake, a real truth that must be opposed to ideology that only masquerades as truth? If so, what follows for a sound political and ethical understanding of torture, and how would your understanding of the Holocaust affect your position on this point? On the other hand, if there is no real truth about torture, where are we left in a post-Holocaust world that is besieged by torture?

RESPONSE BY BJÖRN KRONDORFER

"People can exercise power over others because they can injure others," writes sociologist Heinrich Popitz. "This is the root of power."[39] Deliberate physical injury is the most direct form of violence through which power is exercised. One of the most extreme forms of deliberate violent injury is torture. But torture is more than the infliction of physical pain. It is also the coercive imposition of a particular "truth" in whose name a political regime justifies its actions and proceeds with a deliberate unmaking of both the body and the world of the tortured.

Torture inflicts extreme harm on people under conditions that render them utterly defenseless and choiceless, even though torturers pretend that their victims have a choice—namely, to tell the "truth." One of the disturbing characteristics of torture is that it intimately relates power and truth—a truth that is progressively established in the eyes of the torturer in order for acts of torture to eventually come to an end. This distinct feature differentiates torture from other forms of violence, including genocidal violence.

We can argue, of course, that from the perspective of victims it makes little difference to differentiate between various forms of extreme violence, since the overwhelming experience of pain makes irrelevant the motivations that drive perpetrators to enact their cruelties. But from the perspective of articulating an ethical stance that enables us to intervene in the specific atrocity dynamic of torture, it is important to analyze those differences.

My colleagues perceptively ask about the relationship between the political and the ethical, between power and truth. In particular, I am asked whether "confining" torture to a purely political realm runs the risk of "rendering our response to it ethically bankrupt." Further, if the truth produced in torture is "fictional," as I argue, is it implied that a "real truth" exists, a truth which "opposes ideology that only masquerades as truth"?

The difficulty in determining the relationship between the ethical and the political in the case of torture is that victims and perpetrators have fundamentally different perspectives on what is happening in torture. This difference is due to the radically unequal power relationship that manifests itself in torture through the relentless combination of a primary verbal act (the question/answer in the interrogation) and a primary physical act (infliction/endurance of pain). The gap that opens between the experience of the tortured and that of the torturer becomes unbridgeable. And yet, the slow and methodical process of torture is meant precisely to bridge this gap by forcing the victims into recognizing and accepting a truth that is not theirs. Torture stops when the regime is convinced it has extracted "truth" in the form of confession or information, a truth that conforms to and confirms the ideological conviction of the regime.

When a torturing regime is satisfied with having elicited a "truthful" confession or "valuable" information, torture stops. The torture may even stop when neither a confession nor valuable information is obtained. But this outcome results only when the torturers are convinced that the prisoner has nothing to confess or has no (valuable) information. In such rare cases, torturers still convince themselves that their methods have revealed "truth"—that is, they now presume that their target, due to the rigor of harsh interrogation, is of little or no further value. Irreparable harm, however, has been inflicted on the prisoner—even if the prisoner is now deemed to be of no additional use to the regime.

My colleagues ask: Do we need to assume that in torture there is a "real truth" over against a "delusional truth"? Does the truth of the victim stand in opposition to the fictional truth that is produced in the name of a totalizing ideology?

These are good questions, but I think they miss the point. By phrasing the questions as an issue of "real" versus "delusional" truth, we continue to misunderstand the nature of torture. These queries wrongly assume that there is a power struggle, a battle of wills, that is taking place between two protagonists—the torturer and the prisoner—and that there will be a winner and loser in this contest about truth. Once we think in this way, we are tempted to ask further questions that are misleading: Can the prisoner withstand the pain and withhold the information? Can the torturing regime win the battle by breaking the person? Will the prisoner be broken and betray secrets—or, worse, betray friends and comrades?

Unfortunately, depicting torture as a contest of that sort plays into the hands of those who defend torture as efficient. A torturing regime can always point to the success of its methods, because torture is always efficient in producing results. It always produces some "truth" that is coerced from the victim through the interplay of verbal and physical acts. If we assume that torture is a contest between the power of wills, a case *for* torture could be made on ethical—utilitarian—grounds. Torture, then, is justified as "the best of worst choices," or because "torture is better than execution," or because it is "better to torture one person than to risk the lives of hundreds" (as in the "ticking bomb scenario," for example).

We need to dispel ways of thinking that misperceive the logic and dynamics of torture and thereby lead to seemingly reasonable utilitarian justifications for inflicting it. Torture, after all, is neither forensic evidence gathering nor punishment after a verdict of guilt. Instead, it is a coercive method that operates in the realm of uncertainty, suspicion, and fear. As a violent act of political power, torture becomes necessary in the eyes of a regime when it fears a menacing threat by forces that are invisible, yet thought to be real (or perceived as real). These elusive adversarial forces, which subvert (or are perceived to subvert) the deep ideological convictions of a regime, must be made visible. What a regime does not know—namely the extent, scope, source, location, or timing of its perceived enemies—must be turned into something knowable. When suspects are arrested, the torturing regime has only vague ideas about whether they have valuable information or whether they are guilty of subversion. The torture process fills this lacuna by establishing a "truth" that makes the unknown knowable and even known, albeit not necessarily in ways that are valid or beyond falsification.

Torture, then, is a mechanism that renders meaningless the multiple "truths" of the suspects by and with which they have lived in their own worlds prior to arrest and interrogation. Under torture, the suspects' variegated views and experiences are systematically reduced to a single-minded pursuit of "truth" according to the sincere convictions of the torturer. The *many* worlds of the tortured are made to coincide with the *one* world of the torturer. Success, in the logic of torture, is that at the end of the torture process there is only one truth mouthed by both the victim and the perpetrator. This truth is extracted in a manner that convinces the perpetrator of the accuracy of the victim's confession/information, which, in turn, seems to confirm the regime's truth as well.

Because the torture dynamic correlates power and truth so intimately through the infliction of extreme physical harm, we need to resist the parallel construction that links *power* to the realm of the political and *truth* to the realm of the ethical. The truth production in torture has nothing to do with the ethical: it is inextricably part and parcel of the political. The "truth" established in torture perverts the ethical.

We need to stop asking, then, whether there is a winner in an (unequal) contest over two *truths* in the torture chamber (an assumption, as I have argued, that lends itself to utilitarian justifications of torture). Instead, we must start by asking, and persist in asking, whether it is ethical for *any* worldview to take itself so seriously that it permits and legitimates the infliction of extreme harm.

Once we enter this ethical terrain, we must consider our own reactions to situations when we feel threatened. Unless we refuse to defend our own community by means of torture—especially if and when we are sincerely convinced of our "truth" and its certitude (for example, that democracy, as we know it, represents the best form of political governance)—we remain caught in a self-serving utilitarian argument that can make torture permissible.

Torture always gets some answers—in that sense it is extremely efficient—and the torturer's regime sees those answers as supporting its "truth." The efficiency of such political coercion obliterates distinctions between power and truth. In the realm of the ethical, however, truth cannot be reduced to political expediency or ideological conviction. At the same time, truth can only be discerned in part, embraced provisionally, and defended through open debate, ongoing inquiry, and tested evidence. Recognizing that every political governance must exercise some power, an ethically grounded politics does not negate our need to express and uphold political convictions. Rather, it approaches these convictions with the wisdom of humility and the humbling acknowledgment of one's limitations in understanding how best to regulate human life. An ethically grounded politics does not confuse one's own convictions with "truth" that must be defended at all costs, but rather grants a fair hearing to the insights of others.

In the realm of the ethical, the power we exercise is not to injure others, but to reach consensus through deliberation and dialogue. In such a political system, the practice of torture is unthinkable.

NOTES

1   John Perry, *Torture: Religious Ethics and National Security* (Maryknoll, NY: Orbis, 2005), 92.

2   For example, in *The Lesser Evil: Political Ethics in an Age of Terror* (Princeton, NJ: Princeton University Press, 2004), Michael Ignatieff argues for a restrained counter-violence permissible within democracies.

3   For Dershowitz's comments, see http://edition.cnn.com/2003/LAW/03/03/cnna .Dershowitz/.

4   Quoted in Perry, *Torture*, 51–52. See also Karen Greenberg and Joshua Dratel, eds., *The Torture Papers* (Cambridge, UK: Cambridge University Press, 2005), for a defense of the permissibility of torture in the US war on terror.

5 Michel Foucault, *Discipline and Punish: The Birth of the Prison*, trans. Alan Sheridan (New York: Pantheon Books, 1977), 33.

6 The idea of human dignity originates in secular Enlightenment thinking and forms the basis of the 1987 United Nations Convention against Torture and Other Cruel, Inhuman or Degrading Treatment or Punishment, which is accessible at http://www.ohchr.org/EN/ProfessionalInterest/Pages/CAT.aspx. For strong anti-torture positions, see Richard Matthews, *The Absolute Violation: Why Torture Must Be Prohibited* (Montreal: McGill-Queens University Press, 2008); from a Catholic perspective, Perry, *Torture*; from a Jewish perspective, Jonathan K. Crane, "Torture: Judaic Twists," *Journal of Law and Religion* 26, no. 2 (2010): 469–504. Crane reviews halachic debates and biblical and Talmudic evidence, concluding that in Judaism "torture is neither a bad option . . . nor a less bad option" but "a non-option altogether" (504).

7 Jan T. Gross, *Neighbors: The Destruction of the Jewish Community in Jedwabne, Poland* (Princeton, NJ: Princeton University Press, 2001), 19.

8 Daniel Jonah Goldhagen, *Hitler's Willing Executioners: Ordinary Germans and the Holocaust* (New York: Alfred A. Knopf, 1996), 307.

9 Jerzy Kosiński, *The Painted Bird* (New York: Modern Library, 1965), 139. I include Kosiński's highly controversial novel in this list of well-known historical sources because his fictionalized account had a deep impact on the popular imagination (especially in the 1960s and 1970s).

10 Christopher R. Browning, *Ordinary Men: Reserve Police Battalion 101 and the Final Solution in Poland* (New York: HarperCollins, 1992), 64.

11 Talal Asad, *Formations of the Secular: Christianity, Islam, Modernity* (Stanford, CA: Stanford University Press, 2003), 104.

12 Gross, *Neighbors*, 124. Zygmunt Bauman (*Modernity and the Holocaust* [Ithaca, NY: Cornell University Press, 1989]) and Giorgio Agamben (*Homo Sacer: Sovereign Power and Bare Life*, trans. Daniel Heller-Roazen [Stanford, CA: Stanford University Press, 1989]) argue that the Holocaust is the realization of a particular mode of modernity, not a regression into barbarity.

13 Foucault holds that "public torture and execution must be spectacular" (*Discipline and Punish*, 34). I think he wrongly conflates the evidence-gathering and truth-producing dynamic of torture with subsequent pronouncements of penalty and spectacular torturous executions.

14 Perry shows how dictatorial regimes train recruits to administer torture. Methodic desensitization, initiation rites, secrecy, peer cohesion, rewards, slow induction into increasing administration of pain, and obliteration of empathy are important steps (*Torture*, 88–94).

15 I refer here to Georges Bataille's existentialist notion that sadism is not a form of sexual pathology but "the radical negation of the other" (quoted in Perry, *Torture*, 114). See also Jean Améry's reference to Bataille in *At the Mind's Limits: Contemplations by a Survivor on Auschwitz and Its Realities*, trans. Sidney Rosenfeld and Stella P. Rosenfeld (Bloomington: Indiana University Press, 1980), 35.

16 See Crane, "Torture: Judaic Twists," 471.

17 That torture is performed not by random individuals but by authorized agents is clearly affirmed in the 1987 United Nations Convention against Torture: "Pain or suffering is inflicted by or at the instigation of or with the consent or acquiescence of a public official or other person acting in an official capacity" (Part I, Article 1.1).

18 Asad, *Formations of the Secular*, 104.

19 For a history of torture, see Edward Peters, *Torture*, expanded edition (Philadelphia: University of Pennsylvania Press, 1996 [1985]). For a short survey of Catholic justifications of torture from the 1300s onward, see Perry, *Torture*, 56–58; Crane lists various "motivating reasons for torture" ("Torture: Judaic Twists," 470).

20 See Asad, *Formations of the Secular*, 107–109. Partly because the anti-torture camp has described it as gratuitous and inefficient, torture keeps being misread as any type of gratuitous cruelty that serves no purpose (hence inefficient) or is performed simply for the sake of cruelty (hence gratuitous).

21 See Björn Krondorfer, "Ritual Denied and Read as Truth: From Totalizing Sincerity to the Seriousness of Play," *Journal of Ritual Studies* 27, no.1 (2013): 59–72, where I more fully develop the link between torture and sincerity.

22 Quoted in Martha Huggins, Mika Haritos-Fatouros, and Philip G. Zimbardo, *Violence Workers: Police Torturers and Murderers Reconstruct Brazilian Atrocities* (Berkeley: University of California Press, 2002), 198. That perpetrators understand themselves as acting ethically within their own codes of morality has been examined in the context of National Socialism by Peter Haas, *Morality after Auschwitz: The Radical Challenge of the Nazi Ethic* (Philadelphia: Fortress Press, 1988); and Claudia Koonz, *The Nazi Conscience* (Cambridge, MA: Harvard University Press, 2005).

23 Adam B. Seligman, Robert P. Weller, Michael J. Puett, and Bennett Simon, *Ritual and Its Consequences: An Essay on the Limits of Sincerity* (Oxford: Oxford University Press, 2008), 8.

24 Hannah Arendt, *The Origins of Totalitarianism* (New York: Harcourt Brace, 1976).

25 Torturing regimes are politically unstable, which is why they display and enforce a totalizing ideological sincerity in whose name extraordinary measures are introduced. It is no accident that "harsh interrogations" and the removal of prisoner rights were made permissible precisely at the moment when the United States felt threatened and destabilized after 9/11.

26 Because "truth" in such a system does not refer to accuracy or facticity but to a means of confirming a worldview that a torturing regime regards as truthful, quotation marks should be placed around that term. But for reasons of readability, I often refrain from that practice.

27 Elaine Scarry, *The Body in Pain: The Making and Unmaking of the World* (New York: Oxford University Press, 1985).

28 Quoted in Perry, *Torture*, 25.

29 Améry, *At the Mind's Limits*, 33 (Améry's emphasis).

30 Quoted in Perry, *Torture*, 81.

31 Jacobo Timerman, *Prisoner without a Name, Cell without a Number*, trans. Toby Talbot (New York: Alfred A. Knopf, 1981), 40, 72.

32 Leigh Gilmore, "How We Confess Now: Reading the Abu Ghraib Archive," in *Modern Confessional Writing: New Critical Essays*, ed. Jo Gill (London: Routledge, 2006), 182.

33 William T. Cavanaugh, *Torture and the Eucharist: Theology, Politics, and the Body of Christ* (Oxford: Blackwell, 1998), 2–3.

34 Modern manuals of harsh interrogation methods rely on coercive imposition. The CIA manual *Counterintelligence Interrogation* details how prisoners are made to regress and become utterly dependent through inducement of a "debility-dependence-dread state," which deprives them of "defenses most recently acquired by civilized man," cuts them off "from the known," and plunges them "into the strange" (Mark Danner, "The Logic of Torture," *New York Review of Books*, June 24, 2004, 70–74. See also Perry, *Torture*, 33–36.

35 Quoted in Peters, *Torture*, 124. "Third degree" interrogations meant torture. The phrase is comparable to the euphemistic "harsh interrogation methods," which is used in today's political parlance.

36 See Améry, *At the Mind's Limits*, 35–36.

37 Timerman, *Prisoner without a Name*, 32.

38 Arendt, *Origins of Totalitarianism*, 437–38.

39 Heinrich Popitz, *Phänomene der Macht*, 2nd ed. (Tübingen: Mohr Siebeck, 1992), 25.

3

Speech under Torture

Bearing Witness to the Howl

DOROTA GLOWACKA

> Where violence is inflicted on man it is also inflicted on
> language.
>
> —Primo Levi, *The Drowned and the Saved*

The Oscar for the best film of 2008 went to *Slumdog Millionaire*, a Bolly-wood production directed by Danny Boyle. Amid general enthusiasm, few viewers seemed disturbed by the fact that the backdrop of the film was a torture session, and the main character's life story was presented as a forced confession, extracted from the prisoner by means of repeated beatings, "strappado," electric shocks, and waterboarding.

Arguably indicating the increasing acceptance of such practices, the film is a paramount example of irresponsible representations that normalize and thus help to perpetuate torture. That atrocity has been increasing in the post-9/11 world. The United States bears considerable responsibility for this trend. In the name of a war against terrorism, the United States has violated the United Nations Convention against Torture, a measure—ratified by the United States in October 1994—based on the premise of inalienable human rights that derive from the dignity of the human person. The widespread implementation of torture by American authorities in recent years has been justified by the utilitarian argument that "pain is a lesser and more remediable evil than death" or, in the words of a US interrogating officer, "The screams [of the victims] were for the good of the country."[1]

Much of the literature on torture emphasizes the victims' physical and mental suffering, especially the violation of their bodily integrity. Such accounts fail, however, to examine the disastrous effects of torture's radical assault on the victim's capacity to use language. Protesting every attempt to minimize the victims' screams, a key element in justifications of torture, this chapter focuses on the victim's language-related behavior under torture. In particular, it argues that what happens to human language in these extreme circumstances exposes the limitations of our common conception of the human being as an animal that possesses language. I contend that this widely accepted definition contributes to the acceptability of torture. Therefore, it is imperative to challenge that definition.

Problematic Distinctions

In *Homo Sacer: Sovereign Power and Bare Life*, the Italian philosopher Giorgio Agamben reminds us that, since Aristotle, a person's humanity has been defined not by sheer existence but in terms of a capacity for political life. This outlook means that a human being who is reduced to naked, vulnerable existence—bare life—has zero political power, although that person's life has been absolutely politicized by means of exclusion from what is considered properly human. For Agamben, the contemporary epitome of this exclusion is the *Muselmann* of the Nazi concentration and extermination camps—one not yet dead but so wasted by starvation, disease, and other abuse as to be beyond recovery. In recent years, versions of the politicization of bare life by casting it outside of the law have appeared in places such as detention camps for suspected "terrorists" or "waiting zones" for inadmissible arrivals at airports.[2]

Agamben argues that, according to Aristotle, the conception of proper human life as a life with the capacity for political participation corresponds directly to the metaphysical definition of the human being as the animal that possesses language (*zōon logon echōn*). For Aristotle, the inauguration of the political state corresponded to humanity's passage from the state of nature, in which, like animals, one only had "voice" (*phone*), to a state in which persons could express themselves as political beings, that is, by possessing and using rational language (*logos*). If the polis was founded on the exclusion of bare life, the relation between a person's mere existence and political existence is the same as the relation between voice as such and meaningful language; it is a relation of exclusion: "The living being has logos by taking away . . . its own voice."[3] By positing rational language as the identifying characteristic of the human being, speaking persons then place their own animality outside of themselves, as "already and not yet human."[4] In that sense, Agamben reasons, a person's "mere voice" belongs to his or her self-definition as a human being only in a negative fashion: "Language can subsist only by grasping [and thus excluding] the nonlinguistic."[5] Western metaphysics has constructed a relation between a person's biological life and his or her political life based on the disjunction between voice and language. Within that logic, the humanity of a person who is deprived of meaningful language is called into question since he or she no longer has access to *logos*: the privilege of what constitutes a person as human has been taken away. If human voice as such is excluded from the definition of a human being as a living being who has language, it follows that a cry emitted by a being in the situation in which his or her rational faculties are annihilated by pain can be absolutely negated in the calculations of political power.

Excruciating Pain

Under coercive circumstances, human linguistic behavior can vary widely. A "heroic" cultural ideal, for example, is the subject who remains silent under torture and refuses to disclose vital information. In Nazi-occupied Poland, for instance, Irena Sendler, a member of the Council for Aid to Jews (Zegota), was captured by the Gestapo and repeatedly tortured in 1943. "I would have rather died," she testifies, "than given away what we were doing. What value did my life have compared to the lives of so many people who could have died because of me?"[6] More amply evidenced in torture-related literature is the behavior of those who "break down" under torture and "cough up" the names of their comrades or loved ones, or who make false confessions to stop the pain. Holocaust survivor Jean Améry, who was interrogated by the Gestapo in 1943 after being imprisoned for resistance activities, describes the agony of being suspended from the ceiling by the arms and admits that, had he known the real names of his co-conspirators, he would have most likely given them away, just as he poured out words in which he accused himself of invented political crimes: "I talked . . . dangling bundle that I was."[7] A more recent, post-9/11 example is the case of Maher

Arar, a dual citizen of Syria and Canada, who, while transferring planes in New York in October 2002, was apprehended by officers of the Immigration and Naturalization Service under the provisions of "extraordinary rendition" (stipulated by the Homeland Security Act) and deported to Syria, where, as he says, "during the first two weeks of my stay in Syria, I was physically beaten. What happened during this initial period is I just wanted them to leave me alone, even in that dark and damp underground cell. But after a while, the psychological torture that I endured during this lengthy period, I was ready—I was ready, especially by the end of my stay, by the end of the ten-month period in this underground cell, I was ready, frankly, to confess to anything. I would just write anything so that they could only take me from that place and put me in a place where it is fit for a human being."[8]

Although victims' linguistic behavior during torture may differ, in each instance excruciating pain predominates. Many survivors of torture admit that they groaned, cried, or screamed in pain. In *Prisoner without a Name, Cell without a Number*, which documents the author's experience, including torture, during the Argentine military regime's Dirty War in the 1970s, Jacobo Timerman alludes to his distress: "It is impossible to shout—you howl. At the onset of this long human howl . . . someone sticks his hand in your mouth and pulls your tongue out of it in order to prevent this man from choking. . . . What does a man feel? The only thing that comes to mind is: They're ripping apart my flesh."[9] In George Orwell's *1984*, one of Big Brother's victims, on being told that he is being taken to be tortured in Room 101, "had set up a wordless howling, like an animal."[10] As theorist of pain Elaine Scarry notes, under severe pain such prelinguistic behavior replaces a coherent verbal complaint and consequently destroys the victim's language. For Scarry, this loss is one of the most devastating consequences of pain.[11] The *howl* signals the destruction of the subject's capacity for speech and the implosion of language as a way to communicate meaning. The collapse of language as a consequence of severe pain inflicted by another has lasting effects, and it endures in the survivor's inability to adequately articulate that experience. As Timerman recalls, "In the long months of confinement, I often thought of how to transmit the pain that a tortured person undergoes. And I always concluded that it was impossible. . . . It is a pain without points of reference, revelatory symbols, or clues to serve as indicators."[12] Améry agrees with Timerman: "The pain was what it was. Beyond that there is nothing to say."[13]

The disastrous consequences of the radical incommunicability of pain go beyond pain's resistance to meaningful expression. As Scarry has argued, the expropriation of one's body and voice during torture collapses the boundaries between inside and outside, shattering the subject's sense of self: "Even where the torturers do not permanently eliminate the voice through mutilation or murder, they mime the work of pain by temporarily breaking off the voice, making it their own, making it speak their words, making it cry out when they want it to cry, be silent when they want its silence, turning it on and off, using its sound to abuse the one whose voice it is as well as other prisoners."[14]

Améry also confirms this insight: the collapse of language coincides with the tortured person's being "transformed . . . thoroughly into flesh."[15] The torturer's absolute sovereignty over the victim culminates in the perpetrator's being the master of his victim's scream.[16] Under torture, neither one's body nor one's voice belongs to the self. Thus, as Orwell understood, the objective of torture is not to "obtain information" but to secure power by arrogating the other's capacity for speech: "We are not interested in those stupid crimes you have committed. . . . The object of torture is torture. The object of power is power."[17]

This fundamental insight also guides Timothy Snyder's analysis of the mechanisms of Hitler's and Stalin's totalitarian regimes. In his influential study *Bloodlands: Europe between Hitler and Stalin*, Snyder shows, for example, that the unparalleled effectiveness and speed with which Stalin consolidated absolute power depended on his ability to implement torture. In July 1937, for instance, in fulfillment of Order 00447, "On the Operations to Repress Former Kulaks, Criminals, and Other Anti-Soviet Elements," thousands of individuals were arrested and forced to confess that they were enemies of the Soviet state. According to Snyder, "Confessions were elicited by torture. The NKVD and other police organs applied the 'conveyor method,' which meant uninterrupted questioning day and night," until the individual admitted his or her "guilt."[18] The fact that the main goal of torture is not extracting information but maintaining absolute domination over other human beings has been widely recognized by opponents of torture. In that sense, the violence of torture is ultimately gratuitous; in the words of Auschwitz survivor Primo Levi, such violence is "an end in itself, with the sole purpose of inflicting pain, occasionally having a purpose, yet always redundant, always disproportionate to the purpose itself."[19] Even interrogation experts concede that, insofar as a suspect will say anything the torturers want to hear in order to stop the pain, torture is one of the least effective tools for obtaining reliable information.

The Howl and Human Rights

When a person's capacity for language is destroyed because his or her body is subjected to unbearable pain and degradation, the voice, that is, a person's animal side, which marks him or her as bare life, comes to the fore as a scream or a howl, something *normally* referred to as prelinguistic behavior or animal sounds. With this norm governing how we conceive of what it means to be human, the discourse of human rights, grounded in this metaphysical conception of humanity, reaches an impasse when confronted with a torture victim's cry of pain. The discourse of human rights presupposes that a person is free to use language, that is, to employ it as a tool to communicate meanings or to withhold them. In extreme circumstances, this freedom can be suspended or curtailed but never ultimately revoked. Thus by insisting on human dignity and inalienable rights, including the right to free speech, the UN Convention against Torture enshrines the definition that a human being possesses language which he or she is fundamentally free to use.[20] This definition, however, takes no account of the howl, the nonverbal expression of pain that erupts from a tortured subject, which is usually described as inhuman or as an animal sound. Robbed of the ability to use words, an individual is forced to surrender his or her humanity, to become a mere animal with no language. But the tortured person—especially when his or her howl is in full cry—is neither inhuman nor merely animal. Thus, contrary to traditional metaphysical conceptions, torture reveals the impossibility of a clear distinction between the human and the animal. With the howling victim of torture at its center, the very conception of the human must be reevaluated and rectified.

A fundamental rethinking of what it means to be human, insofar as human beings engage in linguistic behavior, might help us confront and correct the impotence of international efforts to eradicate torture. But the defense of human rights and, in particular, the right to linguistic competence and freedom must be more radical than the solutions proposed by advocates who demand restitution and reaffirmation of the right to linguistic competence and freedom. Efforts to eliminate torture cannot be credible unless they bring focused attention to the howl, to the desperate and disheartening cries of pain that torture intensifies. This focus keeps the spotlight where it belongs: not on a person's rational power to use language and create meaning but on his or her vulnerability to torturous violence.

Agamben's analysis of bare life exposes the failure of a definition of the human based on possession of rational language. It also helps to show some of the steps necessary for effective resistance to the infliction of torture. To fully break through the impasse that stymies human rights discourse about torture, however, Agamben's insights need to be supplemented by Emmanuel Levinas's ethics of responsibility for the other. Levinas rightly underscores that the relationship between human existence and language is fundamentally ethical.

Useless Suffering

In his essay "Useless Suffering," Levinas conceives of the ethical subject through the lens of the phenomenology of pain. This focus shows the pain of "useless suffering" to be irremediable, shocking, and incommunicable. Scarry confirms that insight: "Pain is a pure physical experience of negation, an immediate sensory rendering of 'against,' of something being against one, and of something one must be against. Even though it occurs within oneself, it is at once identified as 'not oneself,' 'not me,' as something so alien that it must right now be gotten rid of."[21] Extreme suffering, says Levinas, is "worse than death"; oddly enough, this observation has been supported by statements from perpetrators of torture. For instance, as specified in the CIA's training manual for interrogators, while the fear of pain must be induced in the subject, "the threat of death has been found to be worse than useless."[22]

Thus intense physical suffering exceeds what can be absorbed and meaningfully processed by consciousness. The sheer evil of pain, its utter negativity, renders useless a person's efforts to put pain "to work," that is, to assign it a purpose or a higher meaning. And *yet*, says Levinas, exactly because the suffering is "pain in its undiluted malignity, suffering for nothing," because the pain is absurd and unmasterable, it has interhuman, ethical meaning in that the other's pain can pry open my egoistic shell. Identifying useless suffering, "*a moan, a cry, a groan or a sigh . . . the original call for aid*," beckons me to act on my basic ethical obligation to help my neighbor.[23] Another's pain can—indeed it must—jolt me out of self-complacency and indifference. The compassion evoked by inherently meaningless suffering does not cancel that suffering's absurdity but does resist it. Meanwhile, if my compassionate resistance causes suffering in me, that suffering, says Levinas, suffering for the suffering of someone else, has immense significance.[24]

In "a moan, a cry," the suffering of the other is "ear piercing" and shatters my deafness to the other's misery. The cry breaks through what Levinas calls the Said, demolishing the word constructs that seek to justify the cry and revealing that such attempts are, at best, rationalizations of indifference. Instead, the suffering of the other demands my response and *solicits me as a witness*. As Scarry notes, however, the tortured subject's suffering is intended to be an unwitnessed event. The torturer's aim includes rendering the victims' screams pointless by ensuring that they will not be heard by compassionate witnesses and thus acknowledged as an expression of human suffering.[25]

Unlike so many of their predecessors, who inflicted torture in public spectacles, contemporary torturers—inflicting atrocities in secret, denying them in public—want no truth-telling witnesses. Nevertheless, their aims do not prevail, at least not entirely. Joel Filártiga, a Paraguayan physician and human rights activist whose seventeen-year-old son Joelito was tortured to death, took some consolation when he underscored that "the dead count when they leave a testimony," that is, when, in spite of the torturer's suppression, cries of pain are heard.[26] The impact of witnessing torture can produce varied forms of resistance. Antonia García, a tenacious opponent of the Spanish dictator Francisco Franco, provides a remarkable example. Having witnessed torture, including the suffering of a mother forced to watch the brutal torture of her son, García vowed that "no human being would ever suffer because of me. No matter what was done to me, I wouldn't say a word."[27] Although she was herself subsequently tortured until her tormentors grew weary, she never uttered a word that might betray others. García's exceptional ability to withstand pain did not stem from some abstract ideal of courage based on the premise of human dignity; rather, witnessing the anguish of another person resulted in a resolution never to contribute, however involuntarily, to another's suffering, regardless of the consequences to herself. In yet another case, Brazilian police inflicted torture on a young man named Murilo Pinto da Silva. He was forced to stand for hours on the sharp edges of open cans. Nevertheless, at the end of a particularly harsh day, he "felt calm, at peace. He knew that, after today, whatever the provocation or the justice of his cause, he would never hurt another human being."[28]

Witnessing Torture

As glimpsed in the examples above, witnessing torture, even enduring it, can intensify ethical responsibility to oppose that atrocity and the political aims invoked to justify it. Judith Butler's *Precarious Life* advances reflection about such responsibility.[29] In the political sphere, she explains, that responsibility entails envisaging "a dimension of political life that has to do with exposure to violence and our complicity in it, with our vulnerability to loss and the task of mourning that follows, and with finding a basis for community in these conditions."[30] Butler expands Levinas's emphasis on the relationship between the self and the other by emphasizing a sociopolitical network within which we are exposed to others who continuously "claim us" and whose losses we grieve. In a political space conceived primarily in terms of interrelationality of selves, *who* we are entails being implicated "in lives that are not our own."[31] On the basis of this essential vulnerability, of being "laid bare" and "given over to the touch of the other," which "signifies primary helplessness and need,"[32] Butler defends a reorientation in politics founded upon responsibility for the physical lives of one another. Arguing against modern states' biopolitical managing of populations, Butler concludes that "to come up against what functions, for some, as a limit case of the human is a challenge to rethink the human."[33] In our times, she contends, this "limit case" includes the "bestialization" of persons in detention camps. Specifically, Butler has in mind a widely publicized photograph from the Abu Ghraib prison in Iraq, where, in 2003, American military and intelligence personnel tortured prisoners in multiple ways, including sexual abuse. In the photograph, military specialist Lynndie England holds a detainee on a leash.[34] Butler observes that this infamous image of the dehumanizing treatment of prisoners presents us with "a figure of the animal against which the human is defined."[35]

Circling us back to issues raised earlier in this chapter, Butler's recognition of the threshold at which the common definition of the human must be questioned underscores the failure of the metaphysical conception of the human as the animal with a capacity for language (*logos*). In stark opposition to Levinas's claim that "a cry, a moan" is interhuman, that metaphysical definition *excludes* from the human realm the cry of pain— the acoustic expression of extreme suffering that reduces a person to mere flesh. Although Agamben does not explicitly make this particular connection in his work, it is in the Nazi camps that the inadequacy of the definition of a person as a speaking being was first revealed, since it was there that "having language" became an inconsequential and insufficient condition for being human. Describing this frighteningly new human condition, Primo Levi asks, "Consider if this is a man / Who works in the mud . . . / Who fights for a scrap of bread,"[36] and he adds that this degradation of the human was inseparable from the fact that, in Auschwitz, "use of the word to communicate thought, this necessary and sufficient mechanism for man to be man, had fallen into disuse."[37] Nevertheless, the human being, though defaced and degraded, was still human—not merely animal—in spite of being bereft of language.

In detention camps, as previously in the Nazi camps, "bare life" results when the prisoner is held *incommunicado* and subjected to torture. What is produced is "a legally unnameable and unclassifiable being," that is, a being whose name does not bind him to any order of belonging: to the state, nation, land, or religion.[38] This radical unnameability of a human being who has been reduced to bare life is indicated in the title of Jacobo Timerman's aforementioned memoir, *Prisoner without a Name, Cell without a Number.* Timerman and countless others among Argentina's "disappeared" were condemned to being nameless. The unnameability epitomized the condition of being deprived of language and reduced to mere voice that does not have a word. In reflecting on the status of prisoners like Timerman, it is crucial, therefore, that we not overlook the utterly dehumanizing and lethal significance of the expression that they are being held *incommunicado.* Implied in the definition of *incommunicado* as "being without the means or right of communicating with others" is the expropriation of the prisoner's voice.

Based on Agamben's political critique of the exclusionary nature of the definition of the human as the animal that possesses language, we must conclude that this definition is an anthropocentric fiction that seeks to establish the essence of the human as distinct from, and dominant over, the animal. Its correlate is the reduction of a person's "mere" voice to an animal sound, which preexists meaningful language. This fiction works to "bestialize," that is, to dehumanize the human. But torture reveals the incoherence of this logic. To exclude the cry of pain, the howl, from the definition of the human is to deny the torture victim recognition as a human being and to consent to his or her status as less than human. If torture is to be effectively resisted, the other's anguished expression of pain must be heard as the ethical foundation of language rather than as prelinguistic behavior that reduces the human to the status of animal. The other's cry of pain, the howl, is useless to her or him, but it is and must be immensely meaningful to me, to us, as an urgent expression of the other's plea for help, a plea that makes and holds me—and you—accountable. This ethical claim must be enacted in the political sphere. As Juan E. Méndez puts it, "Torture will be abolished only when all of us make ourselves responsible for it; for abolishing it and for enforcing its prohibition."[39] This task is urgent because, in Jean Améry's words, "somewhere, someone is crying out under torture. Perhaps in this hour, this second."[40]

CONTRIBUTORS' QUESTIONS FOR DOROTA GLOWACKA

1. Your essay emphasizes that the screams and howls of the individual undergoing torture are the screams and howls of a being who continues to be fully human. You argue that to maintain the dignity of such persons, whose existence under torture is epitomized by the scream or howl, we must rethink what defines us as uniquely human. In particular, you contend, the definition of the human being as "an animal that possesses language" must be questioned. Such definition, you seem to imply, would facilitate torture because its emphasis on language tends "to exclude the cry of pain from the definition of the human" and thereby denies "the torture victim recognition as a human being." Captive to a metaphysical conception of humankind as fundamentally capable of language, those who would condemn torture—even human rights advocates—"enter," you say, "an impasse when confronted with a victim's cry of pain." But is it the case, as you seem to hold, that torture is inextricably linked to the scream or howl? Is it not the case that the pain and suffering of the tortured one, regardless of any kind of vocalization, constitutes the key for moral consideration of torture? Might the scream or howl be only a reaction of the tortured body in and of itself? Furthermore, if we possessed a better understanding about these matters, to what extent, if any, do you think torture would diminish in our world?

2. To shore up your argument that we must not exclude the cry of pain from our understanding of what constitutes a human being, you turn to Emmanuel Levinas to support the claim that "the other's anguished expression of pain must be heard as the ethical foundation of language rather than as prelinguistic behavior that reduces the human to the

status of animal." It is unclear, however, that Levinas can buttress your argument against language as definitive of the human being. For Levinas, what makes the human face *human* is that it *speaks*. Our humanity is manifest in the face-to-face relation, which is fundamentally and inescapably grounded in language. Might it thus be the case that the alleged "inhuman" cry is the human cry for help precisely because the human being is a speaking being? Perhaps the scream or howl implicates us, opens an ethical horizon, because it is the sound of the tearing of the word from the soul of the human being who is, in essence, a speaking being? While considering your responses to these questions, take us further in one more direction: As your essay emphasizes screams and words—during and after the Holocaust—that bear witness to the evil of torture, what do you most want your readers to remember and take to heart as they ponder what you have written here?

RESPONSE BY DOROTA GLOWACKA

Elaine Scarry wrote that the tortured subject's suffering has often been unwitnessed and thus remains unheard. But now we have witnessed and heard: some of the survivors of torture in American detention camps have found their voice; they wrote and published memoirs and poetry, gave interviews and testified in courts and at public inquiries.[41] The images from Abu Ghraib depicting soiled and bloodied bodies—bound, unnaturally twisted in stress positions, sexually humiliated—are now familiar, even too familiar. Recently, those images appeared again on the big screen: the torture extravaganza *Zero Dark Thirty* was an Oscar nominee for best picture in 2012. If few shuddered at the drawn-out scenes of atrocity, some Polish viewers were upset that one of the interrogation scenes took place in Gdańsk.

The face of the detainee can rarely be seen in film images. The framing cuts off the face, or it is covered by a hood that not only impedes breathing but obliterates social identity. Nevertheless, do torture's victims speak to me? Can I hear them suffer? Javal Davis, a military police sergeant stationed at Abu Ghraib, recalled that "for hours and hours, all you could hear was screaming and banging. I know the difference between somebody screaming because they are upset and somebody screaming because they are in pain. I know the difference."[42] What is the difference? What difference does the difference make? Sergeant Davis, for one, continued to perform his duties.

After fleeing from Nazi Germany, Hannah Arendt observed in 1943 that there was nothing inalienably human in a person's naked existence, and therefore nothing in that condition alone guaranteed one's human rights. Underscored by the "detainee crisis" manifest in the American government's difficulty in closing its detention center at Guantánamo and in "processing" the last detainees, Arendt's insight is increasingly recognized. Thus, it becomes imperative to question the philosophical foundations that make it possible for us to understand what it means to be human in terms that are exclusionary and that allow so many human beings to remain unprotected. This questioning does not depend on reading Aristotle, Agamben, or Levinas, although such study may be helpful. Problematic assumptions about what it means to be human permeate our lives, affecting not only what we consciously understand and act upon but also our unconscious perceptual habits, everyday gestures and attitudes, emotions and feelings.

I have located the insufficiency of our understanding of "the human" in the metaphysical conception of a human being as "an animal that possesses language." This definition establishes a boundary between the human and the rest of the animal kingdom. Theodor Adorno once said that, at least for Western consciousness, "nothing is more abhorrent than a reminder of man's resemblance to animals," adding that this was why, for the metaphysical thinking that I am challenging, "animals play virtually the same role as the Jews for fascism": they must be absolutely excluded from what counts as life worthy of living.[43] In an uncanny similarity, it was not just a matter of convenience that the inmates of Guantánamo were transported in cattle trucks, kept in wire-mesh cages that impeded movement, and forced into obedience by the use of specially trained dogs.[44] The detainees at Guantánamo knew that they were excluded from the protection of human rights. Thus, they pleaded to be granted at least the same "rights" as iguanas and tarantulas living on the base or the dogs in the camp because "a dog in the camp had a house, water, food, shade, and grass on which to exercise."[45] Tortured and detained at Guantánamo for five years before being released without explanation or apology in 2006, Murat Kurnaz noted in his memoirs that, in comparison to his detainment situation, "an animal has more space in its cage in a zoo and is given more to eat. I can hardly put into words what that actually means."[46]

It appears, therefore, that a distinction between the human and the animal based on humanity's capacity for language, for *logos*, can also create a border between me and another human being. That is, it favors thinking of others in terms of differences that, in certain circumstances, lead us to exclude them from membership in our own species and thus to withdraw compassion for them. It has made it possible for me to think of my body as a barrier that protects me from being invaded by others, and at the same time to deny that my body's vulnerability and mortality are what I have in common with the animal. In insisting that the animal cannot speak, I both distinguish myself from the animal and allow for the possibility of the bestialization of the human being in whom I do not perceive the same rational faculty.

Yet what if instead of asking whether the animal has *logos*, through which we grant ourselves privileges as humans, we start with a different query, posed by Jeremy Bentham at the end of the eighteenth century: "What else is it that should trace the insuperable line [between human and animal]? Is it the faculty of reason or perhaps the faculty of discourse? The question is not, Can they *reason*? nor, Can they *talk*? but, Can they *suffer*?"[47] It is in this question that I located the kernel of Levinas's ethical conception of language. My capacity for language originates in my ability to hear and recognize the other's cry of pain. Grounded in the vulnerability of my own body to pain, that ability precedes conceptualization of pain in words. Prior to my sense of myself as a singular being, I am immersed in a dense web of affective and sensory attachments with others, many of whom I will not even know. From the moment I am born, and even before my birth, others co-constitute me, and I cannot become human except in this intimacy with others. Those relationships entail that I am always exposed to the pain of the other. Since I always become human with another, my own being is shattered and my humanity crushed when the other is violated, degraded, and exposed to suffering.[48] Levinas's reflection on absolute alterity does not extend to the animal: the other to whom I am responsible is always a human other. Yet rethinking the human with Levinas, starting from my absolute obligation to respond to the other's pain—the obligation that is undeclinable because it constitutes me not only as a rational self but also as a suffering body— could allow us to overcome the ultimately dehumanizing, even deadly, limitations of metaphysical anthropocentrism.

The tortured, humiliated body that I conceptualize as animal-like is a dumb body: I cringe either in disgust or in sympathy, but I do not hear it speak. But this body speaks to me nevertheless, and it speaks to me from within my own capacity for pain. Shortly before her deportation to Auschwitz, the Jewish poet Gertrud Kolmar wrote, "You hear me speak. But do you hear me feel?"[49] Her question points to what I mean by bearing witness to the howl. If I listen, I can hear the tortured body feel, whether that person's howl is literally audible to me or not. The howl sears me also when I see the brute images of torture, just as, if I look, I see a human face rather than a piece of burlap when water is poured over it, gagging the tortured, waterboarded victim to the point of experiencing drowning. Levinas suggests that the other's gagging interrupts my breathing. In a way, *I* find myself gasping under the hood. Bearing witness to the howl does not necessarily mean that I must hear the other's cry of pain. It is enough to know that somewhere, even now, torture is being inflicted and that, in one way or another, a human being is calling my name by crying out, "I am afflicted."[50]

The sound of affliction implicates me in the other's pain and, from within my own body, makes it impossible for me to remain indifferent. But we will not hear what tortured bodies feel and say unless and until we break through the metaphysical deafness that blocks our listening and our discerning that the howl of the tortured ones, in all of its many forms, is profoundly human. To the extent that the howl is heard, really heard deep down, the injustice of torture and the implausibility of its justification will evoke the resistance that they so much deserve.

NOTES

The question of what happens to speech under conditions of torture was suggested to me by my former student, Sara Thaw, who wrote her honors thesis on this topic under my supervision. I thank Sara for allowing me to develop her idea in this chapter.

1   The two quotations in this sentence are, first, from Alan Dershowitz, excerpts from his *Why Torture Works* and, second, from Keith Atkinson, "The Torturer's Tale," both in *The Phenomenon of Torture: Readings and Commentary*, ed. William F. Schulz (Philadelphia: University of Pennsylvania Press, 2007), 235, 108.

2   Agamben explains that such "inclusive exclusion" of bare life from the political has been enabled by the legal concept of the state of exception, which allows for curtailment of civil liberties and suspension of habeas corpus. Agamben's examples include not only Hitler's declaration of the state of emergency after the Reichstag fire in 1933 and the subsequent Enabling Act but also President George W. Bush's implementation of the National Emergencies Act in the United States after the attacks of 9/11.

3   Giorgio Agamben, *Homo Sacer: Sovereign Power and Bare Life*, trans. Daniel Heller-Roazen (Stanford, CA: Stanford University Press, 1998), 8.

4   Giorgio Agamben, *The Open: Man and* Animal, trans. Kevin Attell (Stanford, CA: Stanford University Press, 2004), 35.

5   Giorgio Agamben, *State of Exception*, trans. Kevin Attell (Chicago: University of Chicago Press, 2005), 60.

6   See Anna Mieszkowska, *Matka dzieci Holocaustu: Historia Ireny Sendlerowej* Warszawa: Muza SA., 2005), 196. Translation mine.

7   Jean Améry, *At the Mind's Limits: Contemplations by a Survivor on Auschwitz and Its Realities*, trans. Sidney Rosenfeld and Stella P. Rosenfeld (Bloomington: Indiana University Press, 1980), 36.

8   "'They've Ruined My Life': Torture Survivor Maher Arar Recalls How U.S. Sent Him to Syria Where He Was Jailed and Tortured for 10 Months," *Democracy Now!*, February 27, 2006, http://www.democracynow.org/2006/2/27/theyve_ruined_my_life _torture_survivor. See also Jules Lobel, "Extraordinary Rendition and the Constitution: The Case of Maher Arar," *Review of Litigation* 28, no. 2 (2008): 479–500.

9   Jacobo Timerman, *Prisoner without a Name, Cell without a Number*, trans. Toby Talbot (New York: Alfred A. Knopf, 1981), 33.

10 George Orwell, *1984*, in *The Penguin Complete Novels of George Orwell* (London: Penguin Books, 1983), 879.

11 Elaine Scarry, excerpt from *The Body in Pain*, in Schulz, ed., *The Phenomenon of Torture*, 174.

12 Timerman, *Prisoner without a Name*, 32.

13 Améry, *At the Mind's Limits*, 33.

14 Scarry, in Schulz, ed., *The Phenomenon of Torture*, 174.

15 Améry, *At the Mind's Limits*, 40.

16 Ibid., 35.

17 Orwell, *1984*, 889, 895.

18 Timothy Snyder, *Bloodlands: Europe between Hitler and Stalin* (New York: Basic Books, 2010), 82.

19 Primo Levi, *The Drowned and the Saved*, trans. Raymond Rosenthal (New York: Summit Books, 1988), 106.

20 United Nations Convention against Torture and Other Cruel, Inhuman or Degrading Treatment or Punishment, December 10, 1984, http://www.un.org/documents /ga/res/39/a39r046.htm.

21 Scarry, in Schulz, ed., *The Phenomenon of Torture*, 172.

22 Central Intelligence Agency (CIA), "Coercive Techniques" (from the CIA's *Human Resource Exploitation Training Manual*) in Schulz, ed. *The Phenomenon of Torture*, 159.

23 Emmanuel Levinas, "Useless Suffering," in *Entre Nous: Thinking-of-the-Other* (New York: Columbia University Press, 1998), 98, 93. Emphasis mine.

24 Ibid., 94.

25 Scarry, in Schulz, ed., *The Phenomenon of Torture*, 174.

26 Quoted in Richard Pierre Claude, excerpt from "The Case of Joelito Filártiga and the Clinic of Hope," in Schulz, ed., *The Phenomenon of Torture*, 331.

27 Antonia García, "I Have Nothing to Say," in Schulz, ed., *The Phenomenon of Torture*, 98.

28 John Drolshagen, excerpt from *The Winter Soldier Investigation: An Inquiry into American War Crimes*, in Schulz, ed., *The Phenomenon of Torture*, 131.

29 Judith Butler, *Precarious Life: The Powers of Mourning and Violence* (London: Verso, 2004).

30 Ibid., 19.

31 Ibid., 28.

32 Ibid., 32.

33 Ibid., 90.

34 For the photo as well as commentary about Lynndie England herself, see "Iraq War 10 Years Later: Where Are They Now? Lynndie England (Abu Ghraib)," *NBC News*, March 19, 2013, http://worldnews.nbcnews.com/_news/2013/03/19/17373769-iraq-war-10-years-later-where-are-they-now-lynndie-england-abu-ghraib.

35 Butler, *Precarious Life*, 78.

36 Primo Levi, *Survival in Auschwitz*, trans. Stuart Woolf (New York: Simon and Schuster, 1996), 11.

37 Levi, *The Drowned and the Saved*, 91.

38 Agamben, *State of Exception*, 3.

39 Juan E. Méndez, "Foreword," in Schulz, ed., *The Phenomenon of Torture*, xvii.

40 Améry, *At the Mind's Limits*, 24.

41 Andreja Zevnik argues, however, that despite these powerful speech acts on the part of the former detainees, for the most part torture testimony falls into the domain of the "unspeakable." The dominant power structures control who counts as a speaking subject, and from that perspective, detainees—present and former—fall under an "uninhabitable appellation" of "terrorist" or "al Qaeda," terms that "capture" and ban them from the domain of moral acceptability. Even though the detainees deny such allegations, their claims that they are testifying truthfully about their injury are undermined and deprived of telling power. See Andreja Zevnik, "Becoming-Animal, Becoming-Detainee: Encountering Human Rights Discourse in Guantanamo," *Law and Critique* 22, no. 2 (2011): 167. See also Nina Philadelphoff-Puren, "Hostile Witness: Torture Testimony in the War on Terror," *Life Writing* 5, no. 2 (2008): 219.

42 *Standard Operating Procedure*, directed by Errol Morris (Participant Productions, 2008), at 53 min. This film explores the significance of the torture-related photographs taken by Americans at Abu Ghraib in 2003.

43 Quoted in John Sanbonmatsu, ed., *Critical Theory and Animal Liberation* (Lanham, MD: Rowman and Littlefield, 2011), 10.

44 See, for instance, the film *The Road to Guantánamo*, directed by Michael Winterbottom (Revolution Films Production, 2006).

45 Testimony of Jamal Al-Harith, quoted in Zevnik,"Becoming-Animal, Becoming-Detainee," 157.

46 Murat Kurnaz, *Five Years of My Life: An Innocent Man in Guantanamo*, trans. Jefferson Chase (New York: Palgrave Macmillan, 2008), 99.

47 Jeremy Bentham, *An Introduction to the Principles of Morals and Legislation*, in *The Works of Jeremy Bentham* (Edinburgh: William Tait, 1838), 143.

48 I am guided here by Judith Butler's conceptions of "precarity" and "grievability." See her *Frames of War: When Is Life Grievable?* (London: Verso, 2010).

49 Quoted in John K. Roth, *Holocaust Politics* (Louisville, KY: Westminster John Knox Press, 2001), 57.

50 Sami Al Haj, "Humiliated in the Shackles," in *Poems from Guantánamo: The Detainees Speak*, ed. Marc Falkoff (Iowa City: University of Iowa Press, 2007), 42. Sami Al Haj was imprisoned and tortured in Afghanistan and then sent to Guantánamo.

IS TORTURE JUSTIFIABLE?

P rofessional ethicists, along with laypersons interested in moral issues, are intrigued by the seemingly eternal search for an absolute or unconditioned moral judgment. In the course of this search, key questions demand responses: Are all values relative or can we legitimately posit some moral judgments as absolute? Is every moral conviction subject to conditions of time and place: the epoch in which it is formulated and the culture in which it is embedded? Does social context necessarily determine our value judgments? And if so, do the individual and society at large lack that secure foundation—absolute standards—upon which, according to many thinkers, any firm moral compass must be established? These queries continue to haunt ethical inquiry.

Arguably no better stage exists upon which to view debates regarding "the absolute and the relative" than those settings in which the justifiability of torture is examined. This book, part 2 in particular, is a setting of that kind. The contributors to part 2 would no doubt agree with political philosopher Henry Shue's observation regarding torture that "no other practice except slavery is so universally and unanimously condemned in law and human convention."[1] Yet *ethical* debate on the absolute nature of the evil of torture continues; indeed, such debates have become more widespread in recent years, especially in the post-9/11 world. Some thinkers are inclined to engage in a cost-benefit analysis—the epitome of relativist thinking—regarding whether or not to advocate for the legitimacy of torture. Are there not contexts, they ask, in which torture is permissible, perhaps even morally necessary?[2] The setting most often cited is the "ticking bomb" scenario, in which the good of the many is thought to be served by the torture of an individual who may reveal knowledge of harm intended for multitudes. Philosopher Michael Walzer is among those who argue that there are dire situations in which governments—in the endeavor to translate ethical concerns into law—must "dirty their hands" by allowing acts of torture that in ordinary circumstances would be deemed morally unjustified, indeed reprehensible.[3] The moral quandaries surrounding the question of torture as an absolute wrong are alive and well.

Certain theorists, however, hold that discussion of the right or wrong of torture does not have any place at all in the public sphere. Some so-called absolutists would claim that this section of the book—indeed, the book itself—should not have been written, since any public debate about the rightfulness of torture grants legitimacy to the idea that torture, at least in some instances, may be justified. Social theorist Slavoj Žižek, for example, goes so far as to argue that "essays . . . which do not advocate torture outright, [but] simply introduce it as a legitimate topic of debate, are even more dangerous than an explicit endorsement of torture."[4] Political scientist Jamie Mayerfield speaks about such debate as inevitably "endistancing" the reader from the reality of torture.[5]

Like all contributors to this book, the essayists in part 2 implicitly reject the lines of argument from Žižek and Mayerfield. Torture, they believe, should not be exempt from the Socratic spirit of dialogue and critique that informs the Western philosophical tradition and, hopefully, all ethical debate in the public arena. Indeed, careful Socratic discussion about torture is essential lest problematic arguments, euphemistic discourse, and outlooks that minimize suffering be left to prevail. The four essayists whose work constitutes part 2 refuse to be silent: they engage in a genuine ethical exploration of the legitimacy of torture.

At the outset of her chapter, Suzanne Brown-Fleming notes that "it cannot be assumed that direct awareness of torture will help to bring torturers to justice." She supports that point by examining Bishop Johann Baptist Neuhäusler's silence in the face of acts of torture he could not avoid seeing and hearing from his Nazi prison cell at Dachau concentration camp. Prior to his imprisonment, Neuhäusler showed no aversion to rendering moral judgments: he was a leader of the German Catholic Church, speaking out against Nazi anti-Christian measures. However, imprisoned where he could see and hear beatings and other forms of torture dealt out to prisoners—sometimes leading to their death—Neuhäusler offered no words or acts of protest. Brown-Fleming quotes Neuhäusler as saying that he was very sorry for "not being able to do anything."

Neuhäusler's silence during his imprisonment is easier to understand than his silence in the postwar period, which could be described as deafening. In any case, questions remain: Might he have utilized his special status as a public figure at Dachau to somehow register a protest against Nazi brutality? Instead of speaking out in defense of former Dachau camp guards accused, in the postwar period, of violating the laws of war, might Neuhäusler have served as a prosecution witness? Brown-Fleming claims that more work is needed on this issue, that her chapter "raises . . . more questions than it answers." Yet in response to her interlocutors' challenge to render a moral judgment of behavior, Brown-Fleming states that for her "that question does not feel like the right one." In its stead, her scholarly account of Neuhäusler's life prompts her to reflect on the Holocaust and, in particular, on her responsibility—as the granddaughter of a member of the Nazi Party—to act ethically. She concludes her chapter by posing a critically important question: "How will I act differently than my grandparents did and what will I do to repay the debt?"

Peter J. Haas continues on the path of moral inquiry in a chapter that explores both classical Judaism's discussion of torture and the debate on current practice in the State of Israel. Haas notes that neither the Hebrew Bible nor sources in rabbinic Judaism treat torture "in any systematic way." Although these texts address the dignity of the human being created in the image of God, it was not until Jews could exercise political control in a modern-day state that ethical issues about torture could emerge both with frequency and in depth. Haas claims that the tradition's perspective on human dignity is incorporated both in the Israel Defense Forces' Purity of Arms doctrine and in Israel's Basic Law: Human Dignity and Liberty. Easier to carry out in the abstract than on the battlefield, these moral proclamations were tested early in the current millennium. In response to the 2000 Palestinian Intifada and the first Lebanon War (2006), restraints on the use of torture during interrogations were loosened. Haas quotes law professor David Rosen: "These desperate times call for desperate measures."

Arguments concerning both the morality and the legality of torture have raged—and continue to rage—within contemporary Israel and in the diaspora.[6] Haas notes that "while the growing debate does not directly challenge the general principle of upholding human dignity, it does strongly suggest that in the world of life-and-death terrorism, the preservation of the state of the Jewish people is taking precedence." Fearing a recurrence of catastrophe, survivors of the Holocaust—and younger Israelis, who, in Haas's view, also see themselves in some sense as "survivors"— have helped set the scene for advocacy of torture in certain situations. Haas concludes by noting that the lessons of the Holocaust for a discussion of the morality of torture are complex: the teaching that the "other" must be respected conflicts with the teaching that never again must the Jewish people prove defenseless against those who would attempt to destroy them. Haas leaves the reader acutely aware of how these conflicting views complicate an already complex moral quandary surrounding the justifiability of torture.

Didier Pollefeyt addresses the justifiability of torture head-on. He begins by outlining the moral debate between deontologists (absolutists) and consequentialists (proportionalists). The former, as we have noted, admit no exceptions to the prohibition of torture; the latter most often refer to the "ticking bomb" hypothesis to demonstrate that, in very rare circumstances, torture can be legitimized. Pollefeyt argues that as a Catholic theologian and as a human being striving to live a moral existence, he must denounce torture in "almost every instance." His position, however, opposes any a priori argument that would condemn *all* justifications for torture. Against those who might claim that a proportionalist position on torture would undermine respect for all human life, Pollefeyt claims that he, like absolutists, is motivated by that very fundamental respect. Where he differs from the absolutist position is in his sensitivity to those extremely rare instances when the value of respecting the sanctity of one life comes up against the value of potential preservation of *the lives of many*. In (admittedly) extremely rare ticking bomb scenarios, those who are suspected of having information that, acted upon, might save many lives become, in Pollefeyt's eyes, legitimate targets of torture. In his attempt to preserve the *spirit* of absolutism while denying the *letter*, Pollefeyt notes five "strict criteria" that must be met before extracting information by means of torture could ever be legitimate. He wants the reader to understand that in his view, "torture is always an evil, but sometimes a lesser evil."

Pollefeyt grounds his analysis by examining the ethics of torture in light of the Holocaust. Citing the absolutist views of Nazi perpetrators, he notes "how vulnerable 'ethics' is to manipulation by those in power who are also imbued with a fixed ideology." The Holocaust teaches us that an ideologically driven absolutist ethics can be turned against the value of preserving human life: it can be co-opted into condoning its opposite. Yet Pollefeyt wishes "to stretch the proportionalist argument so far that it becomes almost deontological in nature." He concludes his essay by reiterating his central contention that torture cannot be condemned a priori, that—with fear and trembling—the evil of the torture of one person must be weighed against the potential murder of many. Pollefeyt admits that the legitimate use of torture is more a theoretical than a practical matter because only circumstances extremely rare and urgent would make torture ethically permissible. Legitimate torture remains a possibility—but, paradoxically, an "impossible possibility."

Sarah K. Pinnock's essay concludes part 2. Her chapter begins with a provocative claim: "Defenders of theodicy, the attempt to reconcile God's power and goodness with even the most horrendous evil, are allies . . . of the defenders of torture." Both theodicy and torture, she contends, justify suffering for the sake of some greater good; both understand suffering as merely a means to an end and thus as granting meaning to human torment. Pinnock contends that instrumentalist thinking is integral both to the defense of theodicy as an intellectual undertaking and to the defense of torture as a physical and political act.

The Holocaust grounds Pinnock's reflection. After noting how several Holocaust theologians reject theodicy in responding to the Third Reich's genocide against the Jews, she contrasts the witness to torture of several Holocaust survivors with Nazi justifications of torture as the means to the "higher good" expressed in a "Nazi ethic." In Pinnock's view, the Holocaust "erodes the defense of both torture and theodicy because it confirms . . . not only the disproportionality between suffering and justice but also the sheer uselessness of suffering." Her chapter concludes with reflection on the current debate about torture in the United States.

Far from removing their readers from the traumatic realities of torture, the chapters in part 2 plunge deeply, sensitively, and carefully into issues that are fraught with danger. About that danger there can be no doubt. But the greater danger would be to avoid the persistent and probing inquiry invited by these chapters.

NOTES

1   Henry Shue, "Torture," in *Torture: A Collection*, ed. Sanford Levinson (Oxford: Oxford University Press, 2004), 47.

2   See, for example, Alan Dershowitz, "Torture Reasoning," in Levinson, ed., *Torture: A Collection*, 257–80.

3   See, for example, Michael Walzer, "Political Action: The Problem of Dirty Hands," *Philosophy and Public Affairs* 2, no. 2 (1973): 160–80.

4   Slavoj Žižek, *Welcome to the Desert of the Real: Five Essays on September 11 and Related Dates* (London: Verso, 2002), 103.

5   Jamie Mayerfield, "In Defense of the Absolute Prohibition of Torture," *Public Affairs Quarterly* 22, no. 2 (2008): 112.

6   For illustrations of the range of Jewish views on these matters, see Shlomo M. Brody, "Does Jewish Law Allow Torture?" *Tablet*, December 12, 2014, http://tabletmag.com/scroll/187646/does-jewish-law-allow-torture. Also relevant are the positions taken by the Religious Action Center of Reform Judaism, available at http://www.rac.org/position-reform-movement-torture.

4

Johann Baptist Neuhäusler
and Torture in Dachau

SUZANNE BROWN-FLEMING

By focusing on Bishop Johann Baptist Neuhäusler, a significant but ambiguous German Catholic leader, and his experience in the Nazi concentration camp at Dachau, this chapter employs historical analysis to identify dilemmas about torture during and after the Holocaust. The dilemmas include what to say about advocacy for the torturer instead of the tortured. As Neuhäusler's testimony reveals, it cannot be assumed that direct awareness of torture will help to bring torturers to justice, let alone prove sufficient to eliminate torture from human experience.

Background about Neuhäusler and his circumstances in the Third Reich is necessary to set the scene. Cathedral canon (*Domkapitular*) and doctor of theology Johann Baptist Neuhäusler was born on January 27, 1888, in Eisenhofen, and ordained a priest at the age of twenty-five in Munich, Germany, where he would remain for his long career. He became canon of the Munich Catholic Cathedral in 1932 at the age of forty-four.[1] On February 4, 1941, the Munich Gestapo imprisoned Neuhäusler for ten days. On February 14, Gestapo officials transferred him to the prison Berlin-Alexanderplatz, where he remained until May 24. On that day, Neuhäusler was transferred to Sachsenhausen-Oranienburg and assigned prisoner number 37796.[2] From Sachsenhausen, he was sent to Dachau. Neuhäusler arrived in Dachau on July 11, 1941 at 5:45 p.m., where he was assigned prisoner number 26680.[3] He remained incarcerated in Dachau until April 1945.

Dachau, the only concentration camp that existed from the beginning to the end of the Nazi dictatorship, received its first one hundred prisoners on March 22, 1933.[4] Torture began within months of the SS takeover of Dachau on April 11. By the end of May 1933, "12 prisoners had been either tortured to death or driven to commit suicide."[5] Torture was regulated in Dachau. The camp's first commandant, SS-Oberführer Theodor Eicke, issued a manual in June 1933 "detailing methods of torture to be used as punishment."[6] During Neuhäusler's incarceration, Dachau had three commandants: Alex Piorkowski (February 1940–September 1942), Martin Weiss (September 1943–November 1943), and Eduard Weiter (November 1943–April 1945).[7]

Early in the Nazi period, Neuhäusler acted to preserve the integrity of the Catholic Church. Few priests protested as frequently and publicly against Nazi violations of the 1933 Concordat between the Vatican and the Third Reich, incursions into German Catholic life and practice, and Nazi ideology as incompatible with Catholicism.[8] Following Hitler's accession to the chancellorship on January 30, 1933, it was to Neuhäusler that Cardinal Michael Faulhaber of Munich gave the task of creating "a central collection point from which to disseminate information about the [Nazi] regime's anticlerical and anti-Christian activities."[9] At great personal risk, Neuhäusler established a courier service to disseminate to Austria, the Netherlands, and Rome the information he gathered on violations of the Concordat. Mark Ruff notes that Neuhäusler's "small network of trustworthy couriers worked to ensure his reports ultimately arrived in the hands of [Pope Pius XII], who personally arranged for their safekeeping."[10]

After World War II, in 1947, Neuhäusler was appointed auxiliary bishop of the diocese of Munich-Freising and titular bishop of Calydon. He became the most active of all German Catholic prelates in efforts to commute the sentences of German war criminals convicted in the US Army ("Dachau") trials.[11] Neuhäusler was also the driving force behind construction of the Catholic chapel[12] on the Dachau site in 1960 and the 1963–64 construction of a Carmelite convent adjoining the camp wall.[13] Less discussed and studied are Neuhäusler's experiences in two Gestapo prisons and two concentration camps.

Neuhäusler's Status in Dachau

Inspired by Jan Domagała's *Ci, którzy przeszli przez Dachau* (Those who went through Dachau) (Warsaw: Pax, 1957), Neuhäusler wrote *Wie war das in Dachau? Ein Versuch, der Wahrheit näherzukommen* (What was it like in the concentration camp at Dachau? An attempt to come closer to the truth) in 1960,[14] and in 1967, *Amboss und Hammer* (Anvil and hammer).[15] Among other things, these writings document Neuhäusler's status in Dachau. As a so-called special prisoner (*Sonderhäftling*), a public figure kept as a hostage by the Nazi regime, Neuhäusler was confined to the "Bunker," the prison within the Dachau concentration camp, and as such, did not witness the daily life of the general camp. Nor were his living conditions comparable to those experienced by the majority of camp inmates. Harold Marcuse describes conditions for the so-called special prisoners in the Bunker as follows: "Their cells were not locked; they were allowed freedom of movement within the courtyard separating the Bunker from the nearby service building; their food came from the SS kitchen; and they were taken for walks."[16] Other Dachau special prisoners included Prince Frederick Leopold of Prussia, former Austrian chancellor Kurt von Schuschnigg, former president of the Reichsbank Hjalmar Schacht, Martin Niemöller,[17] and even one of the sons of the controversial Hungarian regent Miklós Horthy.[18]

Neuhäusler's testimony on behalf of Dachau commandant Martin Weiss corroborates the sense of separateness that Neuhäusler and the special prisoners had vis-à-vis other camp inmates. When asked whether he had the "opportunity to speak with the [regular] prisoners in the camp," Neuhäusler responded, "No." When asked whether he "heard from other prisoners in the camp," Neuhäusler responded, "A very few times only. If we went to the dentist, for instance, or if workers came to us to do something." He noted also that "we [special prisoners] were kept apart so much that during the first few months when we were brought to the hospital . . . for examinations it was in closed ambulances and when we were examined all prisoners had to leave the hospital." Neuhäusler also could have visitors. He testified that "more than twenty" of his nephews "were in the army and were permitted to visit when they were home on furlough." Visits generally were of an hour's duration or more, and he was permitted to receive "packages, medicines, and other things." He and the other special prisoners also had access to a doctor upon request.[19]

Additional advantages of Neuhäusler's special prisoner status stood in stark contrast to the deprivation and desperate plight of most camp inmates. Neuhäusler arrived in Dachau on July 11, 1941,[20] with a hat, coat, jacket, waistcoat, trousers, undershirt, underwear, two pairs of eyeglasses, and a pair of socks and shoes.[21] A suitcase with additional clothing and other items was shipped from Sachsenhausen to Dachau: it contained a jacket, waistcoat, pair of trousers, five shirts, four pairs of underwear, one pair of pajamas, sixteen handkerchiefs, one scarf, five pairs of socks, twenty-one [clerical] collars, three towels, one flashlight, three batteries, one box of pills [*Leopillen*], and a cache of letters. The suitcase arrived on July 29.[22] On August 9, camp officials recorded receipt of his watch and fob from Sachsenhausen on the previous day, which Neuhäusler turned over to one SS-Hauptscharfüher Busta on September 9.[23]

The next day, on September 10, the chief of administration (*Leiter der Verwaltung*) in Dachau requested that his colleagues in Sachsenhausen check block 58 for additional property belonging to Neuhäusler.[24] In less than two weeks, the Sachsenhausen administrative office responded with a memorandum listing the missing items: a cardigan, a pair of slippers, a comb, a wallet, five hairbrushes (three of which came in a case), eighteen books, a knife, a change purse, a dust cloth, and writing and sewing utensils.[25] These last missing items arrived in Dachau on October 8, 1941.[26]

Dachau Torture Heard and Seen

The Bunker, or camp prison, was much more than the area of confinement for special prisoners like Neuhäusler. It also was the place where SS guards "tortured individual prisoners to death or drove them to commit suicide."[27] As a Bunker prisoner, Neuhäusler could "see and hear much that happened in the 'Dark Cells' and 'Standing Cells'" in that building, and he could also see and hear "what happened in the yard during [his] first year [in the camp]."[28] Fellow special prisoner and Munich lawyer Josef Müller, who became the Bavarian minister of justice after the war, corroborated these observations, noting that "one of the worst aspects of [his] imprisonment [in the Bunker] was the use of some cells as torture chambers for ordinary inmates and the use of the courtyard as an execution range."[29]

Neuhäusler testified that while he had "only very little" opportunity to know "what was going on in the camp," he "heard beatings which were dealt out since our bunker was separated only by a little yard from the bath house where the beating was taking place," adding that he was "very sorry to say that we not only heard beatings but also the yelling of the prisoners, being able to hear what was going on and not being able to do anything." Especially in 1941 and 1942, he witnessed executions that "took place in the yard next to our yard."[30] He noted the "special poles" that were erected for this purpose and recollected feeling "horror" when he saw those poles and the "three signs" indicating they would be used on a given day. When executions took place, he added, "our cells were locked; a motor truck drove into the yard; the 'Hausl' (name given to the warder, who was a previously convicted prisoner) of the bunker was drunk in the evening; he received a bottle of strong liquor for his 'hangman's service' each time."[31]

Also near the Bunker was the site for "punishment at the stake," carried out in 1941 "on a spot near the Bunker where special posts had been set up." Neuhäusler, who would have seen this form of torture firsthand, wrote about it in the third person: "The punishment (the 'tree') took the following form: The hands of the condemned man were put behind his back, fastened with an iron chain around the wrists and then he was hung up on a hook at such a height that the heels did not touch the ground. According to regulation this punishment lasted one hour. It often happened . . . that he had to hang two hours or longer and was even beaten by the supervising SS-man."[32] In other cases, Neuhäusler could hear, but not see, prisoners being tortured. In describing corporal punishment "on the trestle"—meaning that the prisoner first was "tied in such a way that the upper part of the body lay horizontal and the legs dangled over the sides" and then whipped with leather whips soaked in water—Neuhäusler wrote, "I can hear the moans of the prisoners in my ears to this very day." As for their SS torturers, Neuhäusler recollected that for them "it was a real pleasure when the prisoners screamed, cried, sobbed or fainted from pain."[33]

The Nazi infliction of torture in Dachau's Bunker included the so-called dark cells and standing cells. Neuhäusler described their use as follows:

> To the corrective punishment a period of solitary confinement was also added. It lasted from three to forty-two days. A wooden plank bed served as couch. The confinement could be made stricter by darkening the cell. The worst punishment of all was the "standing bunker." In a room about the size of a telephone kiosk (30 x 30 inches)—I still remember well when it was built—the prisoner was compelled to stand three days and three nights and was given only bread and water; every fourth night he came into a normal cell, ate prisoners' fare and was allowed to sleep for one night on a plank bed. Such were the abominations that the prisoners had to bear from the sadistic Nazis.[34]

Neuhäusler added that torture included hunger and starvation. "The starving of the prisoners," he wrote, "took place so insidiously, so consistently and so systematically that even now one shivers to think of it."[35] While Neuhäusler himself experienced none of these things, he still testified that he felt himself to be "a prisoner without liberty and human dignity, without common human dignity and without my profession." Nevertheless, he noted, for him Dachau was "much better than the prisons of Berlin or Sachsenhausen."[36]

Neuhäusler would have only limited contact with Jewish prisoners in Dachau. In November 1941, most Jewish prisoners from camps in the so-called Greater German Reich were deported to Auschwitz, and only in spring 1944 were Jewish prisoners again sent in substantial numbers to Dachau and other subcamps within the Reich.[37] In his 1946 book *Kreuz und Hakenkreuz: Der Kampf des Nationalsozialismus gegen die katholische Kirche und der Kirchliche Widerstand* (Cross and swastika: The Nazi campaign against the Catholic Church and the church resistance), Neuhäusler included the persecution of Jews in his list of Nazi practices that ran counter to Christian principles.[38] In this two-volume work, he dedicated a section to anti-Jewish measures and speeches.[39] With regard to what he might have witnessed personally, we have no historical account. Meanwhile, a tension exists in *What Was It Like* between Neuhäusler's experience as a special prisoner in the Bunker and that of most Dachau prisoners, including many priests.[40] Memoirs and studies of priests incarcerated in Dachau note forms of torture specific to the nearly three thousand priests incarcerated there, most of them in barracks 26, 28, and 30.[41]

To write *What Was It Like*, Neuhäusler relied heavily on three accounts: the aforementioned *Those Who Went through Dachau* (Jan Domagała); Josef Joos's *Leben auf Widerruf: Begegnungen und Beobachtungen im K. Z. Dachau, 1941–1945* (Life is revoked: Encounters and observations in the Dachau Concentration Camp, 1941–1945), first published in 1946; and François Goldschmitt's five-volume work *Elsasser und Lothringer in Dachau* (Alsatian and Lorrainan prisoners in Dachau), published between 1945 and 1947. In some instances, Neuhäusler could scarcely believe what he read. Domagała, for example, wrote about a transport from Stutthof that reached Dachau on November 14, 1942. On its arrival, he observed, "one could see corpses of prisoners from which parts had been gnawed, because the leader of the transport, a depraved SS-man, had not allowed any food to be given to the prisoners during the journey." Citing this passage, Neuhäusler added,

"On reading this shocking report[,] especially the remark about 'gnawed corpses of the prisoners' . . . I was tempted to doubt if such a thing were at all possible even when hunger had driven the prisoners to the verge of insanity. But an eyewitness, Kohlhofer from Munich, confirmed the statement firmly."[42] Neuhäusler then went on to cite Joos's detailed and harrowing account of the November 1942 transport on which "six corpses were gnawed [and] on several parts of the body the bones were bare."[43]

Persisting Ambiguities, Lingering Dilemmas

Some aspects of Neuhäusler's experiences in Dachau are difficult to decipher. Fragmentary evidence from the holdings of the International Tracing Service (ITS) reveals that Neuhäusler received considerable financial support and regular disbursements. Typically, any money in a prisoner's possession on arrival in Dachau was taken by the camp administration and "credited" to the prisoner, who could draw fifteen Reichsmarks (RM) monthly. In 1942, a "coupon system" was introduced, and prisoners were no longer permitted to "have money in their possession." Monies in their accounts could only be used in the camp canteen.[44] The canteen stocked "beetroot jam, oatmeal, sauerkraut, dried vegetables, tinned mussels and fish, cucumbers, condiments [that were] inedible but avidly consumed," in addition to personal items such as "needles and thread, lotions, creams and perfumes." Few foodstuffs were available at all late in the war.[45]

It is unclear to what extent these regulations applied in Neuhäusler's specific circumstances. ITS-held documentation shows that from the beginning of his incarceration at Dachau, regular deposits ranging from 50 RM to as much as 640 RM were paid into Neuhäusler's account.[46] The disbursements he received ranged from 250 RM to as little as 20 RM.[47] He even received a 100 RM disbursement during his last month in Dachau.[48] By 1944–45, it is unclear what might or might not have been available to purchase with these apparently regular disbursements, and we have no record of how Neuhäusler might have tried to use them, or for what purpose, or, further, what he knew about the depositor.

Also difficult to decipher is how Neuhäusler's experiences in Dachau may have influenced his efforts to commute the sentences of German war criminals, including accused Holocaust perpetrators. Moreover, *What Was It Like* provides little insight about what drove him in the late 1940s to discredit some fellow prisoners. Nor does it explain a letter that Neuhäusler sent to five US congressmen in March 1948, which included statements such as the following regarding "professional witnesses" who allegedly testified for the prosecution in the US Army trials: "I had the impression that, generally speaking, the Nuremberg proceedings were justified, as they concerned those persons chiefly responsible. But there was great anxiety about the Dachau [trials], above all because some former concentration camp inmates appeared as 'professional witnesses,' housed, fed, clothed and so on for more than a year in the Dachau internment camp. In return they made statements at various trials that were strictly rejected by the defendants. But these were given credence and thus many death sentences resulted, the legality of which is very much questioned." Claiming that no fewer than fifty-eight "professional witnesses" testified for the prosecution in the US Army trials, Neuhäusler attached biographies of fourteen. Alleging that these former prisoners were communists, socialists, Jews, homosexuals, criminals, or some combination thereof, he depicted all of them as dishonest and untrustworthy.[49]

Even more puzzling is Neuhäusler's testimony on behalf of the Dachau commandant Martin Weiss, who was tried by the US Army in 1945. In comments notable for their brevity and for what was left unsaid, Neuhäusler testified that on the few occasions when prisoners came to the Bunker for a work assignment, "several times prisoners told us that things were better under [Weiss]." That remark was the entirety of Neuhäusler's specific testimony about Weiss, who governed the camp when some of the torture reported by Neuhäusler had been inflicted.[50] Weiss was sentenced to death by a US military court in 1945 and executed in Landsberg in 1946. In *What Was It Like*, Neuhäusler remembered Weiss:

> I mention the commandant Weiss out of gratitude and as proof that among the despots of the concentration camp there were also some with human feelings. He introduced many pleasant changes in the camp and checked personally if his regulations and orders were observed. He forbade the deliberate beating of the prisoners by the Capos and camp seniors, he personally inspected criminal reports, he himself determined the punishment and was present when it was carried out, lest abuses were introduced. . . . Often he also showed a fundamentally good heart to us "special prisoners" and procured manifold facilities for us. . . . [As inspector general] he did not permit the carrying out of Hitler's command to shell and burn the camp at Dachau together with its inmates on the night

of 28/29 April 1945 yet he was tragically sentenced to death and executed by the Allies after the war, presumably because he signed and executed death sentences which came from Berlin.[51]

Neuhäusler was also one of several Catholic and Protestant clerics, including Martin Niemöller,[52] to write an affidavit (*Eidesstattliche Erklärung*) for Karl Zimmermann, capo in barracks 3, Dachau's infirmary (*Krankenrevier*). The US Army tried Zimmermann in 1947 for "violation of the laws and usages of war" on the grounds that he "participated in and attended the execution of inmates by hanging" and "admitted that he attended executions and participated in them because of orders."[53] Former Dachau prisoner Stanislav Zámečnik, who worked in the infirmary and became a historian after the war,[54] described Zimmermann as "despicable and capable of anything."[55] Inmate Heinrich Stöhr testified that Zimmermann led "a group of the senior nurses . . . into the Bunker," where Neuhäusler was incarcerated, "once or twice weekly." There, Stöhr saw "Zimmerman and the SS-doctor [Hodapp] preparing the injections" used to murder tuberculosis patients from barracks 29. "The injections themselves were administered in a cell near the watch-post within the Bunker," Stöhr testified, "and I myself brought the corpses to the crematorium."[56] Zimmermann knowingly participated in falsifying cause-of-death documentation after inmates were murdered. Hermann Langbein recalled the case of block leader "Wagner," murdered on the order of the camp's Luftwaffe doctor. "In the evening I wrote a toe-tag for [Wagner] and his notification of death. Cause of Death: Heart and circulation failure due to stomach cancer. That was Zimmermann's order," Langbein stated.[57]

Neuhäusler acknowledged only limited contact with Zimmerman, stating that "we were quite strictly separated from the main camp and only entered the infirmary occasionally; rather, the capo of the infirmary, Mr. Zimmermann, came as often as necessary to us [in the Bunker]." From this limited perspective, wrote Neuhäusler, he could testify that Zimmermann "was correct and accommodating toward us and tried to help us to the best of his ability." Further, he wrote, "from our limited contact with the inmates of the main camp, I heard nothing unfavorable about Zimmermann, to the contrary, that circumstances improved [in the infirmary] as compared to his predecessors." Neuhäusler declined to participate in person at the trial due to his many responsibilities as auxiliary bishop.[58] Zimmermann was acquitted.[59]

This brief sketch ultimately raises more questions than it answers. Neuhäusler's accounts of Dachau torture heard and seen, plus his postwar outlook, involve persisting ambiguities and lingering dilemmas. How could such an outspoken opponent of Nazism and its torture defend Weiss, Zimmermann, other former Dachau camp guards, German field marshal Wilhelm List, and high-ranking SS figures such as Oswald Pohl, Paul Blobel, and Otto Ohlendorf?[60] Even when viewed in the broader context of the Catholic clemency campaign and political rehabilitation effort,[61] the fact that we have no satisfactory answer to this question illustrates how much scholarly work remains to be done to reconstruct the world-views and resulting decisions of individuals like Neuhäusler, who, at least in postwar circumstances, could have used their positions to advocate for the tortured rather than for the torturers.

CONTRIBUTORS' QUESTIONS FOR SUZANNE BROWN-FLEMING

1. Your essay about Johann Baptist Neuhäusler concludes by posing this question about him: "How could such an outspoken opponent of Nazism and its torture defend Weiss, Zimmermann, other former Dachau camp guards, German field marshal Wilhelm List, and high-ranking SS figures such as Oswald Pohl, Paul Blobel, and Otto Ohlendorf?" This query is one of many to be found in an essay that, in your words, "ultimately raises more questions than it answers." Yet it may be argued that this question is of a *different order* than others posed throughout the essay. We need you to speak further about this question because of its striking appearance at the end of your analysis. You rightly argue that "the fact that we have no satisfactory answer to this question illustrates how much scholarly work remains to be done to reconstruct the worldviews and resulting decisions made by individuals like Neuhäusler, who, at least in postwar circumstances, could have used their positions to advocate for the tortured rather than for the torturers." But is it just more "scholarly work"—or, if so, what kind—that will clarify what lies at the heart of your concluding question? For example, would further analysis of the *Weltanschauungen* of the time—including the postwar German outlook that sought clemency and amnesty for accused Nazi war criminals—absolve Neuhäusler of culpability for what he did, even if such research were to *explain* why

he acted as he did? Even though the postwar Protestant and Catholic Churches in Germany tried to rescue national autonomy and sought to rebuild their credibility, does it not remain the individual's responsibility to assess the dominant worldview and even, at times, to resist it? Ethical and historical analyses are not identical, but your readers would be helped if you responded to this question: What is your moral judgment of Neuhäusler's behavior?

2. You describe how Neuhäusler bore witness to acts of torture in the Dachau bunker in which he was imprisoned, as well as in the bunker yard adjoining his cell. How else might this "special prisoner" have responded to his witnessing of torture in Dachau? (Certainly his postwar documenting of the horrors of torture was itself an important act of witness.) Especially given the privileges that his special status in the camp gave him, what modes of resistance were available to him and to what extent did he use them? Even though he experienced himself as "without liberty and human dignity," do you think it could still be credible to say that Neuhäusler might have used his position to mitigate the suffering of his fellow prisoners or to take a stand against torture, even within the confines of his cell? As you consider such questions, what do you most want your reader to take away from your reflections about them?

RESPONSE BY SUZANNE BROWN-FLEMING

My own weighted history renders me unqualified to answer these questions. Since that is the case, the reader deserves an explanation about why this is so for me. My grandfather, Eduard Goldermann (1907–1987), joined the Nazi Party on September 5, 1927, at the age of twenty. His low party number was 66979.[62] In December 1935, he formally left the Catholic Church. Heavily involved in building, and ultimately leading, the German Labor Front for the Moselland district, from mid-August 1940 until at least June 1944, he reported directly to Franz Schmidt, the head (*Oberbereichsleiter*) of the Moratorium Commissioner for Organizational Matters (*Stillhalte-kommissar für das Organisationswesen*) in Nazi-occupied Luxembourg. As *Stillhaltekommissar*, it was Schmidt's task to forcibly liquidate businesses, associations, and foundations in that area. According to a memorandum compiled in 1949 for the National Office for the Investigation of War Crimes in Luxembourg, the majority of the holdings of these organizations were purely and simply confiscated for the benefit of the occupying German forces. More than six million RM were confiscated by the Schmidt operation.[63]

For his part, Eduard Goldermann was general commissioner for all savings associations (*Generalbeauftragte für alle Sparvereine*) and thus responsible for liquidating their monetary assets for Nazi coffers. His additional duties included the "safeguarding" and "supervision" of workers' trade unions and associations (*der Sicherung und Überwachung des Vermögens der Gewerkschaften und Verbände*). A third duty was the creation of the administrative infrastructure for the German Labor Front in the *Reichsgau* (Reich District) *Moselland*, officially formed in February 1941 out of the prewar *Gau* (district) Koblenz-Trier, to which Luxembourg was added. In July 1941, Eduard earned the *Kriegsverdienstkreutz* second class for his work as *Gausachwalter* (district chief) of the German Labor Front–Moselland.[64] At the least, the stroke of his pen was necessary for many of the deprivations that followed for his victims. Torture and violence must begin somewhere, and sometimes, many times, organized torture begins with an order or a pen.

My mother was born in Niederlahnstein, a beautiful town on the Rhine River. Its population in 1933 was approximately 15,000. There the Nazi Party won the largest percentage of votes in the national election held on March 5, 1933. During the Nazi period, it was the site of a labor/residential camp for Jews before nearly all of the Jews in this vicinity were forced to emigrate, deported, or murdered. The wartime economy relied on prisoners, POWs, and non-Jewish persons from across western, southern, and eastern Europe who worked in Nazi Germany, sometimes voluntarily but more typically as forced labor. Town records are full of names belonging to citizens of Belgium, Croatia, Czechoslovakia, England, France, Holland, Italy, Latvia, Lithuania, Poland, Romania, Russia, and Yugoslavia—all of these people somehow caught up in the Nazi web and experiencing the war, mostly not of their own volition, in this small place. There is much more to this violent history, all fitting well and properly within a book on torture, all hardly evident to the naked eye in this town today. One must wonder, then, how postwar Niederlahnstein again became an idyllic and enchanting place like the one that captivated Victor Hugo's imagination in the mid-nineteenth century and my own as a child.[65]

So you see, I am born of both Germanies: the Germany of my childhood, of rivers, valleys, castles, neat houses with pristine paint and bright flowers; and the Germany—Germans—of the Holocaust. How can a country that I love, a church that I love, and a family that I love have produced so many who not only did less than they might have to resist Nazism but also participated in and even fervently embraced that cause? I cannot reconcile these two worlds with any amount of historical analysis.

But, a reader may ask, what has all of this to do with Johann Baptist Neuhäusler? For me, everything. I will always owe a debt to every victim of Nazi violence, as will my children after me. I am responsible, I am responsible, I am responsible. I try to produce the fullest possible picture of the participants, victims, and surrounding circumstances of this piece of history, as, above all, a memorial to the victims. Will this be useful? I don't know. Is it enough? No. Will it repay the debt my family owes? No. What is my moral judgment of Neuhäusler's behavior? I condemn him, but because of the crimes my own family participated in with enthusiasm, in condemning him, I condemn a piece of myself. What do I most want my reader to take away from my reflections about him? For me, that question does not feel like the right one. Instead, at least for me, the right question will always be: what will I do to repay my family's debt to Nazism's victims, great, silent, and ever-present?

NOTES

The views I have expressed are mine alone and do not necessarily represent those of the United States Holocaust Memorial Museum or any other organization. I am grateful to Jo-Ellyn Decker and Nicole Dominicus for their aid in obtaining International Tracing Service documentation pertaining to Johann Baptist Neuhäusler, Ryan Bond for his aid in translations, Mark Ruff for providing Neuhäusler's testimony on behalf of Martin Weiss, and Barbara Distel, Jerome Legge, Kevin Spicer, and Sybille Steinbacher for their insightful comments.

1   Harold Marcuse, *Legacies of Dachau: The Uses and Abuses of a Concentration Camp, 1933–2001* (Cambridge, UK: Cambridge University Press, 2001), 229.

2   Central Name Index (hereafter CNI) card for Johann Neuhäusler, 0.1/43991762 /International Tracing Service (hereafter ITS) Digital Archive, United States Holocaust Memorial Museum (hereafter USHMM). See also Johann Neuhäusler, *What Was It Like in the Concentration Camp at Dachau? An Attempt to Come Closer to the Truth,* 2nd ed. (Munich/Dillingen: Manz A. G., 1961), 6.

3   Dachau book of prisoner arrivals, 1.1.6.1/9897057/ITS Digital Archive, USHMM. See Dachau prisoner number book, 1.1.6.1/9894026/ITS Digital Archive, USHMM.

4   Barbara Distel, "Dachau Main Camp," in *Encyclopedia of Camps and Ghettos 1933– 1945,* Volume I, Part A: *Early Camps, Youth Camps, and Concentration Camps and Sub*

Camps under the SS-Business Administration Main Office (WVHA), ed. Geoffrey P. Megargee (Bloomington: Indiana University Press, 2009), 442.

5 Ibid.

6 Ibid.

7 Ibid.

8 Jerome S. Legge, Jr., "Resisting a War Crimes Trial: The Malmédy Massacre, the Churches, and the U.S. Army Counterintelligence Corps," *Holocaust and Genocide Studies* 26, no. 2 (Fall 2012): 235.

9 Mark Edward Ruff, "Johannes Neuhäusler and His Courier Service to the Vatican, 1933–1941," paper delivered during the workshop "The Roman Catholic Church and the Holocaust: New Studies, New Sources, New Questions," United States Holocaust Memorial Museum, August 2012; and Ruff, "The Ambiguities of Vergangenheitsbewältigung: The Unusual Saga of Weihbischof Johannes Neuhäusler," paper delivered at the 2010 German Studies Association Annual Meeting, Oakland, California.

10 Ibid.

11 Suzanne Brown-Fleming, *The Holocaust and Catholic Conscience: Cardinal Aloisius Muench and the Guilt Question in Germany* (South Bend, IN: University of Notre Dame Press, 2006), 88–90.

12 The cylindrical "Chapel of Christ's Mortal Agony" (*Todesangst Christi*) was built at the end of the camp street.

13 Marcuse, *Legacies of Dachau*, 229. Marcuse notes that Neuhäusler's efforts to "break a gate into the camp wall and use the adjoining watchtower to display relics from the camp era chapel in barrack 26" did not come to fruition.

14 The book was a project of the Trustees for the Monument of Atonement in the Concentration Camp at Dachau, and all proceeds from the book were directed to this monument.

15 Johannes Neuhäusler, *Amboss und Hammer* (Munich: G. J. Manz, 1967).

16 Marcuse, *Legacies of Dachau*, 44.

17 Ibid.

18 Affidavit concerning Nikolaus von Horthy, International Information Office Correspondence concerning former prisoners, 1.1.6.0/82100535 and 1.1.6.0/82097009/ ITS Digital Archive, USHMM.

19 Testimony of Johannes Neuhäusler, RG 338, Records of U.S. Army, United States of America, Martin G Weiss et al, November 15 to December 13, 1945, M1174, Roll 2, National Archives II, College Park, Maryland (hereafter RG 338, M1174 Roll 2, NARA).

20 Dachau registration form for Johann Neuhäusler, 1.1.6.2/90421799/ITS Digital Archive, USHMM.

21 Record of property (*Effekten*), 1.1.6.2/90421800-802/ITS Digital Archive, USHMM.

22 Memorandum from the Sachsenhausen administrative office to the Dachau administrative office, July 15, 1941, 1.1.6.2/90421805/ITS Digital Archive, USHMM.

23 Record of effects, 1.1.6.2/90421800/ITS Digital Archive, USHMM. See the reverse side of the document for the transfer of the watch and fob to Busta.

24 Memorandum from chief of administration of Dachau to the administrative office of Sachsenhausen, September 10, 1941, 1.1.6.2/90421804/ITS Digital Archive, USHMM.

25 Memorandum from the administrative office of Sachsenhausen to the administrative office of Dachau, September 22, 1941, 1.1.6.2/90421803/ITS Digital Archive, USHMM.

26 Record of effects, 1.1.6.2/90421800/ITS Digital Archive, USHMM. See the reverse side of the document for the note regarding the arrival of these missing effects.

27 Distel, "Dachau Main Camp," 442.

28 Neuhäusler, *What Was It Like*, 3.

29 Marcuse, *Legacies of Dachau*, 45.

30 RG 338, M1174 Roll 2, NARA.

31 Neuhäusler, *What Was It Like*, 31.

32 Ibid., 46.

33 Ibid.

34 Ibid., 47.

35 Ibid., 48.

36 RG 338, M1174 Roll 2, NARA.

37 Distel, "Dachau Main Camp," 444.

38 Johann Neuhäusler, *Kreuz und Hakenkreuz: Der Kampf des Nationalsozialismus gegen die katholische Kirche und der Kirchliche Widerstand* (Munich: Verlag Katholische Kirche Bayern, 1946), 19.

39 Ibid., 316–30.

40 The number cited in Domagała for imprisoned priests is 2,720, of whom 2,579 were Catholics of varying nationalities.

41 Adelbert Ludwig Balling and Reinhard Abeln, *Martyr of Brotherly Love: Father Engelmar Unzeitig and the Priests' Barracks at Dachau* (New York: Crossroad, 1992), 43. Broken down as follows, 2,720 clergy were incarcerated in the Dachau concentration camp: 2,579 Catholics, 109 Protestants, and the remaining a mixture of Orthodox, Muslim, Old Catholic, and Mariavite. Of the 2,720 clergy, 447 were of German nationality.

42 Neuhäusler, *What Was It Like*, 49.

43 Ibid., 50.

44 Paul Berben, *Dachau 1933–1945: The Official History* (London: Comité International de Dachau, 1975), 60.

45 Ibid., 68–70.

46 Dachau card recording deposits and withdrawals of *Reichsmarks* for Johann Neuhäusler, 1.1.6.2/90421806/ITS Digital Archive, USHMM. See also the record of payment vouchers for Dachau pertaining to Neuhäusler: 1.1.6.1/9945753, 9946195, 9946774-5/ITS Digital Archive, USHMM.

47 Ibid., 1.1.6.1/9947027, 9947316, 9947475, 9947838, 9948069, 9948117, 9948269, 9948418, and 9948485/ITS Digital Archive, USHMM.

48 Ibid., 1.1.6.1/9949092/ITS Digital Archive, USHMM.

49 Brown-Fleming, *The Holocaust and Catholic Conscience*, 88–90; Legge, "Resisting a War Crimes Trial," 236.

50 RG 338, M1174 Roll 2, NARA.

51 Neuhäusler, *What Was It Like*, 16–17.

52 Declaration in lieu of an oath by Martin Niemöller on behalf of Karl Zimmermann, September 10, 1947, 5.1/82308230-31/ITS Digital Archive, USHMM.

53 Review and recommendations, *United States versus Rudolf Adalbert Brachtel et al.*, February 26, 1948, 5.1/82307854-56/ITS Digital Archive, USHMM; part of the records of Case Nr. 000-50-2-103 (*Prozess* Brachtel-Zimmermann, 24 November to 11 December 1947). A complete copy of this trial's transcript is available in the ITS Digital Archive. SS-Obersturmführer Rudolf Brachtel was head of the tuberculosis barrack in Dachau (*Leiter, Tbc Versuchsstation*).

54 Stanislav Zámečnik, *Das War Dachau*, trans. Peter Heumos and Gitta Grossmann (Frankfurt am Main: Fischer Taschenbuch Verlag, 2007), 284. Zámečnik wrote the first history of the camp.

55 Ibid., 170.

56 Ibid., 222–23.

57 Ibid., 273, quoted from Hermann Langbein, *Die Stärkeren: Ein Bericht aus Auschwitz und anderen Konzentrationslagern* (Frankfurt am Main: Bund-Verlag, 1982).

58 Declaration in lieu of an oath by Johannes Neuhäusler on behalf of Karl Zimmermann, August 4, 1947, 5.1/82308210/ITS Digital Archive, USHMM. Original German: "Aus dieser beschränkten Eigenerfahrung kann ich bezeugen, dass Herr Zimmermann sich gegen unks korrekt und entgegenkommend benahm und nach Kräften uns zu helfen suchte."

59 Review and recommendations, *United States versus Rudolf Adalbert Brachtel et al.*, February 26, 1948, 5.1/82307855/ITS Digital Archive, USHMM.

60 Ruff, "The Ambiguities of Vergangenheitsbewältigung," 2.

61 For more information on these developments, see Brown-Fleming, *The Holocaust and Catholic Conscience.*

62 File on "Goldermann, Eduard, 25.10.07," in Record Group 242, Berlin Document Center Microfilm, Partei Korrespondence, Roll D109, NARA, College Park, MD.

63 Memorandum from L'auditeur militaire délégué Kauffman for the attention of the National Office for the Investigation of War Crimes in Luxembourg, 23 January 1949, Archives de L'etat Grand-Duché de Luxembourg.

64 File on "Goldermann, Eduard, 25.10.07," in Record Group 242, Berlin Document Center Microfilm, Partei Korrespondence, Roll D109, NARA, College Park, MD.

65 Suzanne Brown-Fleming, *Nazi Persecution and Postwar Repercussions: The International Tracing Service Archive and Holocaust Research* (Lanham, MD: Rowman and Littlefield, 2016), ch. 2.

5

The Emerging Halachic Debate about Torture

PETER J. HAAS

Classical rabbinic sources concerning torture are understandably sparse. From the beginning of rabbinic Judaism in Roman times down to the middle of the twentieth century, Jews as a community did not exercise political control and so were not in a position to imprison others, let alone torture them. Questions about imprisonment or torture came up only in theoretical legal discussions such as commentaries on certain biblical passages.

The situation changed with the 1948 creation of the State of Israel. The emergence of Jewish political control has necessitated inquiries that were absent from classical discussions. One of those inquires involves legal reflection about the relationship between the defense needs of the state and its obligation to the continuity of the Jewish people, on the one hand, and the Jewish legal and moral heritage, on the other. In what follows I look at the emerging discussions on torture as these take shape in contemporary Israeli and Jewish discourse. The issue of legalized torture is still a rather theoretical and marginal topic in the history of Jewish thought, but the fact that it surfaced post-1945 allows us to see how the topic is taking rhetorical shape in light of the lingering trauma of the Shoah.

To contextualize my analysis, I need to address the complex relationship between traditional Jewish law and the practice of law in the modern State of Israel. The State of Israel was established as an independent, multiethnic, secular, parliamentary democracy with its own sovereign legislative body, the Knesset. At the same time, it was expressly established as a

homeland by, for, and of the Jewish people. One of the foundational questions facing the state, then, is whether the Jewish legal tradition (halacha, as
it is known in the religious community, or Hebrew law, as it is called among
secularists) should have any role at all in Israeli law and, if so, what that
role should be. Surprisingly, the historical experiences of the Jewish people
in general, and of Jews during the Holocaust in particular, have not been
significant factors in how this debate has taken shape in either secular or
religious settings. In fact, the influence of traditional Jewish law in Israel
has been largely indirect and relatively marginal except for issues of personal status (that is, the determination of Jewish identity and thus the
regulation of marriage, divorce, burial, and the like), where it has predomi-
nated. Otherwise, Israeli law is a complex mixture of Knesset legislation,
Israeli common law, British common law from the Mandatory period, and
even Turkish law, especially as regards land ownership issues.

In this multifarious legal landscape, the issue of the legal use of torture
rose to the level of significant public discourse beginning only in 1987,
when the Palestinian uprising called the First Intifada broke out. After a
scandal erupted over the deaths of two Palestinians in police detention,
the government established the so-called Landau Commission (chaired
by former Supreme Court Justice Moshe Landau) to investigate the use of
torture in Israeli detention facilities. The report, released publicly in 1991,
banned torture but did allow the application of a "moderate measure of
physical pressure" when dealing with terrorist organizations.[1] The report
has since been the subject of intense debate within Israel and internationally both for its limitations on torture and for its allowance of "moderate"
physical pressure. Whatever its shortcomings, the Landau report has become
the foundational document for all subsequent Israeli discussions of torture. Over the years, a number of methods of torture have come under
judicial scrutiny (pivoting around the question of what counts as "moderate"), and most, if not all, such methods have been declared illegal by
the Israeli Supreme Court (often acting as the High Court of Justice). In
other words, the court has systematically restricted what kinds of torture are deemed moderate and thus permissible. Of particular importance was a decision by the Israeli High Court of Justice in 1999. It held
that while officers of the Israeli security services did have legal authority
to torture inmates under their control, this power was limited, absent
specific legal warrant, to the same laws that applied to police and other
civil investigations.

It should be noted, however, that the High Court of Justice also ruled that security agents who exceeded their legal authority in such matters were not necessarily criminally liable if their actions were taken in good faith and under "proper circumstances."[2] The decision is complex and introduces its own ambiguities (such as what counts as proper circumstances), but it reflects the court's effort to strike a balance between legal authority, the need to extract information when faced with terrorist threats, and the obligation to preserve human dignity. The 1999 decision sparked a wider discussion of torture within Jewish law, tradition, and ethical teaching. Before turning to those discussions, however, consider some of the classical Jewish attitudes and teachings that inform the debate.

The Classical Sources

The Hebrew Bible does not address the topic of torture in any systematic way. When we do find references to torture or the intentional infliction of pain or humiliation, the biblical text does not so much condone or condemn torture as it reports on instances of the use of violence and degradation without drawing explicit broader implications. One of the few biblical laws regarding torture (or at least severe judicial punishment) is the acceptance of flogging as a standard sentence for certain infractions, although the flogging itself is limited to forty blows, lest the guilty party be "degraded before your eyes."[3] In terms of actual biblical legislation, little support exists for torture or mistreatment outside of strictly limited juridical situations and even then not to the point of public degradation. Otherwise, the Bible mostly reports on the mistreatment of people without addressing the question of legal or moral norms. King David, for example, reportedly subjected conquered people to various forms of humiliation and even what sounds like slave labor.[4] A more egregious example occurred during the return from the Babylonian exile when Nehemiah reports that he dealt severely with people who had intermarried, cursing them, flogging them, and even having their hair pulled out.[5] The book of Proverbs also deserves mention because it notoriously recommends using the rod lest the child be spoiled and seems to suggest that beating fools is a matter of course.[6] These latter cases seem to consider such acts more as chastisement for the victim's own good than as torture in the sense of punishment, revenge, or interrogation. Overall, then, the biblical texts do not contain sustained and systematic discussions about torture. This trend continues in rabbinic literature, which is intriguing because that literature is known for exploring exhaustively virtually all areas of the human experience.

The classical rabbinic literature does distinguish between torture as a mode of punishment and torture as a means of extracting information or confession. By and large, however, the traditional literature has scarcely anything to say about torture per se, and when it does speak to that topic, the analysis is mostly situated in the context of repeat offenders. The Babylonian Talmudic tractate Sanhedrin, which deals specifically with rules concerning how the ideal rabbinic court (*Beth din*) should function, does allow for a certain amount of mistreatment in specific cases. Sanhedrin 46a, for example, says,

> It has been taught: R. Eliezer b. Jacob said: I have heard that the *Beth din* may, [when necessary,] impose flagellation and pronounce [capital] sentences even where not [warranted] by the Torah; yet not with the intention of disregarding the Torah but [on the contrary] in order to safeguard it. It once happened that a man rode a horse on the Sabbath in the Greek period and he was brought before the Court and stoned, not because he was liable thereto, but because it was [practically] required by the times. Again it happened that a man once had intercourse with his wife under a fig tree. He was brought before the *Beth din* and flogged, not because he merited it, but because the times required it.[7]

Another relevant passage occurs in Sanhedrin 81b, which deals with a serial recidivist who committed several crimes worthy of having him "cut off" (*karet*), that is, expelled from the Jewish people. Such a one, the Babylonian Talmud tells us, may be put in a "cramped cell that has no room for him either to stretch or lie down." He is then fed bread and water until his stomach shrinks, and then barley and water until his stomach bursts, causing his death.[8]

In the *Mishneh Torah*, the monumental Code of Jewish Law from the twelfth century, Maimonides argues ("Laws of Murder" 2:4–5),

> All of these murderers and those like them who cannot be put to death in court, if the king wishes to kill them simply for justice's sake or for the benefit of society, he may do so. Also, if the court determines that it is necessary for the times that this person be put to death, they may do

so at their discretion. If the king does not kill this person and the court determines that the times do not demand an extra-judicial execution, still the court is required to severely beat them within inches of their lives and to incarcerate them in horrible conditions for a long time, and to cause them to suffer in many different ways in order to instill fear in all of the rest of the evil folks so that it should not be a stumbling block that they say, "I will kill my enemy in a round-about way just as so-and-so did, and I will be free from punishment."

On the other hand, the use of torture to elicit information or confessions almost never comes up, and when it does, it is dismissed immediately. The basis for denying the use of torture to obtain evidence is the biblical law that requires the testimony of two independent witnesses to effect a conviction, a rule that eliminates the testimony of the accused.[9] Again in his *Mishneh Torah*, Maimonides underwrites what is often regarded as the definitive halachic position (see Sanhedrin 18:6), when he states that "the ruling of Scripture is that the court does not put a person to death nor impose flogging on a person on the basis of his own admission, but only on the testimony of two witnesses."[10]

In contrast to the paucity of discussions regarding torture, the rabbinic literature is replete with passages that mandate the preservation of human dignity. A few examples provide a sense of the whole. The late Mishnaic tractate *Ethics of the Patriarchs* stresses human dignity several times: verse 2:10 notes, "Let your fellow-man's honor be as dear to you as your own," and 4:1 begins, "Who is honored? One who honors his fellow human being." The Jerusalem Talmud states that "one who gains honor through the degradation of his fellow human has no share in the World to Come" (Chaggiga 2:1). Likewise, the Babylonian Talmud holds that "the value of human dignity is so great that it supersedes a negative commandment of the Torah" (Berachot 19b–20a), likens shaming to snuffing out someone's soul (Bava Metzia 58b–59a), and argues that shaming someone is worse than stealing from them or committing adultery. In a similar vein, Maimonides notes that "a rabbinic prohibition is always and everywhere superseded for the sake of human dignity. And even though we are explicitly enjoined in the Torah not to depart from the Sages' teaching either to the right or to the left, this negative precept itself is set aside in the interests of human dignity [*kvod ha-bri'ot*]" (*Laws of Kilayim* 10:29).

In addition, there are prohibitions against causing unnecessary pain to animals (*tsa'ar ba'alei hayim*). These prohibitions are based on various biblical passages, such as Exodus 23:5, and are expanded upon in the Talmud.[11] The argument is often made that if the Torah is concerned with the unearned suffering of animals, how much more must it be concerned about suffering inflicted on human beings.

From Classical Sources to the State of Israel

As the overview indicates, Judaism's classical sources explore torture in penal contexts, where punishment for repeat offenders is the issue. Those sources also dismiss torture as a reliable means for obtaining information or confession. On the whole, however, the classical tradition has relatively little to say about torture. Much more common are texts that highlight the dignity and sacredness of human life. These passages place a strong halachic emphasis on preserving the honor due to human beings, who are created in the image of the divine.

Early on, this traditional Jewish moral perspective became encoded in the Israel Defense Forces (IDF) as part of the doctrine called Purity of Arms (*Tohar HaNeshek*). This doctrine attempts to define *jus in bello* (morality in fighting a war) with regard to specific operational conditions facing the Israeli military. The norms of military ethics are easier to maintain in classrooms than on battlefields, and the IDF's Purity of Arms doctrine is no exception to that reality. But it has been and continues to be a significant standard for moral thinking and conduct in the ranks of the IDF. Its basic declaration is that "the soldier shall make use of his weaponry and power only for the fulfillment of the mission and solely to the extent required; he will maintain his humanity even in combat. The soldier shall not employ his weaponry and power in order to harm non-combatants or prisoners of war, and shall do all he can to avoid harming their lives, body, honor and property."[12]

In addition, Section 277 of the Israeli Penal Code stipulates that "a sentence of up to three years in prison can be imposed for using, or threatening to use, violence against a person for the purpose of extorting a confession of, or information related to, an offense." The one exception, contained in Article 34, excludes criminal liability for acts that are "immediately necessary" to save the life, freedom, person, or property of oneself or another from a "concrete danger stemming from the conditions at the time of the act."[13] For most Israelis, this doctrine has signified that the IDF is "morally superior" to the enemy, and thus the IDF has enjoyed a kind of iconic status in mainstream Israeli society.

More broadly, Judaism's traditional concern for human dignity has also been encoded in Israel's Basic Law: Human Dignity and Liberty (*kvod ha-Adam ve-heruto*). Adopted in 1992, it begins with the statement that "basic human rights in Israel are based on the recognition of the value of the human being, and the sanctity of his life and his freedom, and these will be respected in the spirit of the principles of the Declaration of Independence of the State of Israel."[14]

Given this background, it is hardly surprising that discussions about the use of torture, let alone arguments in favor of the practice, remained marginal in the State of Israel for fifty years. The situation changed early in the twenty-first century. Pivotal events included not only the al-Aqsa Intifada, whose launch in September 2000 included a massive campaign of suicide bombing directed against Israeli civilian targets, but also the 2006 war in Lebanon, which included Hezbollah's traumatic rocket attacks on northern Israel. These events raised concerns among many Israeli and American Jewish thinkers, especially on the political right, that the IDF's Purity of Arms doctrine and the state's Basic Law: Human Dignity and Liberty were not fully compatible with, and in fact might be harmful to, the ongoing struggle against the asymmetric war being waged against Israel, the homeland of the Jewish people.

Recent arguments reconsidering Israeli use of torture are largely based on the premise that moral restraints on the army and other security forces as they battle terrorist organizations are endangering the lives of Jews, and as a result such restraints are in fact prohibited by halacha. One of the first challenges along these lines was launched by Rabbi Itamar Warhaftig against the 1999 High Court of Justice ruling noted above. In an article published in 2000, Warhaftig used halachic grounds to defend the use of torture as an interrogation technique.[15] In addition to assuming that sound reasons existed for thinking that the person on whom torture was to be inflicted actually possessed relevant information, Warhaftig's argument rested on several premises: that the target of the torture could end the torture by giving up information; that the information sought was meant to save innocent lives; and that in any case the requirement to preserve human dignity did not apply to someone intent on killing others.

In a long essay published in 2003, David Rosen, a law professor at Emory

University, provided a more extensive analysis that also defended a hala-chic basis for torture. Rosen contended that "in the future, the creation of a just Palestinian society is a noble goal. In the meantime, as the Noahide commandments continue to be defied and the sanctity of life is rendered meaningless, Israel has an obligation to engage in whatever actions neces-sary to maintain law and order and protect the Jewish people from danger, wherever and however it may arise."[16] In a word, he argued that "these des-perate times call for desperate measures."[17]

By early 2004, some Jewish Israeli settlers in the occupied West Bank were beginning to complain openly that the Purity of Arms doctrine should be abandoned in light of the grim animosity of the surrounding Pales-tinian population. The argument, put forward by a number of rabbis con-nected to West Bank and Gaza rabbinic councils and yeshivas, was that security forces could not fight Palestinian terrorism if they were forced to operate under artificial bans, such as avoiding harming civilians at all costs.[18] This call to abandon *Tohar HaNeshek* received some notice and condemnation in the general Jewish press, but at the time did not garner broad attention. While the settlers were not advocating torture per se, they were firmly asserting that sometimes the need exists to use extreme physi-cal force in defense of the state and the Jewish people. These arguments gained traction in the wake of the sustained rocket attacks and disappoint-ing ground results of the Lebanon War of 2006. Significantly, memories of the Shoah lurked in the background of all sides of this dispute, especially as regards the overriding need to prevent what was feared to be another "holocaust" of the Jewish people.

A striking example of this change in attitude even among American Jews can be seen in a statement released by a delegation of the Rabbinical Council of America, who visited northern Israel in the wake of the Hez-bollah rocket attacks during the 2006 war. The delegation's statement declares that "speaking from within our own Judaic faith and legal legacy, we believe that Judaism would neither require nor permit a Jewish soldier to sacrifice himself in order to save deliberately endangered enemy civil-ians. This is especially true when confronting a barbaric enemy who would by such illicit, consistent, and systematic means seek to destroy not only the Jewish soldier, but defeat and destroy the Jewish homeland. New reali-ties do indeed require new responses. Especially when it comes to such matters involving life and death, self-sacrifice and the fundamental right to life and limb."[19]

In a similar vein, and in light of international concern over the high toll of Lebanese civilian deaths during the war, a group of American Orthodox rabbis called for the IDF to ignore international criticisms and to focus on accomplishing its mission. In particular, they urged the IDF to be "less concerned with avoiding civilian casualties on the opposing side when carrying out future operations."[20] This growing appeal was bolstered by Michael J. Broyde, another law professor at Emory University and, at the time, leader of the Young Israel Synagogue in Atlanta. In an article published in *The Jewish Week* (July 7, 2006), Broyde carefully reviewed the Jewish halachic approach to war, both in terms of entering a war (*jus ad bellum*) and in terms of how a war may be conducted (*jus in bello*). He argued that during war in which Jewish lives are at risk, Jewish law can be read to allow wide moral license, depending on the specifics of the case. Following this interpretation, Broyde concluded that the halacha does not specifically prohibit outright either collective punishment or torture. This lack of prohibition means that such measures are in fact allowable under the halacha. Broyde explicitly moved in this direction: "Similarly, what might otherwise be considered outrageous pressure in extracting the information needed to save a soldier that the government is seeking to rescue might well be permissible according to Jewish law, assuming, first, that it would be effective in extracting the information, second, that less outrageous pressures would not be as effective, and finally, that it is ordered by the army (or an equally responsible branch of government) through a duly authorized military order following the 'chain of command' and did not violate international treaties."[21]

Broyde acknowledged that his approach at times makes him uncomfortable,[22] but nonetheless he argued that "all conduct in war that is needed to win is permitted by halakhah."[23] Broyde's article provoked harsh negative responses, many citing the halachic stress on human dignity, but his analysis still carries considerable weight.[24]

Thus the issue of the halachic permissibility of using torture to elicit information is now openly on the Jewish table for the first time in nearly two thousand years. It is impossible to predict how matters will pan out over years and decades, but it is clear that the debate's emergence and intensification signal that new territory in halachic discourse has been entered. Halachic reasoning on a topic that was barely even recognized as existing in premodern times is now taking place in considered seriousness.

While the growing debate does not directly challenge the general principle of upholding human dignity, it does strongly suggest that in the world of life-and-death terrorism, the preservation of the state and of the Jewish people is taking precedence. Whether stated explicitly or not, behind such arguments is the specter of the near extermination of the Jewish people during the Shoah. One lesson being drawn from the Shoah is that the threat of genocide is real and a lack of forceful response can be catastrophic. On the other side, of course, another lesson of the Holocaust is the importance of maintaining a strict separation between military use of force and even torture, on the one side, and the infliction of unnecessary torment, degradation, and humiliation upon nonmilitary populations, on the other. At stake is not only the preservation of human dignity in general terms but also the preservation of the humanity of the soldiers inflicting the pain. Caught in the middle are average Israelis who regard themselves in some sense as survivors of the Shoah and who see themselves under concerted assault once again.

The Shoah shows how far human beings can go in degrading and tormenting their enemies if given "permission" to do so by governing authorities. But the Shoah also shows the damage such license ultimately inflicts on the perpetrators. Thus, while the Shoah remains part of the context when the issue of torture comes up in Israel, and in broader Jewish discussions too, that catastrophe does not—indeed probably cannot—settle the questions that torture raises for Jews in Israel and elsewhere. The Shoah does, however, add immense emotional and cognitive clout to an emerging topic of Jewish legal discourse.

CONTRIBUTORS' QUESTIONS FOR PETER J. HAAS

1. Your essay recounts contemporary statements regarding the conduct of the Israeli army, including comments by American Orthodox rabbis and, in particular, by Rabbi Michael J. Broyde. The Orthodox rabbis want the Israel Defense Forces to be "less concerned with avoiding civilian casualties on the opposing side when carrying out future operations." Broyde thinks that the halacha (Jewish legal tradition) cannot be read as specifically prohibiting either collective punishment or torture. Both statements significantly qualify the Israeli army's traditional emphasis on Purity of Arms. Do these contemporary interpretations imply that the rights of the Jewish people either supersede or

stand in opposition to declarations of universal human rights? You suggest that the Holocaust shadows the current halachic debate about torture. As far as torture is concerned, what are the most important—and the most problematic—consequences of that shadow? Although one important lesson of the Holocaust is that never again will Jewish blood be shed with impunity, does not the Holocaust also remind the Jewish people of the necessity to preserve human dignity—a value you cite as fundamental to both biblical and rabbinic Judaism?

2. You maintain that important rabbinic writings—themselves based on a variety of biblical passages—contain "prohibitions against causing unnecessary pain to animals." In addition, you note the rabbinical perspective that "if the Torah is concerned with the unearned suffering of animals, how much more must it be concerned about suffering inflicted on human beings." Such statements indicate not only that it is wrong to abuse animals but also that the human person has a privileged position as far as prohibitions against inflicting unnecessary pain are concerned. Significant questions lurk in this discourse. Where animals or human beings are concerned, what distinguishes unnecessary pain from other kinds of human-caused pain? When is it necessary, if it ever is, for human beings to cause pain and suffering? What implications for torture would your responses contain? The rabbinical perspective would seem to make the torture of an animal a clear instance of the prohibited causing of unnecessary pain. Would the situation be any different where the torture of a human being is concerned? Does the rabbinic concern for animals undergird an even stronger concern for the human person, one that would prohibit any and all torture of a human being? How would the shadow of the Holocaust affect your responses to these questions?

RESPONSE BY PETER J. HAAS

These questions focus further the issues I identified in my essay. As the questions indicate, I have several vectors of discussion going on simultaneously, all of which influence each other at various points. One vector is the overarching question of what influence traditional halacha should have on current Israeli law. A second involves *jus in bello*, how to fight a war justly. On the one hand, traditional rabbinic law, as I pointed out, all but dismisses the use of torture for anything outside of judicial punishment, although such law does not discuss warfare all that much in any case. These circumstances allow Michael Broyde to be technically correct in saying that halacha does not explicitly prohibit the use of torture in wartime. On the other hand, the State of Israel sees itself as being in a permanent state of asymmetric warfare with enemies some of whom have shown themselves willing to inflict mass civilian casualties, whether through suicide bombings or rocket barrages. This situation changes the whole "just war" discourse. A third vector underscores the role of diaspora voices—Broyde, after all, is American, not Israeli—in shaping Israeli law, society, and culture. Finally, all of these debates take place nowadays within the shadow of the Shoah. That reality complicates matters, including the question of whether, and to what extent, international or other outside law should or can play a role in the torture-related discussions.

I could add yet another dimension, namely, that for the most part, opposition to torture and the absolute need to protect innocent civilians remain strongly entrenched in more liberal Jewish communities (especially those of the Diaspora), both religious and secular. My point in the essay, then, is not so much to justify, condemn, or advocate for this, that, or the other position in the discussion of torture as it is to document that the topic of torture has become a focus of serious and committed debate in the Jewish community. I maintain that the emergence of this debate is recent and largely unprecedented.

Turning to the questions themselves, it seems to me that halachic discussions have traditionally occurred in something of a self-contained universe of discourse. Throughout the history of rabbinic Judaism, there have been arguments about whether to include non-Jewish sources in essentially Jewish deliberations. While technological and scientific advances are routinely known and dealt with in halachic literature, the resistance to using outside philosophy or law as guides or models has largely stood over time. The reason, to be overly simplistic, is the supposition that Torah law is revealed and therefore is totally self-sufficient. Turning to other philosophical or legal sources would compromise or diminish the purity of that which is revealed. That constraint, however, does not necessarily apply to historical events (the devastations of the Shoah, for example, or the security needs of the State of Israel). In certain circles of traditional Jewish halachic thinking, as represented, for example, by Broyde, such events can and indeed must be taken into consideration. But "outside" legal principles, such as those articulated in the United Nations Declaration on Human Rights, can be dismissed as irrelevant and dangerous.

But even working solely within the confines of the Jewish halachic tradition does not handle completely the dilemmas that torture puts into bold relief. Comparison of the ban on inflicting suffering on animals and on humans serves as a good example. This comparison can be made in more than one way. One could say that the avoidance of inflicting pain on humans as creatures of the divine is so foundational that we learn from it that we must ban the unnecessary suffering of animals as well. On the other hand, it could be argued that if the infliction of pain on an animal is banned, similar infliction on a human being should be banned even more. In other words, it is hard to adduce from the argument itself whether it is humans or animals that are privileged in this regard. While this is an interesting philosophical conundrum, in practical halacha up to now it has been largely a moot point. The bottom line is that inflicting undeserved or unnecessary punishment on either an animal or a human being is wrong. Only now, with the torture debate, is it even possible to ask about the moral and logical relationship between the two bans and, importantly, the relationship among suffering, punishment, and torture.

In addition, the interpretation and meaning of key terms comes into play. *Undeserved* and *unnecessary* are two examples. When one considers suffering, punishment, or torture—and their relationships—how should *undeserved* and *unnecessary* be understood, both in terms of the person who experiences those things and in terms of the person who may be causing them. It seems to me, for example, that amputating a limb with inadequate anesthetics in order to prevent the spread of gangrene (as was often done during the American Civil War) could produce "necessary" pain, whereas violently fracturing the leg of a peaceful political protester could not. Most actual real world incidents are hardly this clear cut, however, and in dangerous, tense, or stressful situations, moral clarity is hard to achieve on the spur and in the narrowness of the moment. And of course what appears deserved or necessary at the time may, considered in a larger scope or upon deeper reflection, turn out not to be that way at all. Perhaps a classic example is a battle of the American War of 1812, in which it appeared to General Andrew Jackson absolutely necessary to drive off British invaders at New Orleans. Jackson's efforts to secure the city, which he succeeded in doing, resulted in massive casualties, American as well as British. In retrospect it turns out that the killings on the battlefield were totally unnecessary since the Treaty of Ghent, which ended the war, had been signed before the battle. In those days, however, word traveled slowly. Was Jackson guilty of a war crime?

I think that reflection on the prohibition against inflicting undeserved or unnecessary pain on an animal should proceed as follows: would you do to an animal what you are now intending to do to this person? In general, such logic should preclude all torture on a human being. But of course the analogy is not a truly good one: people are not animals in important ways. One would never think of torturing an animal to elicit information, for example, but one could (arguably, at least) do so with regard to a person. So at the end of the day I would have to say that the prohibition on inflicting undeserved or unnecessary pain on an animal, like arguments about "the lessons" of the Holocaust, can cut both ways.

The Holocaust has affected, is affecting, and hopefully will continue to affect ethical reflection, including deliberation about torture. But *the* lessons of the Holocaust have not yet been universally identified and prioritized. Often, different lessons have been adduced by different communities at different times and in different contexts. The effects of the Holocaust on Jewish thinking in every area (legal, halachic, moral, political) shed important light on the impact that extrahalachic events can or should have on internal halachic debates. In the wake of the Shoah, the Jewish community is probably still suffering from a kind of posttraumatic stress syndrome. In debates within the Jewish community, the "lessons" of the Holocaust are summoned to justify many different positions. The Holocaust is about both the horrific consequences of totally "othering" the Other and of the necessity of the Other to resist such "othering." So perhaps the conundrum that Israel faces about torture is whether Israel is "othering" or being "othered" and thus which Holocaust lesson most appropriately applies. Put another way, what counts most: moral purity or survival? That dilemma is fraught, partly because the either/or may be oversimplified, but I think arguments such as Broyde's highlight crucial issues that the State of Israel, the Jewish community, and other communities too can only avoid at their peril.

NOTES

1   The Landau Commission report can be found at http://www.hamoked.org/files /2012/115020_eng.pdf. Further information is available at the Israeli Ministry of

Foreign Affairs web site: http://mfa.gov.il/MFA/AboutIsrael/State/Law/Pages/Israel
-s%20Interrogation%20Policies%20and%20Practices%20-%20De.aspx.

2   *Public Committee Against Torture in Israel v. The State of Israel and The General
Security Service*, in HCJ 5100/94. See http://www.btselem.org/english/torture/HCJ
_Ruling.asp.

3   Deuteronomy 25:2, for example.

4   II Samuel 12:31.

5   Nehemiah 13:25.

6   Proverbs 22:15 and 29:15, for example.

7   Sanhedrin 46a, available at http://www.come-and-hear.com/sanhedrin/sanhedrin
_46.html.

8   Cited in Dov S. Zakheim, "Confronting Evil: Terrorists, Torture, the Military and
Halakhah," *Meorot* 6, no. 1 (2006), http://www.yctorah.org/component/option,com
_docman/task,doc_view/gid,304/.

9   See, for example, Deuteronomy 17:6 and 19:15.

10 For further discussion on this thread in Jewish law, see Steven H. Resnicoff, "Criminal Confessions in Jewish Law," *Jewish Law Commentary*. The article is available at
www.jlaw.com/Commentary/crimconfess.html.

11 See the Babylonian Talmud, tractate Bava Metzia 32b, for example.

12 The official doctrine of the Israeli Defense Forces can be found at http://www.idf
.il/1497-en/dover.aspx.

13 See Alexandra L. Wisotsky, "Israeli Interrogation Methods Legitimized by Court,"
The Human Rights Brief (1997). The article is available at http://www.wcl.american
.edu/hrbrief/v4i3/israel43.htm.

14 Full text available at http://www.israellawresourcecenter.org/israellaws/fulltext
/basiclawhumandignity.htm. The last phrase was added as an amendment.

15 Itamar Warhaftig, "Investigations by the Security Service in Light of Halachah"
(in Hebrew), *Techumin* 20 (2000): 145–50. A detailed critique of Warhaftig's article
can be found in Mark Warshowsky, "Torture, Terrorism and the Halachah," in *War
and Terrorism in Jewish Law: Essays and Responsa*, ed. Walter Jacob (Pittsburgh,
PA: Rodef Shalom Press, 2010), 13–50.

16 David Rosen, "Does Ariel Sharon Consult His Rabbi? How Israeli Responses to Terrorism Are Justified under Jewish Law," 54. The article is available at http://www
.jlaw.com/Articles/responseTerrorism.pdf.

17 Ibid., 53.

18 See http://www.adl.org/PresRele/IslME_62/4561_62.htm.

19 See http://www.rabbis.org/news/article.cfm?id=100826.

20 Reported in the *Jewish Daily Forward*, August 25, 2006. See http://forward.com
/articles/1438/rabbis-israel-too-worried-over-civilian-deaths/?.

21 Michael J. Broyde, "The Bounds of Wartime Military Conduct in Jewish Law: An
Expansive Conception," Herbert Berman Memorial Lecture, November 3, 2004
(Flushing, NY: Center for Jewish Studies, Queens College, City University of New
York, 2006), 38.

22 Ibid, 42.

23 Ibid., 38.

24 See, for example, Rabbi Aryeh Klapper, "Torah Does Not Support Torture," *Edah*, http://www.edah.org/klapperb.cfm. See also Rabbi David Rosenn, Rabbi Jeremy Kalmanofsky, and Rabbi Melissa Weintraub, "Torah against Torture: A Sample OpEd," *Jewish Week*, October 6, 2006.

6

Torture in Light of the Holocaust

An Impossible Possibility

DIDIER POLLEFEYT

This chapter explores whether a proportionalist approach to torture can pass the test of a post-Holocaust Catholic understanding of good and evil. To begin, one can distinguish two basic positions in dealing with moral issues about torture: a deontological approach and a proportionalist one. The former is taken by "absolutists," who contend that torture is intrinsically evil and can never be legitimized or accepted. Deontologists defend this position by emphasizing the integrity—physical and mental—of the human being who is tortured. Torture denigrates the victim's autonomy and human dignity; it often regards the individual as little more than a source from which information is to be extracted. Deontologists stress that torture undermines the moral universe itself and therefore must always be prohibited. Such an interpretation can be found in the fifth article of the Universal Declaration of Human Rights (1948).[1] It has been made even more explicit in the 1949 Convention Relative to the Treatment of Prisoners of War, Geneva: "The following acts are and shall remain prohibited at any time and in any place whatsoever . . . violence to life and person, in particular murder of all kinds, mutilation, cruel treatment and torture."[2] The Catholic Church also holds a clear deontological view about torture. The 1992 *Catechism of the Catholic Church* states that "torture which uses physical or moral violence to extract confessions, punish the guilty, frighten opponents, or satisfy hatred is contrary to respect for the person and for human dignity."[3] In addition, Pope John Paul II's encyclical *Veritatis Splendor* calls torture "intrinsically evil" (*intrinsece malum*).[4] Emphasizing that the prohibition against torture must never be contravened, Pope Benedict XVI supported that judgment in his 2007 address to the Twelfth World Congress of the Commission of Catholic Prison Pastoral Care.[5]

Accentuating consequences, not absolute prohibitions, the proportionalist outlook is different. Where torture is concerned, it weighs moral value by considering that good outcomes may sometimes entail choices between the lesser of evils, if not decisions in favor of necessary evils. Proportionalists often use the "ticking time bomb" scenario to show that urgent circumstances can legitimize the use of torture in rare cases. They invoke a thought experiment in which a terrorist in custody possesses critical knowledge, such as the location of a "ticking time bomb" that will soon explode and cause great loss of life. Proportionalists claim that in a case like that—where timely information about the bomb's location may be obtained—sound reasons exist to inflict torture. The consequence of doing so, they contend, is a lesser evil than murder. Indeed, to avert that calamity, torture may be a necessary evil. Hence, while proportionalists do not deny that torture is evil, they are prepared to argue for the conditional possibility of torture based on a contextual assessment of costs and benefits. Torture is then acceptable only when the benefits of torture exceed its costs. The "ticking time bomb" scenario seems both to illustrate and to invoke that principle.

Avoiding the Slippery Slope

A major objection to the proportionalist approach is the slippery slope argument: once we decide to torture a single person, we cross a moral line and will be willing to torture anytime it seems necessary. Eventually we may create a "culture of torture." As a Catholic theologian trained in the proportionalist intellectual tradition, I think there is a crucial difference between an ethics that legitimizes a culture of torture and an ethics that—while condemning torture in almost every instance—will not argue, a priori, that torture is never morally necessary. To be clear, I am not defending any broad justification of torture. Rather, I support the argument that would legitimize "restricted" or, better, "restricting" torture. This position demands taking the greatest possible caution in ever defending the morality of torture. The argument does not deny reality by taking a theoretical, deontological position but is sensitive to the possibility of conflicts between values and antivalues. It tries to discern honestly and critically when the radical respect for the dignity of the human person is limited by the right to life and the integrity of other people and communities. In this way, a proportionalist understanding of torture can also be motivated by a radical respect for human dignity.

Proportionalists contend that torture is legitimate only in extremely rare cases to gain vital information in what is considered a supreme emergency—for example, when one is faced with the choice between the torture of one or a few people and the potential death of innocent people. Therefore, proportionalists employ strict criteria to legitimize use of torture: (1) the danger should be imminent and very severe; (2) fundamental values should be at stake; (3) no other options can be available to gain access to the necessary life-saving information; (4) there should be reasonable evidence that the captured individual knows the information, that the information will be useful, and that the pain inflicted will lead directly and immediately to the vital information; (5) the torture must not cause death or irremediable harm in the long term to the person who is tortured.

The foregoing does not imply that in the proportionalist view torture becomes a good in itself. On the contrary, torture is *always* an evil, but sometimes a lesser evil. Thus the possibility of a justified act of torture can never be excluded a priori. Michael Walzer has argued that sometimes a moral politician with high ethical standards will acquire "dirty hands" because he may be obliged under certain circumstances to opt for torture to avoid a much greater evil. This individual recognizes all the while that torture remains a moral evil: "He commits a determinate crime, and he must pay a determinate penalty. When he has done so, his hands will be clean again, or as clean as human hands can ever be."[6] The proportionalist position also holds that this legitimation of torture in isolated and extreme cases is not the same as accepting institutionalized torture as a legal and ongoing practice of the state. It also implies that governments can never take torture "off the radar," that any act of torture should be undertaken by someone who has the juridical authority to do so, and finally, that each decision should be made public and thus be open to democratic judgment, including harsh critique and insistent protest.

Taking the Holocaust into Account

Whether this proportionalist approach to torture passes the test of a *post-Holocaust* Catholic understanding of good and evil depends, at least in part, on taking the Holocaust itself explicitly into account. Consider, then, the perspectives of Holocaust victims, perpetrators, and bystanders. Tortured by Nazis before deportation to Auschwitz, the Jewish philosopher Jean Améry described torture as an essential aspect of Nazism. His reflection offers unique insight into the experience of torture under the swastika, but not only there. For Améry, torture is an experience of being physically overwhelmed that is equivalent to an existential consummation of destruction. The person being tortured is completely isolated in his or her own body. When writing that one's mind and soul "are destroyed when there is that cracking and splintering in the shoulder joints," Améry makes clear that there is no proportionality in torture: the nature of torture is such that it inflicts pain without proportion.[7]

Against this line of thinking, one can argue that the intention of a torturer in one situation can be very different from the intention in another. Améry's testimony suggests that his bodily and psychological integrity was violated for no other reason than the satisfaction gained by his sadistic torturers. But it is also possible, as I have argued, to cause pain with the intention of obtaining information that might save human lives. Although one can argue that pain is not always the deprivation of a basic human good—pain is often present, at least to some extent, in even the best human experiences—what we learn from Améry is that in the experience of *all* torture, whatever the intention, the pain itself transcends every kind of proportionality. This awareness does not mean that torture cannot be judged according to a proportionalist ethic; rather, it implies that alternative goods or evils that are at stake should also be disproportionate in nature.

A decisive question follows immediately: who will decide when torture is acceptable? This issue leads me to seek responses from the perspective of perpetrators of the Holocaust. In his groundbreaking book *Morality after Auschwitz*, Peter Haas questions not why the Nazis committed such evil as the torture of Améry, but why they did not recognize this evil as evil.[8] The answer to this question, in Haas's view, is that *good* and *evil* had been given a new interpretation in Nazi Germany. Millions of Germans were no longer capable of seeing evil as evil. The Germans did not lose their ethical faculties; rather, they adopted new modes of moral evaluation. Many Germans were well aware of what was happening to the "enemies of the people," but they found the actions undertaken by the Nazis to be morally acceptable and acted consciously and enthusiastically in accordance with this new moral interpretation. This "moral" Nazi logic goes far toward explaining how the Holocaust was maintained for years without much meaningful opposition from German political, judicial, medical, or religious leaders. How could torture—as brutal as it is—be judged to be moral? Haas would say that the difficult emotions which may have arisen in the minds of the torturers were the "necessary price" that had to be paid if one wanted to contribute to a higher Nazi goal. Arguably, every morality asks people at certain moments to give up feelings generally understood as "human." Nazi ethics praised mercilessness as a moral virtue.

What we learn from Haas's analysis is how vulnerable "ethics" is to manipulation by those in power who are imbued with a fixed ideology. How merciless can ethics become when traditional moral values are excluded from such ideologies. The Nazis thought there were good reasons to torture their victims, such as the alleged need for medical experiments or the ruthless implementation of war goals. Of course, not every ethical legitimation of violence is automatically a misuse of ethics. Should we show mercy, an important human virtue, to those who show no mercy? Should we tolerate the intolerable? From this perspective, there is a radical difference between torture in Amery's case and torture in the "ticking time bomb" scenario. Nevertheless, we learn that not every ethical argumentation leads to a morally correct decision. We learn that we always risk falling into the trap of a situational ethics that claims the end justifies the means. In Amery's case, torture could never pass the test of this moral rigor since it violates almost all criteria of proportionality reasoning, starting with the fifth one I noted above: no permanent, irredeemable harm may be inflicted on a human being.

A third perspective garnered from a study of the Holocaust is related to the position of bystanders and the "dynamics of indifference" that often characterized their position.[9] We learn from Holocaust studies how bystanders were not always adequately informed—or how they neglected to inform themselves—about what was happening around them. They remained passive, avoided involvement, and felt powerless. Responsibility for the evil that was occurring was spread so wide that most people did not feel accountable. Of course, in a totalitarian system, even when evidence of evil's being committed was obvious, bystanders had relatively few possibilities for protest that did not put them and their families in dire straits. In a democratic context, bystanders can play a more critical role if they have access to the necessary information and if moral weight is given to good deeds in the larger society. But even in a democratic context, bystanders can easily be paralyzed and rendered powerless.

The argument that those who would otherwise be called bystanders can abandon that role to protest the immorality of torture presupposes that such situations are clear and relatively easy to judge. In most cases when moral dilemmas come into play, we are confronted with many uncertainties; options for acting are often unclear. This dilemma exists even in the "ticking time bomb" scenario. Will there ever be a situation where everything is certain and where bystanders will have no moral questions when confronted with the complexities at hand? With regard to the "ticking time bomb" scenario, it would be difficult to judge if there was a bomb and if the tortured person had the requisite information that would lead to its dismantling. Therefore, some call the "ticking time bomb" situation merely hypothetical, a "fraud scenario."[10]

What, then, do we learn from study of the Holocaust with regard to moral issues surrounding torture? We learn that comparing deontological and proportionalist approaches to the morality of torture can be a merely intellectual exercise. But there is much more to be learned. Study of the Holocaust requires us to give more attention to the radical experience of torture itself. As Améry indicates, the perspective of the victims of torture shows that there is no continuous passage from "normal" human suffering to torture, but rather a radical discontinuity, a complete disproportionality.

Another Jewish philosopher, Emmanuel Levinas, echoes and extends Améry's insights in reflecting on the meaning of torture in the context of *incarnation*.[11] Even if our human freedom is characterized in principle by an infinite invulnerability, says Levinas, the nexus of spirit with body—our incarnation—makes us extremely vulnerable beings. Because of our "carnal condition" (*condition de chair*), we are defenseless against instruments of torture that penetrate both body and spirit. For this reason, our human will is not heroic, but rather precarious and fallible; in the end, our will can only be characterized as a "derisory freedom" (*une liberté dérisoire*). On the one hand, according to Levinas, the will is created free, divine, and inviolable; on the other hand, especially because of its corporality, the will is vulnerable. This condition implies that torture not only aims to force the victim to confess secret information; it also destroys the human person as at once soul and flesh. In torture, the human will is brought to and kept at the border of its own decay—this is the immorality of torture. Torture reveals the vulnerability of the will in the sense that even the greatest mind, the greatest hero, can be forced to become a betrayer. This humiliation is the deepest one that the tortured person has to undergo and bear. Torture makes one into an object but at the same time maintains the person's subjectivity. One cannot "steal the secret" of the other if one kills or renders the other unconscious.

Study of the Holocaust also reveals the dangers of torture from the perspective of the perpetrators, whose core of being is also destroyed by this act. One becomes contaminated by the evil that one does to the other. This evil does not remain external to the perpetrator, but precisely because the perpetrator is also incarnated, evil enters into his or her body and soul. The torturer who destroys the freedom of the victim also destroys his or her own freedom from within. In this sense, torture is contagious: it destroys the dignity of freedom in both victim and perpetrator. The study of Nazi torture shows how the practice of torture has a deeply dehumanizing impact on the torturer; it also teaches us not to expect too much of bystanders, who might otherwise be thought of as those who could prevent such an abuse of power. As I have argued, both in totalitarian and democratic societies, bystanders are often not well informed and not directly engaged in the acts of the torturer. Bystanders may be morally confused, divided, powerless, or indifferent when confronted at a distance by torture.

Revisiting the Proportionalist Argument

Taking the Holocaust into account, my proportionalist argument remains a critically important approach to an ethics of torture. Given the many conditions that must exist for a "ticking time bomb" scenario to come into play, this approach rejects facile acceptance of torture as a moral act. Indeed, through exploration of Holocaust-related torture, including especially the disproportionality of the pain caused by torture, my outlook is constrained almost to a deontological position. I believe this is what the Catholic teaching wishes to express by its deontological condemnation of torture. Nevertheless, I would not go so far as to conclude that torture is "structurally" disproportional. Even if I am almost moved to the deontological position,

I continue to opt for a proportionalist approach. As I have argued, a "just cause" can be at stake here: there could be a more grave injustice in play. A post-Holocaust exploration of torture, however, demands that we tremble in the face of such dilemmas. It warns against ever feeling satisfied with regard to these matters.

These latter insights lead to my central conclusion: torture cannot be excluded a priori as a moral possibility, but as a moral possibility, torture must be questioned time and again in terms of the consequences at stake. On the one hand, torture can never be prohibited in advance in every context; since it is not an absolute evil, torture should always be weighed proportionally in light of potential murder. A greater evil may come about, in very rare contexts, if torture is not administered. On the other hand, it is impossible to imagine at this moment, except theoretically, any circumstances that would be so clear and urgent that a proportionalist judgment justifying torture could be offered. For this reason, I term torture an *impossible possibility*. However, evildoers must know that a proportionalist judgment may need to be made in circumstances in which it is warranted. One can never be certain a priori that torture cannot, in certain circumstances, be justified. The concept of *impossible possibility* serves as a cautionary measure, requiring us to hesitate, question, criticize, and postpone torture as long as possible in the search for alternatives. Still, we must be open to the possibility that in certain circumstances, there may be no moral choice other than to engage in acts of torture.

This position can be understood and criticized as a paradox. It is, however, also the position taken by the Catholic Church with regard to capital punishment. The *Catechism* does not condemn capital punishment on deontological grounds as a universal evil, but says rather that "cases of absolute necessity for suppression of the offender today . . . are very rare, if not practically non-existent."[12] Thus the traditional approach of the church does not exclude by definition all recourse to the death penalty, at least not when it appears to be the only possible way of effectively protecting human lives against an unjust aggressor. If nonlethal means are sufficient to protect the lives of other human beings, one has to limit oneself to those means that speak directly to the common good and the dignity of the human person. And as a consequence of the ability of the modern state to protect potential murder victims through an adequate system of imprisonment, the death penalty, according to church doctrine, is in fact almost never necessary—and thus almost never morally acceptable. This line of argument is similar to my proportionalist approach to torture, recalling the distinction articulated above between the a priori (in principle) impossibility of torture and the empirical near impossibility of torture that a sound consequentialist approach requires. Cases in which torture would be considered inevitable are "very rare, if not practically non-existent."

CONTRIBUTORS' QUESTIONS FOR DIDIER POLLEFEYT

1. You want to curb and eliminate torture. Nevertheless you oppose a blanket condemnation of it. While criticizing deontological and consequentialist positions, you argue that the "ticking time bomb" scenario could justify torture under "very rare, if not practically non-existent" conditions. Thus, you contend, a total condemnation of torture would be a *static* absolute. Are you arguing instead for what might be called a "living absolute," one *enacted*—rather than *posited*—by our facing, with fear and trembling, the choice between the torture of one or more people and the murder of others?

    The parameters giving rise to such a choice can never be known in advance of the moment of *enactment* of that choice, but at the same time you articulate five "strict criteria" that must be met prior to the infliction of torture if torture is ever morally justified: (1) the impending danger to innocents must be "imminent and very severe"; (2) "fundamental values should be at stake"; (3) "no other options" are available; (4) useful information can be obtained; (5) "the torture must not cause death or irremediable harm in the long term to the person who is tortured." But how *imminent and severe* must the danger be? How should *fundamental values* be defined? Are not other options *always* available? How *useful* must the information be? When does torture *not* cause irremediable harm? Who gets to decide when your "strict criteria" are met, and what happens if the interpretations/decisions are contestable or contested? Furthermore, how would you respond to the following dilemma: Once criteria for judging the morality of torture are cited in advance of the critical moment of decision, has not a "living absolute" become fixed in the expectation that the unanswerable can be answered?

2. Your position requires you to keep your balance on a precarious high wire with no safety net. For example, it is well known that the "ticking time bomb" scenario is a carefully constructed thought experiment that arguably no actual circumstances ever match. Even if you do not

fall off the high wire when confronting the dilemmas posed by your "strict criteria"—especially the "who decides?" problem—you have not met the objection that the real world does not contain the finely tuned "ticking time bomb" scenarios that would be legitimate occasions for torture to extract life-saving information. You feel the pressure of that problem because you acknowledge that your position is almost stretched into one that rejects torture outright. Yet you allow "ticking time bomb" possibilities—scarcely realistic though you admit they are—to trump outright rejection of torture. How, then, do you respond to the proposition that perpetrators of torture will take comfort from the fact that you keep the torture chamber door unlocked, especially when they see that, your objections to the contrary notwithstanding, your "strict criteria" provide convenient interpretive ways to justify torture?

Given the "impossible possibility" of maintaining balance on the high wire of your own construction, why not reject torture outright? That question looms ever larger as you develop your analysis of the racking pain and relentless suffering caused by torture, a part of your essay that brings to mind lines from the Polish poet Wisława Szymborska. "Nothing has changed," her poem "Tortures" repeats five times. "The body is a reservoir of pain . . . its bones can be broken; its joints can be stretched. In tortures," she understates, "all of this is considered."[13] You are at your best when you share Szymborska's firm ground. On the high wire, your moral balance is too shaky.

RESPONSE BY DIDIER POLLEFEYT

Post-Holocaust ethical reflections on torture can indeed be described as calling for keeping one's balance on a precarious high wire. Holocaust scholars know very well that there is no safety net underneath when they fall off the wire in the confrontation with evil. In my view, this predicament requires a carefully nuanced consideration of torture. A central moral concern in that inquiry, especially in the post-Holocaust world, poses a key question: who is the victim? During the Holocaust, the answer to that question often would have been "a Jewish prisoner in a Nazi camp, tortured for whatever reason or for no reason at all." In such cases, the moral issue is simple and clear: torture is a moral evil and should be condemned without any hesitation or restriction. But my analysis suggests, in the form of another query, a different answer to the question posed above. Would it be morally legitimate to torture a Nazi perpetrator for the sole purpose of eliminating the possibility that yet more victims would suffer as a result of a *failure* to torture the perpetrator? In this case, I believe that an absolute moral position rejecting torture in all instances—whatever the circumstances—involves serious problems. A proportionalist moral position offers more opportunities to exercise justice toward large numbers of potential victims implicated in a "ticking time bomb" scenario.

A proportionalist position underscores that one is often confronted with the clash between two moral evils. In such cases, I contend, one has to choose the lesser evil. For example, the act of amputating a leg to save a human life is an act with a double effect: the leg is lost, but the person's life is saved. The amputation is not a good in and of itself; it is and remains an evil. The amputation saves the life of the person, but the loss of the limb is not redeemable, at least not completely. Instead, that loss remains irreversible, tragic, and even shocking. Morally speaking, the act of amputation can therefore never be chosen for its own sake. That is why we say that in such an instance, the negative (evil) effect may never be intended, but only tolerated in light of a higher good to be attained. The amputation itself can never be called redemptive, even if the consequence is that a person's life is redeemed. The saving of the person can never make the amputation itself a good.

As applied to the issue of torture, therefore, proportionalist reasoning leads to moral complexity. On the one hand, this approach attempts to delay the use of this form of extreme violence as long as possible; on the other hand, this mode of argument does not deny the possibility that exceptional circumstances may exist in which not to torture may result in murder. It is only with "fear and trembling" that this line of argument attempts to realize its ethical call within the complexity occasioned by a realization that a potentially exceptional case may indeed become a reality.

I hold that any justification of torture should be made in the course of employing the strictest intellectual rigor, taking into account all those goods and evils that are at stake in a given context at a given moment. In fact, I agree with my respondents that I am arguing for a kind of "living absolute" rather than a "static absolute." In any discussion with those who would want to torture for a higher moral good, I would introduce criteria against which the legitimacy of torture must be measured so rigorously that, in practice, acts of torture will almost never be morally acceptable. These criteria are based on a long and solid tradition in Catholic moral theology, including, for instance, the just war theory developed by Augustine and Thomas Aquinas. This theory holds that the use of violence ought to meet rigorous philosophical, religious, and political criteria, which are indeed very strict and severe. These criteria are at work in key questions that test whether torture approaches moral legitimacy: How near and severe is the danger? How fundamental are the values at stake? Are no alternatives available? How useful will the eventual information be? How sure is it that torture will not cause death or irremediable harm? If the United States government had persistently raised these questions, and carefully applied the criteria embedded in them, not one person would have been tortured at Guantánamo.

Given my very restricted defense of torture as an *impossible* possibility, my respondents wonder why I do not reject torture outright. In short, they want me to be an absolutist, and I think they do so because they fear that my position plays into the hands of relativism and too easy "justifications" of torture. I reject that implication, and in doing so, I want to point out that absolutism is not necessarily the antidote for easy "justifications" of torture. For instance, one can claim to be absolutely opposed to torture on moral grounds but end up justifying torture by calling it something else— "enhanced interrogation techniques," for example, or other euphemisms such as "waterboarding." Absolutist discourse is no guarantee against torture. To the contrary, such discourse can be rendered powerless or, even worse, help to mask torture by calling it something other than what it is, all the while proclaiming "absolutely" that torture is never justifiable. The Holocaust drove home this lesson, for Nazism succeeded in combining ethical absolutism with moral relativism in a monstrous way.

Absolutists—including Nazi absolutists—strive to avoid uncertainties, but a proportionalist approach to torture learns to deal with moral uncertainty, complexity, and ambiguity. Advocates of proportionalism have no expectation that the unanswerable can be answered with perfection. Avoiding euphemistic language and speaking openly about torture, my proportionalist position emphasizes that even in the "ticking time bomb" scenario, we will never know *with certainty* that a bomb exists or that the person to be tortured is the right person, the one who possesses the necessary and exact information sought. We will never know *for sure* that torture will generate useful information and whether that information can be obtained in a timely manner. My approach to torture is put forward for *uncertain* situations and, in particular, for those in which every decision is likely to have an undesirable outcome, at least to some extent. It also recognizes that situations exist in which not acting becomes itself an act with severe moral implications. Thus, this approach is made for a world in which there are no finely tuned scenarios that can categorically legitimize or reject torture.

This brings me to yet other questions posed by my critics: Who gets to decide what's what in the circumstances I have noted? What if there are different interpretations as to the nature of a moral decision to be made? First, I emphasize that any moral decision to inflict torture can be made only in extreme circumstances that are always unique and contextual. Further, I argue that no government should be given the right to make a decision that would apply to each and every case in which the legality of torture is at issue: there is always a risk that governmental power may be misused. One can hope and pray that one will never be confronted with a situation in which torture seems justifiable. Yet virtually every human being, every group, every community can imagine circumstances in which that terrible dilemma could be real. If such situations do occur, one should know that all those involved will be held accountable for the choices they have made or not made; they will be held accountable also for the evils that may prove to be the outcome of these choices. Individual and public accountability is a central element in the proportionalist approach to torture. In addition, even if one finally decides not to torture in a circumstance of this sort, it must be understood that this is not necessarily a neutral act. A decision *not* to torture can also give rise to evil consequences.

It is true that my position is so strongly driven by the desire to avoid torture that it almost rejects torture outright. And indeed, I allow not so much for the possible occurrence of a "ticking time bomb" scenario per se, but rather for the eventuality that somewhere, sometime, an extreme and tragic situation may arise, a situation in which the suffering of others is so imminent that torturing the likely perpetrator or accomplice can be deemed the lesser evil. But this restricted view of torture is completely different from leaving the door of the torture chamber unlocked and wide open for perpetrators of torture, providing them with "convenient interpretive ways" to justify atrocity. Employing a proportionalist approach, there is simply never a "convenient" way to defend torture, nor any easy way to unlock—or permanently lock—torture's doors. My position demands that perpetrators of torture never feel comfortable, that they will always be held accountable for the evil they cause.

Paradoxically, one of the most telling reasons not to reject torture outright lies with the victims of the Holocaust, those whose bones have turned into dust and ashes. Levinas, I believe, would put the point as follows. Facing the question "Why not reject torture outright?" his response would emphasize four words: *because of the Other.*[14] Levinas stressed the importance of face-to-face relationships, but he did not interpret them as if there were only two persons in the world. He spoke about "Third Parties" too. The experience of the face of the Other is not the only relationship in which one must hear the commandment "Thou Shalt Not Murder." Levinas emphasized that we must address issues of social justice. Many others exist beside the Other. Properly understood, Levinas's philosophy is attentive to the presence of this third party. Sometimes, when we do something for the Other, it has a known or unknown effect on others. Levinas is sensitive to the difference between the interhuman relationship, where we only have moral concern for one another, and relationships with the larger society in which we have to be concerned with *all* others.[15] That consideration is the reason I do not embrace moral absolutism about torture: we should leave open—at least in theory—the possibility of torture in extreme cases precisely because of care for the suffering of others.

Following Levinas, I have made a clear choice to stay with an ethics grounded not in the heaven of theoretical moral principles but in a conflicted and violent world where people suffer unjustly. No one, I contend, should put his own moral comfort so far above the well-being of others that he would be opposed a priori to torture. Should a Nazi perpetrator captured by Allied Forces in the middle of World War II be a priori safe from torture if, theoretically, such a person could provide vital information that would lead to a highly effective attack on an extermination camp? Of course, this scenario also assumes that the decision would be made at a moment when the perpetrator is unwilling to give the necessary information even though he would be at no risk in doing so. In response, one can say that no such Nazi was ever captured in specific circumstances of that kind. My point is that a reflection on such a hypothetical situation should at least change, in theory, the nature of our argumentation about torture when the welfare of others is at stake. It should be clearly understood, in conclusion, that my advocacy of a proportionalist argument is completely different from any blind and random legitimation of torture.

NOTES

1   United Nations General Assembly, Universal Declaration of Human Rights, http://www.un.org/en/documents/udhr/index.shtml.

2   International Committee of the Red Cross, Convention (III) Relative to the Treatment of Prisoners of War, Geneva, 12 August 1949, accessible at http://www.icrc.org/ihl.nsf/COM/375-590006?OpenDocument.

3   Vatican, *Catechism of the Catholic Church*, para. 2297, http://www.vatican.va/archive/ENG0015/_INDEX.HTM.

4   Vatican, *Veritatis Splendor*, no. 80, http://www.vatican.va/holy_father/john_paul_ii/encyclicals/documents/hf_jp-ii_enc_06081993_veritatis-splendor_en.html.

5   This speech is available at http://w2.vatican.va/content/benedict-xvi/en/speeches/2007/september/documents/hf_ben-xvi_spe_20070906_pastorale-carceraria.html.

6   Michal Walzer, "Political Action: The Problem of Dirty Hands," in *Torture: A Collection*, ed. Sanford Levinson (New York: Oxford University Press, 2004), 72.

7   Jean Améry, *At the Mind's Limits: Contemplations by a Survivor on Auschwitz and Its Realities*, trans. Sidney Rosenfeld and Stella P. Rosenfeld (Bloomington: Indiana University Press, 1980), 40.

8   See Peter Haas, *Morality after Auschwitz: The Radical Challenge of the Nazi Ethic* (Philadelphia: Fortress Press, 1988).

9   See Victoria Barnett, *Bystanders: Conscience and Complicity during the Holocaust* (Westport, CT: Greenwood Press, 1999).

10   David Luban, "Torture and the Ticking Bomb," in *The Torture Debate in America*, ed. Karen J. Greenberg (Cambridge, UK: Cambridge University Press, 2006), 84–97.

11   Emmanuel Levinas, *Totalité et infini: Essai sur l'extériorité* (Paris: Kluwer Academic, 2001 [1961]), 100–104; Emmanuel Levinas, *Liberté et commandement* (Paris: Livre de Poche, 1999), 36–38.

12   *Cathecism of the Catholic Church*, para. 2297.

13   Wisława Szymborska, "Tortures," in *Poems New and Collected 1957–1997*, trans. Stanislaw Baránczak and Clare Cavanaugh (New York: Harcourt, 1998), 202.

14   The word *other* in Levinas's corpus is sometimes capitalized. The capitalization refers to persons insofar as they are understood in the essence of their being as other.

15   Emmanuel Levinas, *Otherwise Than Being or Beyond Essence*, trans. Alphonso Lingis (Dordrecht: Kluwer Academic, 1991), 159.

7

The Justification of Suffering

Holocaust Theodicy and Torture

SARAH K. PINNOCK

Defenders of theodicy, the attempt to reconcile God's power and goodness with even the most horrendous evil, are allies—unwittingly perhaps
but allies nonetheless—of the defenders of torture, for both justify suffering in the name of a greater good. At first glance, that proposition may
seem problematic, if not offensive. Focused on philosophical and theological inquiry about God's nature and the reasons for evil and suffering,
theodicy is primarily intellectual. On the other hand, while moral and
legal analyses of torture lie in the realm of the intellect, torture itself is
physical and psychological. It entails the deliberate infliction of bodily and
mental harm. These differences notwithstanding, I argue that those who
engage in theodicy and those who inflict torture share what can be called
a similar hermeneutic of instrumentalization: both theodicy and torture
interpret suffering as a means to an end.

Their knack for rationalizing and legitimating pain shows that the
practitioners of theodicy and torture not only participate in but also exert
considerable influence on the social construction of reality.[1] Imposing a
positive justification on the suffering of others, both discourses serve to
silence those who view their suffering as purposeless. I will highlight
Holocaust-related writings that vividly illustrate these claims. These writings provide valuable insight into diverse rationales for suffering, includ-

ing the perpetrators' self-justifications as well as the victims' interpretations of perpetrator motives. The Nazis assumed that their infliction of torture served worthwhile goals, but those who survived such torture emphasize the gratuitous and useless suffering it produced. Theodicy's attempts to account for evil and suffering are not restricted to the Holocaust and the torture it entailed, but that fact drives home all the more that the practitioners of theodicy and torture have much in common, because they impose meaning on misery.

Grounded in reflection on the Holocaust, this chapter compares and contrasts justifications of suffering in the discourses of torture and theodicy, drawing on perpetrator and victim perspectives as well as philosophical and theological responses. Beginning with the problem of God and evil, I discuss objections to theodicy by Jewish and Christian Holocaust theologians. Next, I contrast National Socialist justifications for torture with responses from Holocaust survivors Primo Levi and Jean Améry as well as from the philosopher Jean-Paul Sartre. The essay draws to a close with my response as a Holocaust scholar and as an American citizen to the use of "enhanced interrogation"—a pernicious euphemism for torture—by the United States after the terrorist attacks of September 11, 2011. My conclusion revisits parallels between the justificatory discourses of theodicy and torture, and questions whether theodicy can be good in a world so rife with torture.

Theodicy

The Holocaust raises pervasive theodicy questions, such as those articulated in the classic memoir *Night* by Elie Wiesel. On Rosh Hashanah 1944, teenage Eliezer prays with difficulty, asking: "Where are You, my God? How do You compare to this stricken mass gathered to affirm to You their faith, their anger, their defiance? What does Your grandeur mean, Master of the Universe, in the face of all this cowardice, this decay, and this misery?"[2] Older Jewish prisoners, such as Hasidic sage Akiba Drumer, affirm that God is testing faith and punishing sin or that suffering is preparation for the Messiah, yet Eliezer refuses to believe that God would condone mass murder. The narrator observes, tellingly, that if Drumer had been able to maintain the belief that his suffering was a divine test, he would have lived longer, but "as soon as he felt the first chinks in his faith, he lost all incentive to fight and opened the door to death."[3] *Night* points the reader toward a protesting response to suffering that maintains Jewish observances but questions their meaning. In later writings, Wiesel ponders why God accompanies his people into exile, and he finds it plausible that God weeps and lacks the power to intervene. But ultimately, Wiesel prioritizes faith questions over theodicy responses and insists that "nothing justifies Auschwitz."[4]

Among post-Holocaust Jewish thinkers, Richard Rubenstein is notable for his opposition to theological claims that God allows the Holocaust to fulfill divine purposes. In the first chapter of *After Auschwitz*, he reflects on his encounter with Pastor Heinrich Grüber, dean of the Evangelical Church of Berlin, a Protestant clergyman well known for his wartime opposition to National Socialism. They met in 1961, the same year that Grüber served as a witness for the prosecution in the Jerusalem trial of Adolf Eichmann, a key perpetrator of the Holocaust. Grüber's advocacy on behalf of Jews in Nazi Germany made it all the more shocking when Rubenstein heard him respond strongly in the affirmative to the question "Was it God's will that Hitler destroyed the Jews?"[5] Yes, Grüber answered, the Holocaust was part of God's plan. Rubenstein admired Grüber's logical consistency in applying the Christian doctrine of providence, but he was horrified at its meaning.

Not only did Grüber justify the deaths of six million Jews as fitting into salvation history, he also held that God gives the Jews a special destiny and used Hitler accordingly. Although Grüber was an ally of Jews, his conviction that Jews play a special or "mythical" role in history is problematic.[6] It may even have antisemitic implications. While scores of theologians agree with Grüber about the role of Israel and the lordship of God over salvation history, they typically blame human free will and sin for the Holocaust rather than holding God accountable, as Grüber did. In my view, however, even these more moderate theodicy claims fall under Rubenstein's critique because if God is creator and redeemer (as affirmed in Christian confessions), then God permits the Holocaust in redemption history. Rubenstein declares that such theodicy is immoral, and his conclusion is shared by other significant post-Holocaust Jewish writers, such as Emmanuel Levinas, Emil Fackenheim, and Eliezer Berkovits.[7]

Some post-Holocaust Christian theologians stringently object to theodicy and agree with Rubenstein that theodicy has scandalous implications. Those offering dissenting understandings of God's role in history include Johann Baptist Metz, John Roth, and Kenneth Surin.[8] The German Protestant theologian Dorothee Soelle is another notable example. In her

1970s response to the Holocaust, Soelle argued that theologians offer a sadistic view of God if they claim that all suffering is punishment for sin, and she observed that this point is made forcefully in the book of Job. Exploring the writings of the sixteenth-century Protestant reformer John Calvin on human unworthiness and submission to God, she deplored his conclusion that suffering is God's chastisement for sin. Soelle noted that theologians often try to balance authoritarian images of God with claims about divine love for humanity, but if God's love requires human suffering for a higher good, such as testing faith or strengthening character, that proposition raises more questions than it answers.[9]

This notion of divine omnipotence and human subjection to absolute power raises troubling parallels with Nazi ideology. To illustrate her point, Soelle quoted SS leader Heinrich Himmler in an address he gave to his officers on October 4, 1943, which justifies suffering as building strength. "Most of you know," said Himmler, "what it means to have 100 corpses lying side by side, or 500 or 1000. To have endured this and to have remained decent men in the process—except for exceptions caused by human weakness—this has made us hard as nails. This is a glorious page in our history that has never been written and never will be."[10] Utterly rejecting Himmler's position, Soelle finds that admiration of ultimate power is idolatrous, whether that power belongs to God or humanity. She observes that any "explanation of suffering that looks away from the victim and identifies itself with a righteousness that is supposed to stand behind the suffering has already taken a step in the direction of theological sadism, which wants to understand God as the torturer."[11] Political or divine, authoritarian control manifests abuse of power. Rejecting divine omnipotence, Soelle develops a theology of divine immanence, resistance to suffering, and mystical encounter with God that enables faith to endure despite pain.

While Rubenstein and Soelle advance theological opposition to theodicy, Emmanuel Levinas makes strong ethical objections in his philosophy of interhuman relationships. His landmark essay "Useless Suffering" develops a phenomenology of the suffering subject that displays suffering's excesses and the ethical imperative to see the suffering of the Other as useless.[12] Levinas observes that the logic of theodicy victimizes the victims after the fact by denying their witness to suffering, and he concludes with vehemence that "the justification of the neighbor's pain is certainly the source of all immorality."[13] In the framework of relation to the Other,

Levinas holds that the suffering of the other person is a call or an appeal that should evoke my responsibility. Faced with a suffering victim, I should respond as a person with the intention to give aid—or in Soelle's terms, with resistance to suffering—not with rationalizations that make pain useful. Levinas finds only one exception to suffering's uselessness: suffering in me generated in response to the Other. Compassionate or loving attention to the suffering Other can produce suffering in the person who gives care. This suffering is not the same as that of the suffering Other. Indeed, not even the communication of suffering is transferable, but responsibility for the Other makes one vulnerable.[14] Levinas's critique of theodicy clearly applies to situations of torture where pain is deliberately justified and the tortured person is dehumanized.

Torture

Under National Socialism, justification of torture exposed political reasoning based on racial definitions and genocidal prejudices. Special courts were created outside of the existing judicial system to apply exceptionally harsh penalties for crimes against the state and the German *Volk*. In 1934, for example, the *Volksgerichtshof* tribunals prosecuted cases of "treason," which was broadly defined as any activity harmful to the nation.[15] Especially after World War II began in 1939, theories of race offered legal justification for cruel treatment of Jews, gypsies, Poles, Slavs, and other eastern Europeans who were defined as *Untermenschen*, inferior mentally and physically.[16] In 1942, Heinrich Himmler ordered special interrogation policies for use "only against communists, Marxists, Jehovah's Witnesses, saboteurs, terrorists, members of resistance movements, antisocial elements, refractory elements, or Polish or Soviet vagabonds. In all other cases, preliminary authorization is necessary."[17] These regulations presumably established differences between torture applied to members of the *Volk* and torture applied to alien enemies, but they scarcely eliminated "unauthorized" actions. Himmler's orders might require a doctor to be present if more than twenty strokes were to be administered in an interrogation beating, but the purpose of that measure, far from having a humanitarian impulse behind it, was to keep a prisoner alive to prolong the interrogation. Favored torture methods—including sleep deprivation, starvation, whipping, trussing, pressing, and burning—differed among commanders and countries, but suspicion typically was a sufficient reason for inflicting torture.

The involvement of Nazi doctors in torture demonstrates its social normativity in the Third Reich. During the war, for example, the Germans believed that the Soviets had developed a drug to facilitate confessions. Convinced that such a drug could be immensely useful in combination with torture to obtain information from the Polish resistance, Nazi physicians in Auschwitz's Hygiene Institute conducted experiments to determine whether morphine and barbiturates could advance information extraction.[18] Other scientific investigations created conditions of torture for concentration camp subjects, including high-altitude and freezing experiments conducted in Dachau in 1942 on behalf of the *Luftwaffe* to determine the fate of pilots parachuting from damaged airplanes.[19] In retrospect, these so-called scientific investigations were mainly examples of a specialized type of torture.

For the perpetrators, torture was useful for building group cohesion and proving the "toughness" of SS guards and other officials. As early as 1933, Dachau camp commander Theodor Eicke issued regulations requiring prisoners to be treated with extreme brutality as enemies of the state, since "whenever the interests of the Fatherland are at stake, only ruthless measures are appropriate."[20] To inflict torture and conceal pity was a matter of honor and duty. Participating in acts of severe violence and observing them stoically became a mark of distinction and a source of group bonding, which is why Eicke ordered the torture of prisoners to take place in front of his men. Infliction of torture was supposed to harden and strengthen them, while the dehumanization of victims reinforced ideologies of superiority. Like other forms of brutality employed under National Socialism, torture intensified a sense of group belonging within a culture that glorified violence.[21]

Yet enthusiasm for torture could sometimes be deemed indecent. SS officer Wilhelm Boger of the Political Department at Auschwitz was famous in the camp for concocting the "Boger swing"—a torture device that suspended helpless prisoners and exposed them to vicious beatings that usually ended with the victim's death.[22] In Boger's 1949 trial, witnesses testified to his sadism, and trial research uncovered a 1943 reprimand from his superiors in Berlin for "excessive cruelty" and overstepping his authority. Boger received a heavy sentence from the postwar West German judiciary that convicted him—life plus five years—because there was evidence that he acted brutally on his own initiative. Ironically, the same courts were more lenient toward other SS camp guards who obeyed orders to torture, assuming that since their actions were routine, their superiors were mainly responsible. In the postwar denazification process, rather than deem as criminal all acts of those volunteer SS guards involved in torture, German courts and the public singled out sensational and grotesque cases of torture like Boger's for punishment, thus protecting the more ordinary perpetrators of torture from blame.

In addition to individual torture, a defining feature of National Socialism was the torture of large populations, which was enacted through social engineering. In contrast to the ratio of torturers to victims in a prison cell, victims in the concentration and death camps far outnumbered those who tortured them. Examining the purposes of the camps, Primo Levi observed that cruelty and misery far exceeded what was necessary for the mass murder that the Nazis committed. What Levi called "useless violence" prevailed. Since these excesses took considerable effort on the part of perpetrators, much above what was needed for simple extermination, motives for this useless violence seem enigmatic. Struggling to make sense of useless violence, Levi concluded that the underlying rationale was to make suffering an end in itself.[23] Choosing what he considered mundane examples instead of more dramatic ones such as medical experiments or torture devices like the Boger swing, Levi details boxcar transports, latrines, roll calls, senseless bed-making requirements, enforced nudity, malnutrition, tattooing, untreated diseases, and redundant physical labor. From the prisoners' point of view, he writes, "all these sufferings were the development of a theme, that of the presumed right of a superior people to subjugate or eliminate an inferior people."[24] This institutionalized torture physically concretized theoretical claims regarding the nature of the *Volk* and its enemies.

Jean Améry corroborated Levi's insights about useless violence in his analysis of the torture he endured in the Nazi internment camp at Breendonk, Belgium. Reflecting on his loss of dignity and trust in the world, Améry concluded that torture was the essence of National Socialism. While other regimes used torture as an expedient way to suppress resistance or extract confessions, Améry argued that for National Socialism torture was an absolute. To become "a fully valid representative of the Führer and his ideology," followers of Hitler "had to *torture*, destroy, in order to be great."[25] The fundamental justification of torture was the higher purpose of exalting the *Volk* and subjugating other peoples.

In the postwar period, the torture meted out by the Third Reich showed the regime's depravity and seemed to horrify the public. Thus there was widespread shock in the late 1950s when it became known that the French colonial government was using torture to suppress the revolt in Algeria. In the introduction to Henri Alleg's *The Question*, an autobiographical account of the torture of Alleg by the French in Algiers, the philosopher Jean-Paul Sartre drew a provocative parallel between the screams heard on the street from Gestapo headquarters in Paris in 1943 and those resulting from prison torture by the French during the Algerian War (1954–62). He wonders how the resistance of the French could be transmuted into silent complicity, how the French could move from victim to perpetrator in one decade. Reports like Alleg's eventually broke the silence, and Algerian independence was achieved, but the struggle on both counts was long and anguished.

Sartre concluded that, depending on the occasion and the opportunity, "anybody, at any time, may equally find himself victim or executioner."[26] I am concerned, however, that this statement underestimates power imbalances that exclude some oppressed groups from "equally" playing the role of executioner. The experience of gypsies and Jews during the Holocaust is a case in point. Nevertheless, from my standpoint as an American citizen in the aftermath of the terrorist attacks of September 11, 2001, I identify with Sartre's admonition. Under President George W. Bush, my government approved so-called enhanced interrogation techniques for use on terrorist suspects in the Guantánamo Bay detention camp and elsewhere, thus violating the humanitarian principles of the 1949 Geneva Conventions. To my dismay, I am a beneficiary of torture (euphemistically disguised) that is supposed to ensure my safety. I am uncomfortable admitting my proximity to perpetrators and question whether voting to oust the Republican government was sufficient resistance to what I consider morally wrong. While the United States justified enhanced interrogation for the sake of homeland security, from my position as a Holocaust scholar and US citizen, I cannot help remembering the association between torture and Nazism. I suspect that, in general, the use of torture is a sign of moral corruption in politics and society—that of my own country included.

Justification of Suffering

Theodicy and torture produce discourses that commonly justify the infliction of pain by blaming the victim, alleging character benefits for perpetrators, and contending that suffering advances higher purposes. In this section I argue that such justifications cannot withstand criticism, and I respond to some possible objections to my argument.

It is evident that defenses of torture and theodicy employ and arguably even depend upon justifications of suffering. In many instances of torture, the victim is considered to be subversive, criminal, or asocial—threatening in one way or another because he or she withholds information or is simply deemed alien and "other"—even though such accusations may be unfounded. The victim's "guilt" may be "explained" by something he or she allegedly has done or knows about, such as terrorist activity, or by some conferred negative ontological status, such as racial inferiority. In any case, causing the victim to suffer is justified, either as a means to extract information or punish behavior or as a confirmation of the victim's threatening inferiority. In theodicy, justifications of suffering work in different but related ways; they depend on claims that suffering is (1) the result of actions done—or improperly left undone—by human beings and (2) an ingredient—arguably an essential ingredient—in salvation history. Depending on how salvation history is understood, God may or may not bear responsibility for the suffering that results from human thought and action. The Holocaust erodes the defense of both torture and theodicy because it confirms, again and again, not only the disproportionality between suffering and justice but also the sheer uselessness of suffering. It is not plausible that Jewish concentration camp inmates were more collectively sinful than German Christians, nor that among prisoners, victims were tortured because they deserved it. Divine goodness and justice are called into question since God apparently permits massive, unnecessary, and unjustifiable suffering in the history of redemption, even if humans are the agents of evil.

Alternately, torture may be justified based on its benefits for perpetrators and for society at large. Under National Socialism, infliction of torture purportedly increased the torturer's might and bravery. This interpretation is an especially disturbing and perverse reversal of the maxim—problematic in its own right—that suffering makes one stronger. Supposedly, the perpetrators' infliction of suffering enhanced the nation by extracting useful information, ridding society of blight, and giving victims what they deserved. The analogue in theodicy would be that suffering is redemptive, and therefore those who inflict suffering—including those who torture—play a part in the realm of salvation history.

Some readers may object to any position that implicates God in torture. In response, I do not equate the agency of God with that of human torturers who are directly responsible for their acts, but that distinction does not altogether absolve God of responsibility. Admittedly, the theodicy attributed to Dean Grüber is extreme in affirming that Hitler was God's henchman. But like Rubenstein, I take seriously how the Jewish and Christian traditions make strong claims about God's role in the world. God is almighty, good, and just, and yet God at least permits overwhelming kinds and degrees of unnecessary suffering that can credibly be called nothing other than useless. God has overarching responsibility for the design of creation and the realization of redemption. According to the Bible, God has the power to intervene in the world, and God can reward and punish. Hence the Holocaust, including the unmitigated torture and suffering it entailed, raises serious questions about God's power, presence, and plan.

Some post-Holocaust Jewish and Christian thinkers propose to limit if not remove God's responsibility for suffering by contending that God has limited power, God suffers, and God depends on humanity for redemption. These debates about God are complex, and the multiple forms of theodicy cannot be completely covered here. In broad strokes, however, I maintain that because it defends God's goodness and justice, theodicy ends up justifying suffering and even torture.

Defenders of torture often appeal to "higher purposes" and the ways in which torture can benefit society by supporting them. Through the confessions it produces, the intelligence it gathers, and the national security it protects, torture allegedly benefits society. It is a means to ideal ends. As Améry so effectively argued, torture was integral to National Socialism. In the post-9/11 "war on terror," so-called enhanced interrogation has been dedicated to the aim of security at home and abroad. Like torture, theodicy also appeals to a higher purpose: for example, divine redemption referred to in biblical terms as the messianic age or the kingdom of God. This teleology of universal goodness and justice is ethically admirable, whereas state-sponsored torture is practiced under conditions of authoritarian control. Admittedly, there are vast differences in the content of these goals, but what is formally similar is the cost-benefit reasoning that instrumentalizes suffering. In discourses of both theodicy and torture, the ends justify the means, and the means, in one way or another, often involve and even entail suffering—even useless suffering.

My position is that every person is a moral and spiritual being, and therefore the suffering of others should never be viewed as the means to an end. While this concept of personhood and human dignity can be found in many sources, my views are influenced particularly by Emmanuel Levinas's ethics of responsibility for the Other, the interpersonal philosophies of Martin Buber and Gabriel Marcel, and Jewish and Christian moral teachings.[27] The seminal text in the Bible that grounds this standpoint is the statement that human beings are created in God's image (Gen. 1:27). I object to torture under all circumstances as a violation of human dignity. Moreover, I hold that use of torture has negative repercussions not only for victims but also for perpetrators, societies, and nations.[28] My commitment to the worth of each individual leads me similarly to argue that it is morally wrong to defend theodicy and, in particular, its proclivity to justify suffering as a means to redemption. It is better to protest against the Holocaust as an irresolvable moral scandal and enigma than to offer religious justifications for torture and other horrendous suffering.

I appreciate that there are readers who may accept some of my objections to theodicy but yet have faith that God has good reasons for permitting suffering, even if God is inscrutable and mysterious. I also realize that it is possible to approve of theodicy and oppose torture, despite my argument that theodicy justifies the suffering of others in morally objectionable ways. However, I am concerned that theodicy hinders recognition of useless suffering—including the useless suffering that torture inevitably produces—and discourages active protest against such harm. Theodicy lessens the scandal of suffering by giving it spiritual purpose and fails to provide the moral leverage needed to resist it. The indifference of many individual Christians and churches during the Holocaust illustrates my point.

On behalf of the victims of useless suffering, I conclude that it is logically consistent and morally right to oppose torture and theodicy simultaneously. More than half a century after the Holocaust, we can easily express disapproval of torture committed in the Nazi era. But we should also examine our proximity to contemporary uses of torture and find the courage to speak out against them. We can feel grief for the dead millions and question God, but we should not diffuse our present ethical responsibility with justifications of torture and suffering.

CONTRIBUTORS' QUESTIONS FOR SARAH K. PINNOCK

1. In addressing the relationship between torture and theodicy, you turn to Emmanuel Levinas's claim that the suffering of the other evokes responsibility in me. True, if I witness the suffering of another, I

should feel a need to respond. However, it seems that the perpetration of intended torture requires a different and more severe kind of responsibility than that associated with so-called natural suffering. You point to some of the rationales employed by Nazi torturers, whose ideological perspectives made torture a means to build social cohesion, advance medical experimentation, and exalt the *Volk*. From these perspectives, torture was much more than a method of obtaining information against a person's will; it was itself a key part of a specific regime and its goals. Given your position that one can no more justify divinely ordained suffering of any kind than one can justify the suffering caused by torture, what does the particularity of torture, especially in its Nazi forms, require people to do if they seek to be ethically responsible? As one considers the victim of torture inflicted by Nazis, or by anyone for that matter, what does ethical responsibility entail with regard to the victim, the perpetrator, and also with regard to God?

2. You argue that "the practitioners of theodicy and torture have much in common, because they impose meaning on misery," drawing on "a similar hermeneutic of instrumentalization." In a post-Holocaust world, is each and every justification of suffering suspect? You seem to agree with Levinas's judgment that teleological interpretations of suffering are "the source of all immorality." How far should critiques of teleology be taken? Are all attempts to justify evil equally reprehensible? Specifically with regard to torture, how might the world be different if our thinking about evil and suffering more closely reflected your outlook about them?

RESPONSE BY SARAH K. PINNOCK

My essay analyzes discourses about suffering and the rhetoric of rationalization. It objects to torture and theodicy because both validate suffering as serving good purposes and thereby silence the testimonies of victims. The questions above ask me to pursue two lines of reasoning that expand my analysis into applied ethics and constructive theology. What does reflection on the Holocaust suggest about how to act responsibly in situations of torture? If some theodicies are problematic, are all teleological justifications of suffering or God unacceptable?

I agree with the 1984 United Nations Convention against Torture, which calls torture "cruel, inhuman, and degrading," and with the prohibition of torture proclaimed in the Geneva Conventions of 1949. The particularity of Holocaust torture is important today because it underlines a key distinction between two types of justification: (1) a political justification when torture was inflicted on members of the "Aryan" *Volk* by the Nazi regime, and (2) a racial, ideological justification when torture was inflicted on people deemed "non-Aryan" by the Nazi regime. Imprisoned Germans could be tortured if special authorization was given, and the main purpose of this torture was to increase the severity and success of interrogation. Torture was applied particularly to those who threatened the state, such as members of the resistance and political opponents. In contrast, the very existence of non-Aryan peoples was seen as detrimental to the state, and torture was deemed appropriate to underscore their alleged subhuman status regardless of guilt or innocence with respect to specific actions. Their degraded status was sufficient to justify inflicting torture upon them. More than that, their degraded status arguably necessitated that torture should be inflicted upon them. This distinction remains crucial today if we are to grasp how torture works and why it is so prevalent in situations of extreme hostility and violence, especially in circumstances where ethnic, racial, religious, or national conflicts may approach genocidal proportions. Thus the Holocaust prompts examination of the close connections between torture and genocide in locations such as Rwanda and Bosnia. In such situations, action to end torture must occur within the primary framework of action to end genocide.

The Holocaust also helps to show that the distinction noted above is neither absolute nor exclusive. The lines can be blurred between torture for political reasons and torture rooted in ethnic or racial discrimination. For example, in the US-led "war on terror" after September 11, 2001, "enhanced interrogation" was employed for intelligence purposes at locations such as Guantánamo Bay and Abu Ghraib prisons and defended as a political tactic. Although the torture of suspected terrorists had political ends in view, the resulting dehumanization underscored that these suspects were deemed undeserving of human respect. Their degradation was justifiable even if they had no valuable intelligence to give. Indeed, their tortured status perversely served to brand them further as alien "others." Because al-Qaeda terrorists were Muslims, torturing them was more acceptable to the public in America and Europe because religious and ethnic as well as political identities distanced the victims as foreign and threatening.

My ethical reflections on torture draw on Levinas's model of interpersonal responsibility and his objections to theodicy as immoral. I think his framework of self and other means that an ethical response to torture must take into account the degree of separation between myself and people directly involved in torture—perpetrators and victims alike. As an American educator, I am sheltered from direct contact with torture. For me, encountering the tortured other or the torturer involves reading witness accounts or watching videotaped testimonies. But responsibility requires more than that. Responsibility to victims entails witnessing about and for them and registering political objections against their treatment. In addition, responsibility includes doing what I can to stop the perpetrators but also attempting to understand the historical and institutional conditions of torture and the range of choices of the agents of torture, who may have varying degrees of responsibility within a military or political system of authority. Levinas's ethics provides a response to torture with an extended sense of responsibility that reaches over distances and beyond differences.

Are there acceptable teleological justifications for the suffering that torture always produces? Two scenarios are frequently noted in contemporary debate. One involves the possibility of retributive justice, which could entail justifying torture as punishment, retaliation, revenge, or deterrence directed against, for example, a known perpetrator of atrocities. Another, a version of what is often called the ticking time bomb scenario, involves cases where torture might yield information that could save lives before it is too late, a rationale used by American officials to justify enhanced interrogation of suspected terrorists.

I disagree with both of these justifications of torture. Retributive justice cannot really be just if it entails the cruel, inhuman, and degrading methods that are part and parcel of torture. As for being a deterrent to terrorism and other forms of violence, torture is unlikely to be effective. To the contrary, its use is likely to inflame violence rather than reduce it. As far as defusing ticking time bombs is concerned, the information extracted by torture is rarely, if ever, sufficiently accurate or timely to produce the intervention that purportedly is available in no other way. Meanwhile, all uses of torture—including those in ticking time bomb scenarios—corrode the ideals of legal justice and democracy.

Theodicy may attempt to justify suffering in teleological ways by maintaining that it can serve good ends, such as punishing wrongdoing, developing character, or being among the sometimes unavoidable consequences of the unparalleled value of human freedom. Perhaps even the suffering caused by torture could lead to "positive" outcomes such as strength or resilience for victims, regret or apology from perpetrators, or political initiatives to delegitimize and prevent torture. But such rationalizations are unconvincing, especially if one gives the testimony of torture victims the respect it deserves. After being tortured, Jean Améry went on to write a profound essay on torture, which inspired ethical outlooks like mine. But does Améry's witness against torture justify his suffering as serving a good end? Does his suicide at age sixty-five militate against such justification? My point is that to instrumentalize suffering condones cruelty, which is wrong in itself, and no positive results can make such justifications ethical. Teleological interpretations of torture are never acceptable.

NOTES

1   On this point, see Elaine Scarry, *The Body in Pain: The Making and Unmaking of the World* (Oxford: Oxford University Press, 1985), esp. 56.
2   Elie Wiesel, *Night*, trans. Marion Wiesel (New York: Hill and Wang, 2006), 66.
3   Ibid., 77.
4   Elie Wiesel, *All Rivers Run to the Sea: Memoirs* (New York: Alfred A. Knopf, 1995), 105.
5   See Richard L. Rubenstein, *After Auschwitz: History, Theology, and Contemporary Judaism*, 2nd ed. (Baltimore, MD: Johns Hopkins University Press, 1992), 9.
6   Ibid., 13.
7   For an excellent study of Jewish antitheodicy, see Zachary Braiterman, *(God) after Auschwitz: Tradition and Change in Post-Holocaust Jewish Thought* (Princeton, NJ: Princeton University Press, 1998), 94.
8   John K. Roth, "A Theodicy of Protest," in *Encountering Evil: Live Options in Theodicy*, ed. Stephen T. Davis (Louisville, KY: Westminster John Knox, 2001); Johann Baptist Metz, *Faith in History and Society*, trans. David Smith (New York: Seabury, 1980); Kenneth Surin, *Theology and the Problem of Evil* (Oxford: Blackwell, 1986).
9   Dorothee Soelle, *Suffering*, trans. Everett R. Kalin (Philadelphia: Fortress Press, 1975), 24.
10   Quoted in ibid., 28.
11   Ibid., 32.
12   Many scholars who comment on Levinas's philosophy in English capitalize the word *other* (French, *Autrui*) to denote persons insofar as they are understood, in the essence of their being, as other.
13   Emmanuel Levinas, "Useless Suffering," in *The Provocation of Levinas: Rethinking the Other*, ed. Robert Bernasconi and David Wood (New York: Routledge, 1988), 163.
14   Ibid., 159.

15 Edward Peters, *Torture*, expanded edition (Philadelphia: University of Pennsylvania Press, 1996), 123.

16 Duncan Forrest, ed., *A Glimpse of Hell: Reports on Torture Worldwide* (New York: New York University Press, 1996), 24.

17 Peters, *Torture*, 125.

18 Robert Jay Lifton, *The Nazi Doctors: Medical Killing and the Psychology of Genocide* (New York: Basic Books, 1986), 290.

19 George J. Annas and Michael A. Groden, *The Nazi Doctors and the Nuremberg Code* (Oxford: Oxford University Press, 1992), 71–75.

20 Thomas Kühne, *Belonging and Genocide: Hitler's Community, 1918–1945* (New Haven, CT: Yale University Press, 2010), 66.

21 Ibid., 91.

22 Thomas C. Hilde, *On Torture* (Baltimore, MD: Johns Hopkins University Press, 2008), 11.

23 Primo Levi, "Useless Violence," in *The Drowned and the Saved*, trans. Raymond Rosenthal (New York: Vintage Books, 1988), 106.

24 Ibid., 115.

25 Jean Améry, "Torture," in *At the Mind's Limits: Contemplations by a Survivor on Auschwitz and Its Realities*, trans. Sidney Rosenfeld and Stella P. Rosenfeld (Bloomington: Indiana University Press, 1980), 30. The italics are Améry's.

26 Jean-Paul Sartre, "Preface," in Henri Alleg, *The Question*, trans. John Calder (Lincoln: University of Nebraska Press, 2006), xxviii. Alleg's book was originally published in French in 1958.

27 For analysis of objections to theodicy, see Sarah K. Pinnock, *Beyond Theodicy: Jewish and Christian Continental Thinkers Respond to the Holocaust* (Albany: State University of New York Press, 2002), esp. 97.

28 On this point, see Derek S. Jeffreys, *Spirituality and the Ethics of Torture* (New York: Palgrave Macmillan, 2009), esp. 139.

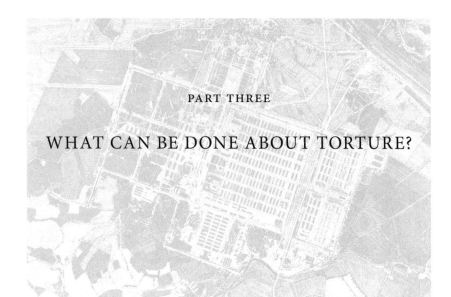

WHAT CAN BE DONE ABOUT TORTURE?

The question "What can be done about torture?" haunts this book. Reflections about a world in which all torture is condemned, or in which some torture might be legitimate, thread their way through the two previous parts. In this final section of *Losing Trust in the World*, the essayists explicitly raise questions about the prospects for healing and justice in a world that continues to be racked by torture. They try to identify and encourage at least some of the steps that are especially necessary and important to stanch the loss of trust that torture inevitably bleeds away.

Responses to this question fall into several categories. Some people concentrate on micro-level activities, working as individuals to advance the seemingly unending work of eliminating torture. Realizing respect for the "other" in day-to-day life; parenting the young to resist all forms of racism; educating students to honor the personhood of all their fellow humans—these are some of the ways for each of us to bear witness and give support on behalf of those who have suffered, and still suffer, at the hands of the torturer.

Although responses to suffering may emerge from the conscience of individuals, no person alone can do everything that is needed to curb, let alone eliminate, the scourge of torture. Thus the contributors to part 3 emphasize that communal cooperation and political action are critical to keep torture in check. Indeed, every person who holds this book, plus many more, can participate in movements committed both to healing those who have been tortured in the past and to preventing acts of torture in the future. Organizations such as the Center for Victims of Torture, the World Organisation against Torture, the Association for the Prevention of Torture, and the National Religious Campaign against Torture are only a few of many institutions that provide opportunities to work on a macro-level to eliminate torture in near and far corners of the earth. One need not choose between micro- and macro-level paths. Torture can be fought on the personal and the political fronts at the same time.

The contributors to *Losing Trust in the World*—including the essayists in this final section—have not randomly banded together. What binds us is a commitment to Holocaust studies, which in turn confers upon us the responsibility to reflect on torture, which was rife during the Shoah and is endemic now. Confronting torture during the Holocaust made it imperative to respond to the question "What is to be done about torture today?" This book's three final chapters try to envision how at least some trust in our fellow human beings might be regained in a still tortured post-Holocaust world. While these authors acknowledge the hideous ongoing presence of torture—and although they are not immune to the despair that led Jean Améry to contend that at times it might seem that Hitler had won a post-humous victory—the essayists in part 3 set themselves the task of reflecting on what can be done to deprive Hitler of that triumph.[1] The three authors approach this task in different ways: Margaret Brearley addresses the presence—and absence—of therapeutic care for torture victims; David Patterson warns us about those who are the successors of the Nazi enterprise of collective torture; and John K. Roth concludes the volume with a discussion that calls the reader to join those who commit themselves to "the responsibility to protect."

Margaret Brearley begins by noting the birth of a small number of rehabilitation centers established in the 1980s for survivors of torture. Although only a small fraction of these survivors have had access to treatment, those able to escape the tyranny of their governments and secure safe haven elsewhere often found therapists employing resourceful healing strategies. Just as the torturer often invents destructive acts, so must the healer outdo the torturer's "creativity" in his or her medical and psychological treatment of survivors. Brearley documents the challenges of the therapist, over decades, to restore dignity to those who suffer both a shattered body and a broken spirit.

In the second half of her essay, Brearley underscores that therapists working with torture victims have often learned much from the testimony of Holocaust survivors. Brearley, however, warns against simply grouping survivors of the Holocaust with other survivors of torture: those who survived the Holocaust had often developed "patterns of resilience, courage, and survival mechanisms . . . in ghettos and camps," thus aiding their own postwar integration and mitigating—at least in their own eyes—a need for psychiatric help. In lieu of seeking such help, many Holocaust survivors bonded with fellow survivors in the endeavor to establish informal self-help support communities. In the 1980s and later, large survivor organizations appeared, emphasizing the need for both individual and small group therapy. "Collective strengthening," Brearley contends, has militated against the hopelessness felt by these survivors of the Holocaust. She concludes that the survivors' experiences of collective torture can shed light both on other victims of torture and, by extension, on those who suffer from other and diverse forms of traumatization.

David Patterson's essay begins with the claim that torture in the post-Holocaust period has assumed those special characteristics that belonged, as Jean Améry claims, to the essence of the Third Reich. Nazi torture, in Patterson's words, has "spilled into what is now one of the most pervasive post-Holocaust assaults on the holy . . . , namely Islamic jihadism." Indeed, the central message of Patterson's essay is that we must remain vigilant in combatting what he perceives to be elements held in common by Nazism and jihadism. Patterson details the linkage between these two ideologies, contending that the latter has been deeply influenced by the former. The Nazis singled out Jews because of their racial identity; jihadists demonize Jews qua Jews in a similar manner.

Patterson further contends that the centrality of torture in both regimes stems from the desire to "negate the flesh-and-blood being of the victim" to impose their ideologies onto both the body and the spirit of the Jew. The Jew as Jew is called by "an absolute, transcendent commandment" to honor the sanctity of his or her fellow human, an outlook that negates the worldviews of both Nazis and jihadists. Thus for both Nazi and jihadist, hatred of the Jew is necessary and essential, "for the Jew most fundamentally undermines everything they respect." Those exclusionary worldviews, according to Patterson, understand race hatred not simply in biological terms but as protection against the "metaphysical category" of respect for the other person embodied in Judaism. Patterson concludes his essay by calling for moderate Muslims to oppose extremist Islamic jihadists and their seemingly total assault on the holiness of the human being.

Améry likened torture to rape.[2] Amplifying that relationship, John Roth begins this book's final chapter by stating that "no book on torture can pass muster if it fails to concentrate on rape/torture" and, in particular, on what he calls "rape/torture-as-policy—intentional and systematic use of rape/torture as a weapon of war and genocide." Although torture is a larger category, rape and torture, Roth reminds us, are "closely related and intertwined." Recognition of rape/torture, especially as it manifests itself in genocidal policy, is a necessary condition for responding to the "What can we do?" question put to the contributors to part 3. But more than that is needed, and thus Roth brings this book to a close by discussing "the responsibility to protect"—R2P, as it is frequently abbreviated. "As an international norm," Roth indicates, "R2P is in its infancy," but since 2005 it has had a least a foothold in international law. Strengthening support for R2P could help curb, if not eliminate, torture, including rape/torture as policy.

Whenever torture takes place, Jean Améry emphasized, "trust in the world breaks down."[3] Healing responses to that disaster require individuals and communities that protest and resist torture using every resource at their disposal—political, religious, medical, educational, and more—to keep that atrocity at bay. The chapters that bring this book to a close strive to move in that direction, encouraging, in Améry's words, "all those who wish to live together as fellow human beings."[4]

NOTES

1   Jean Améry first published *At the Mind's Limits: Contemplations by a Survivor on Auschwitz and Its Realities* (originally titled *Jenseits von Schuld und Sühne* [Beyond Guilt and Atonement]) in 1966. About a decade later, not long before Améry committed suicide, the book was reissued with a new preface by the author. It began as follows: "Between the time this book was written and today," wrote Améry, "more than thirteen years have passed. They were not good years. One need only follow the reports from Amnesty International to see that in horror this period matches the worst epochs of a history that is as real as it is inimical to reason. *Sometimes it seems as though Hitler has gained a posthumous triumph*. Invasions, aggressions, torture, destruction of man in his essence" (emphasis added). Jean Améry, *At the Mind's Limits: Contemplations by a Survivor on Auschwitz and Its Realities*, trans. Sidney Rosenfeld and Stella P. Rosenfeld (Bloomington: Indiana University Press, 1980), vii.
2   Ibid., 28.
3   Ibid.
4   Ibid., xiv.

8

Assuaging Pain

Therapeutic Care for Torture Survivors

MARGARET BREARLEY

Thou shalt not stand idly by the blood of thy neighbor.

—Leviticus 19:16

The Holocaust survivor Jean Améry called torture the "most horrible event a human being can retain within himself . . . an existential consummation of destruction."[1] As Améry emphasized, the torturer exercises "total sovereignty" to create terror and annihilation within individual victims and populations.[2] Regimes that routinely employ torture, Michael Taussig observes, control populations "through the cultural elaboration of fear" and by crippling "a people's capacity to resist."[3] They use torture in the name of a so-called higher good. "Every regime that tortures," Ariel Dorfman rightly underscores, "does so in the name of salvation, some superior goal, some promise of paradise," with torturers generally thinking of themselves as "guardians of the common good."[4] Torture inverts truth, goodness, and all normality; victims are reduced by intolerable pain to nonhuman animals, and torturers become inhuman savages. Indeed, said Améry, "torture becomes the total inversion of the social world, in which we can live only if we grant our fellow man life, ease his suffering, bridle the desire of our ego to expand."[5]

Care for Torture Survivors

In the early 1980s, medical centers for the care of torture survivors began to be founded, their establishment inspired by Amnesty International's 1972–73 campaign against torture and its 1984 report, *Torture in the Eighties*, as well as by public opposition to torture that mounted in the mid-1970s with support from the World Medical Association, the International Council of Nurses, and the World Psychiatric Association. In 1981, the General Assembly of the United Nations created a Voluntary Fund for Victims of Torture. By 2016, a global network of more than 140 torture rehabilitation centers existed, each a member of the International Rehabilitation Council for Torture Victims.[6] Established in 1982, the oldest is the International Rehabilitation and Research Centre for Torture Victims (RCT) in Denmark. Soon after, in 1985, the London-based Medical Foundation for the Care of Victims of Torture (now called, and hereafter identified as, Freedom from Torture) was founded by Helen Bamber, surgeon Elizabeth Gordon, and other doctors.[7] Therapeutic centers were subsequently created throughout Europe, the United States, South America, Southeast Asia, and elsewhere. A few discreet organizations operate in countries still using torture.

Only a tiny minority of torture victims can access such centers. Typically, countries that practice torture do not have torture rehabilitation centers. If such centers exist in those places, they operate under severe difficulties and are sometimes attacked. Edward Peters assesses the situation accurately: for the vast majority of torture survivors "who cannot escape their country, or where there has been no governmental change from the time of their torture, rehabilitation is almost impossible."[8] However, torture survivors are often among those who do manage to flee to safe havens in exile. In the early twenty-first century, lawyers representing asylum applicants in the United States estimated that that at least 50 percent of their clients were torture victims.[9]

Rehabilitation centers for torture survivors seek to reverse torture's catastrophic inversions of normality and human wholeness. Their medical and psychological therapists try to restore dignity to survivors, to heal where possible and encourage acceptance of what cannot be mended, and to publicly resist torture. Psychiatrist and psychotherapist Johan Lansen, who has treated torture victims in Berlin and Copenhagen, notes that "torture and psychotherapy are antithetical to each other. Where therapy aims at liberating people from pain, torture wants to oppress fellow human beings and consciously cause pain. Therapy promotes personal autonomy, while torture aims at total dependence. Therapy means growth; torture, deprivation of the psyche's brilliance and mutilation of the body. For that very reason, therapists and torturers are each other's mortal enemies."[10]

Consequences of Torture

Torture uses many physical devices and psychological techniques to inflict maximum pain and to break a victim's will and personality. Consequently, torture survivors are left with complex physical and psychological conditions that require treatment by varied specialists. Many torture rehabilitation centers employ not only medical staff, psychotherapists and psychiatrists, physiotherapists, and a range of psychoanalysts, but also therapists who use music, art, crafts, or writing. For, as Dori Laub observes, a torture survivor is "a whole person, a person whose life has been shattered on multiple levels. . . . A shattered life needs multiple levels of intervention in striving to become whole again."[11] Consequently, at Freedom from Torture and other centers, "treatment is as flexible and imaginative as the ingenious cruelty that it undermines."[12]

Torture takes many forms: "A myriad of techniques are used to inflict pain, including suspension by the limbs for prolonged periods; mock executions; mock drowning; electric shocks; deprivation of sleep, food, water and light; unrelenting beatings with fists, studded belts, batons and rifle butts; and rape, a torture inflicted on both men and women."[13] Extreme forms of torture, such as falanga (beating of the soles of the feet), as well as sexual violence, can cause catastrophic and long-lasting physical injuries. Permanent damage can include fractured or mutilated limbs, broken backs, deep internal trauma, major difficulties in walking, damaged nerves, brain trauma, loss of cognition and memory, migraines, and epilepsy. Virtually all survivors suffer from chronic pain.

The psychological as well as physical damage can be catastrophic. Probably the majority of torture survivors suffer from posttraumatic stress disorder (PTSD), and virtually all have deep-seated psychological wounds, often including profound depression. As Améry observed, "Torture has an indelible character. Whoever was tortured, stays tortured. Torture is ineradicably burned into him, even when no clinically objective traces can be detected."[14] Therapists stress that torture survivors' complex psychological reactions are normal human reactions to extreme, abnormal, and inhuman acts. The torturers' hatred is inscribed on the survivors' bodies. Usually the survivors' inner worlds are deadened by the torturers' violence. As psychotherapist Mary Raphaely notes, "For so many, torture is experienced as a rupture which they cannot reach behind, disrupting the core of their identity."[15] Torture ruptures not only bodies but lives; for many survivors, it obliterates memory of past happiness, denies hopes for the future, and scars all sense of selfhood in the present.

The physical and psychological losses experienced by torture survivors are by no means the end of that sad story. Survivors likely have lost "work, status, family, and credibility" as well.[16] Often their family and friends have also been tortured or killed, and survivors have lost community, homeland, and language. Devastatingly, they have lost trust in their fellow man and inhabit a world that now seems meaningless. Many live in a state of chronic fear, hopelessness, and what psychotherapist Jeremy Woodcock termed "a terrifying existential loneliness."[17] Helen Bamber aptly echoes Améry when she sums up the consequences by emphasizing that "there is no end to the effects of torture."[18]

Attributes of Therapists

During and immediately after the extreme violence of torture, the "tortured person," declared Améry, "is only a body, and nothing else beside that."[19] The therapists' long-term challenge, however, is not only how to bring physical healing to the wounded body but also, and above all, how to restore and heal the broken spirit. Gaining the trust of survivors is challenging, because torturers can use apparent kindness in the process of destroying a victim's will. Having experienced "sadistic interrogators and friendly ones," says Behnam Behnia, "survivors are likely to respond to service providers with a great deal of suspicion and trepidation."[20] Therapists must not only demonstrate their trustworthiness but also create an environment for healing that differs as much as possible from places of imprisonment and torture. "Non-conventional space," explains Mary Raphaely, "is absolutely essential."[21] (At Freedom from Torture, the main waiting area, overlooking a garden, is colorful, lined with pictures, and filled with the sound of a fountain. The corridors used by survivors are curved rather than straight.)

Another obstacle to trust-building in the recovery process is that torture victims know medical professionals are frequently part of the torture process.[22] Therefore, doctors involved in caring for torture survivors must proceed with special sensitivity. The "medical examinations must be part of the therapeutic relationship," Bamber stresses, and they must be conducted with maximum thoughtfulness—especially when victims have endured sexual torture.[23]

Therapeutic centers for torture survivors, such as the Primo Levi Centre in France, emphasize that, because the "symptoms which follow torture . . . are multiple, complex and deep-rooted," the therapeutic response must be interdisciplinary and take place on multiple levels, with the aim of offering "containment and accompaniment of such intense suffering."[24] The therapeutic act of "walking *with* people"[25] involves "understanding who the person really is."[26] For some therapists, working with torture survivors is "almost a religious act. . . . One therapist says he feels almost like a priest."[27] Some therapists have had their own torture experiences. Many have parents who were Holocaust survivors or war refugees. Still others have themselves gone into exile. Marion Baraitser, a writer who has worked in London with the Baobab Centre for former child soldiers and trafficked children, stresses the empathy deriving from such pain-filled personal histories. "To have been wounded," she states, "can be used to identify with others who are wounded . . . can create a pathway that is very genuine and can help to heal. . . . One's own suffering opens up a vein to everyone else's suffering."[28] Here again, healers and victims, on the one hand, and torturers, on the other, stand at opposite poles. As Elaine Scarry underscores, "There are no two experiences farther apart than suffering and inflicting pain."[29]

Therapeutic Approaches

Nowhere more than during torture, says Scarry, "does language come so close to being the concrete agent of physical pain. . . . The question, whatever its content, is an act of wounding; the answer, whatever its content, is a scream."[30] Torture survivors often protect themselves by retreating into deep silence and muteness, but a listening, responsive voice can eventually bring release from that self-silencing. Some survivors suffer from memory impairment due to cognitive changes brought about by beatings to the head, but most must cope with memories of pain, shame, and utter vulnerability, which intrude agonizingly into daily consciousness. The unbearable past renders the present unbearable too. Working toward healing torture survivors demands extraordinary patience and tact. Eliciting a survivor's story can take many months, involving a gentle mode of slow, attentive listening rather than direct questioning.

While all therapists aim at enabling torture survivors to voice their suffering in speech, thus rediscovering and affirming their own unique identity through the spoken word, some counselors encourage more permanent expression. For example, several professional writers in London, influenced by Dori Laub's pioneering testimony therapy with Holocaust survivors and Viktor Frankl's logotherapy, have helped torture survivors to express themselves in writing. Sonja Linden, playwright, theater director, and 2001 writer-in-residence at Freedom from Torture, notes the beneficial effects for survivors participating in the Write to Life project. "To re-visit the experience of torture and degradation is to re-enter the darkest tunnels of memory," Linden observes. "It needs not just courage and determination but faith—faith that there will be light at the other end. The hope of being read is one such light."[31] Sheila Hayman, filmmaker, writer, and long-time leader of the Write to Life project, maintains that for torture survivors writing is "a powerful and subtle tool." When read in public, she states, their words—factual or fictionalized accounts of their own suffering—"bounce off the audience like a mirror, an echo chamber." This experience provides assurance "that *they* [the torturers] have not managed to destroy me. Reading [aloud] is a fortress, a playground, a movable home—one can take it anywhere, it cannot be taken away."[32]

Therapists try to unlock sources of resilience within survivors by reaching behind the trauma to evoke memories of a pretraumatic past and also by fostering skills and human bonding in the posttraumatic present. Freedom from Torture's Natural Growth Project is an innovative example of such resilience building. Mary Raphaely, who works within the project, notes that "nature provides a continuum between a client's pre- and post-traumatic states."[33] Some of the most mute and fragile survivors are given psychotherapy through gardening, either in Freedom from Torture's garden or, for those who are more robust, in rented allotments. The aim of such therapy, Sonja Linden and Jenny Grut explain, "is for the client to be able to remember the past within the present, without being overwhelmed."[34] Pleasant childhood memories of gardens, grandmothers, and village life may be kindled by certain herbs or particular flowers. The minute acts of gardening—planting and pruning, spacing plants and weeding—can absorb clients in a creative present. As one survivor commented, "When I garden, I feel I have a painkiller medicine to make me strong."[35]

Therapeutic centers for torture survivors, cognizant of the self-healing potential inherent in community bonding, also foster the gradual building of new relationships through therapy in small groups. Workshops for music, painting, cooking, crafts; family therapy groups; groups based around a homeland or language; multiethnic groups—these can break through the intense isolation endured by tortured persons and may renew their creativity. Within such groups, the individual discovers that he or she is not alone in being consumed by the anguish, self-condemnation, grief, and shame imposed by torture. The groups can allow a protected space for mourning the dead, for gradual empathy with others' pain, for the rediscovery of laughter, song, and joy in life. At their best, therapists give torture survivors what Naomi Stadlen calls "heartroom."[36] Realizing the survivors' pain and becoming vulnerable themselves, therapists, like good parents, try to affirm each survivor's distinctive identity. Where possible, they restore language and memory, summon awareness of beauty and new life options, and create protective yet sociable space.

Deep Parallels

Some therapists have observed deep parallels between torture survivors and survivors of the Holocaust. Early on, the Israeli psychiatrist Shamai Davidson discerned that torture survivors could be better understood "through the paradigm that has emerged from our understanding of the prolonged suffering and after-effects of survivors who emerged from the Holocaust."[37] Dina Wardi is another psychotherapist who probes parallels between the experience of survivors of torture and Holocaust survivors. "The primary purpose of the Nazi psychological warfare," she writes, "was the destruction of the Jewish people as a collective . . . realized partly through the destruction of the identity and personality of each individual as a person and as a Jew."[38] Virtually all Holocaust survivors endured multiple forms of massive and prolonged collective trauma, experiencing, in the words of genocide scholar Israel Charny, the "persecutory brutalization and systematic torture of the Holocaust odyssey of evil."[39] These survivors were subjected to multiple torments amounting to torture, which, in Jean Améry's words, was the "essence" of the Third Reich.[40] Virtually all camp survivors experienced starvation, unspeakable terror, multiple violent and sudden bereavements, constant pain, and systematic degradation that included what Terrence Des Pres called "excremental assault."[41] Survivors of Nazi extermination camps had "experienced particularly intense and destructive forms of traumatization."[42] All had been destined for eventual annihilation in camps that reduced individuals to agonized particles of one vast, collectively tortured body. None remained unscathed at the hands of the SS, who functioned, individually and collectively, as torturer and executioner.

In the primitive conditions and often harsh restrictions of Displaced Persons (DP) camps in Germany immediately following World War II, those survivors of extermination camps, concentration camps, and death marches who could be saved from starvation or disease were slowly nursed back to physical health. That treatment, however, could not erase the fact that each survivor bore a unique individual burden of massive loss, physical pain, psychological trauma, and often suppressed rage. Some of the most traumatized committed suicide. Each Holocaust survivor had experienced the total isolation of the torture victim, for, in Dori Laub's words, at the very core of Holocaust trauma lies "the complete failing of the empathic human dyad; the executioner does not heed the victim's plea for life and relentlessly proceeds with execution. Human responsiveness came to be non-existent in the death camps."[43]

For many years after their liberation, most Holocaust survivors were given no therapeutic care, but they commonly formed intense social communities that helped to reestablish and sustain identity. Sometimes fragmented survivor groupings grew into spontaneous therapeutic communities. For example, speaking of the 45 Aid Society, created by over six hundred "boys" brought from concentration camps to Britain in 1945, Buchenwald survivor Ben Helfgott told me, "We were each other's therapy."

Virtually everyone who survived the Holocaust did so because of human reciprocity between victims, even in the most extreme conditions. Nearly all camp survivors had been in mutually supportive pairs or small groups. Such relationships often strengthened morale and encouraged the will to live. As Jewish survivors gradually regained physical strength and therapeutic solidarity in postwar DP camps, an essential "we" was built through the creation of schools, the restoration of religious rituals and festivals (though often reinterpreted in the light of the Holocaust), "mourning academies" to gather the survivors of particular towns or regions on key dates (including anniversaries of Nazi liquidations of ghettos), and cultural activities, including newspapers and reenactments of Holocaust experiences.[44]

By 1951, the majority of survivors had emigrated to Israel or elsewhere. All but the most traumatized integrated into society, energetically immersed themselves in work, and created families. Generally faced with uncomprehending or indifferent populations, silence about their traumatic past was common outside of groups of fellow survivors. Deep psychic pain— though often manifest in unusual behavior and family relationships lived in the shadow of murdered relatives—was seldom verbalized. By the 1950s and 1960s, psychiatrists working in Europe, the United States, and Israel encountered in many Holocaust survivors massive and sometimes irreversible psychological traumatization. The Norwegian psychiatrist Leo Eitinger, himself a Holocaust survivor, called this traumatization "concentration camp survivor syndrome." Typical manifestations included chronic anxiety, depression and irrational fears, perpetual feelings of loss, emptiness, mourning for murdered family members, inability to enjoy life, feelings of depersonalization, and "living as if dead."[45] Psychiatrists were unprepared "for the experiences of multiple loss and the severity of the trauma suffered by Holocaust survivors. The scope and scale surpassed the imagination."[46] While, in the face of such deep trauma, psychiatrists generally recognized the inadequacy of current clinical terminology, drug-oriented psychiatric practices, and traditional Freudian neurosis-oriented psychoanalysis, some avoided recognizing the clear links between psychiatric symptoms and the collective torture endured during the Holocaust. In many hundreds of Holocaust survivors, states Dori Laub, "trauma-related illnesses were neglected in diagnosis and decades-long treatment."[47]

Yet there were psychiatrists, especially those who were themselves Holocaust survivors or children of survivors, who did recognize such links. Some became convinced that psychological symptoms found in virtually all Holocaust survivors were "actually logical responses to a bizarre and extreme trauma" and that, while some psychic damage was so catastrophic as to be irreversible, empathic therapists could bring considerable healing.[48] They pioneered new and influential therapeutic approaches. Elie Wiesel noted that Leo Eitinger did "wonders in exploring the wounded soul and the burning memory of survivors before bringing them relief and consolation."[49] Laub and others championed intense listening to survivor testimony, a "very special alertness to subtle cues and mostly unintended signals, to the resonances of the traumatic event."[50] Attentive listening to survivors elicited important insights. Davidson saw that flashbacks and other symptoms labeled as PTSD often represented valuable integrative "episodes of . . . cathartic working through of traumatic memories while at the same time struggling . . . to find meaning in life."[51] It was recognized that certain patterns of resilience, courage, and survival mechanisms developed in the ghettos and camps had aided postwar integration—so much so that, although nearly all Holocaust survivors had experienced deep psychological traumatization, the majority did not feel the need for psychiatric help. Conversely, certain consequences of massive trauma, such as psychic numbing, had led to long-term dissociation and emotional and cognitive disturbance in some survivors. Davidson and others realized that child survivors suffered especially profound long-term psychological damage, and that many survivors' children had been deeply affected by their parents' traumatic past.

One insight—that reciprocal sharing lessens pain and that self-help survivor groups, acting as a substitute for lost families and communities, are profoundly therapeutic—encouraged the formation of large survivor organizations during the 1980s and 1990s: Amcha (Israeli Center of Holocaust Survivors and Their Families) in 1987, the psychotherapeutic Shalvata Mental Health Center (1990, also in Israel), the purely social Holocaust Survivors' Centre (1993) in London, along with several others in North America and elsewhere. Such organizations emphasized small group therapy in addition to highly individualized counseling. Therapists noted that as Holocaust survivors aged and experienced new vulnerabilities in illness and bereavement, traumatic memories of horror that had been suppressed or controlled would "return in reinforced strength" and disrupt normal life.[52] Survivor centers proved to be invaluable therapeutic sources of friendship, shared ritual, creative activity, and memorialization of the dead. Judith Hassan, director of Shalvata in London from 1991 to 2010, wrote that although "there can be no cure for the deep wounds that exist, . . . there is a sense of collective strengthening through being together which challenges the chaos, the darkness and the hopelessness in the aftermath of trauma."[53] For so long "outsiders" to the host community, in such centers, Hassan observed, survivors became "insiders"—powerful, self-determining, and mutually supportive.

Both Davidson and Hassan urged that psychotherapists working with the "living witnesses of unimaginable terror" *must* be affected by what they heard. If necessary, they ought to cross professional boundaries "in order to convey trust and a sense of immersion [in] . . . the unique experiences of each survivor."[54] Moshe Teller, a psychotherapist who has worked both at Shalvata and at Freedom from Torture, speaks of the need for therapists to "hold survivors emotionally in difficult times" and to have "a zealous responsibility for the other."[55]

Elie Wiesel praised Eitinger's "capacity to pierce the wall of silence that surrounds the voices of so many Jewish Holocaust survivors."[56] Now being replicated to assist torture survivors, the healing, helping Holocaust-related work of Eitinger and other therapists reflects Elaine Scarry's profound hope that "these . . . acts that restore the voice become . . . almost a diminution of the pain, a partial reversal of the process of torture itself."[57] Through a "secular holiness" that opposes the darkest evils of the Holocaust and torture, one glimpses at least partial fulfillment of the psalmist's hope: "God is with me through my helpers; therefore I can face my foes" (Psalms 118:7).[58]

CONTRIBUTORS' QUESTIONS FOR MARGARET BREARLEY

1. You argue that perhaps more than other victims of torture, Holocaust survivors early on formed their own networks and relied on one another for healing. Left to their own devices, without the benefit of rehabilitation centers or other organized forms of therapeutic care, many of the Holocaust's torture victims nevertheless found healing. You quote one Holocaust survivor as saying, "We were each other's therapy," and you state that "by 1951 . . . all but the most traumatized integrated into society, energetically immersed themselves in work, and created families." You add that although nearly all survivors of the Holocaust experienced trauma, "the majority did not feel the need for psychiatric help." Your analysis offers hints about what the experience of Holocaust survivors can teach us about rebuilding life after torture, but can you be more specific about that relationship? In what ways might the experience of Holocaust survivors influence contemporary therapeutic care for victims of torture?

2. Given your findings regarding Holocaust survivors' healing processes, how might these perspectives apply to those of us who neither were victims of torture during the Holocaust nor are professional therapists who continue the work of healing them? How might laypersons who

have not been subjected to torture stand with and support Holocaust survivors and victims of torture? In a post-Holocaust world, how might concerned people take responsibility for strengthening the relationships that foster mental health? Could your research help to create a moral universe in which torture becomes unthinkable?

RESPONSE BY MARGARET BREARLEY

Torture destroys and aims to destroy: it desecrates. As Elaine Scarry noted, civilization creates artifacts to shelter and protect humans, to reduce pain; torture uses artifacts to destroy humans, to create maximum pain. In Scarry's words, "Torture *begins* at precisely the point where [civilization] has left off: it starts by appropriating and deconstructing the artifacts that are the products of creation—wall, window, door, room, shelter, medicine, law, friend, country, both as they exist in their material form and as the created contents of consciousness. Torture *ends* at what is the other's starting point; it "produces" the pain that has not only been eliminated by the act of creation, but whose very existence had been the condition that originally occasioned the act of creation."[59] For Scarry, torture reverses the process of creation at the heart of civilization.

To counter the destruction of torture, the "ongoing work of civilization" is, according to Scarry, "making making . . . 'remaking making,' rescuing, repairing, and restoring it to its proper path each time it threatens to collapse into, or become conflated with, its opposite."[60] This insight has profound significance. For, as Scarry stresses, "these same interpretive categories would, if themselves unfolded and developed, also make it possible to enter and understand other concussive events."[61] In other words, this pattern of re-creation, renewing all means of easing pain as the obverse of the destruction of torture, opens the possibility and intensifies the moral impetus for each of us to become co-creators in the reduction of pain. So, while relatively few may know Holocaust survivors and far fewer still knowingly meet torture survivors, all of us encounter those who have suffered "concussive events." The homeless, the newly bereaved (especially bereaved parents), those enduring mental breakdown or disorder are among the many victims of catastrophic rupture and loss who can feel inwardly "tortured."

Scarry's vision offers practical hope to us as individuals. For just as organizations helping survivors of intense man-made trauma use artifacts—walls, shelter, medicine, law, friendship, country—to help repair and restore, so can each of us do so. The open door; the laid table; walls and rooms that welcome guests within them; homes as shelter not only for family and friends but for strangers and those suffering; offering friendship to the other, to those who are isolated or distressed, to those from ethnic communities other than our own—all these make for healing.

John Schlapobersky, himself a torture survivor and a long-standing group analyst and therapist working with survivors of torture, stresses the key value of the therapist's "therapeutic presence."[62] That presence contrasts with the absence of compassion in the wider world, exemplified for Schlapobersky in W. H. Auden's poem "The Fall of Icarus," which notes how "everything turns away / Quite leisurely from the disaster."[63] Attentive "presence" is one key to understanding how Holocaust survivors supported each other by being "for the other," creating a group "therapeutic presence." This compassionate self-help in groups can be deeply healing, as Schlapobersky has noted: "A small group of suffering people can help to relieve the problems for each of them. . . . The key to this process has something to do with generosity."[64]

Margi Abeles, a London therapist who has long worked with Holocaust survivors, found that in the early postwar years, the conventional wisdom was "don't go there."

> Survivors had somehow survived the prolonged traumatization and torture of the Shoah, where black was white and dehumanization was planned. . . . Holocaust survivors just got on with their lives and put the experience "somewhere else," as they had no audience other than one another and no one else would listen. . . . They did not have the luxury to mourn. . . . The "survivor syndrome" was pathologized; it was labelled psychiatrically and treated as a mental health category. . . . Only when there were people who *could* listen did the realization come that the telling, the validating and normalizing of their experiences, and the affirmation that survivors have every right to feel deep emotions about their past experiences of trauma, *are* therapeutic."[65]

This tradition of mutual support and therapeutic listening has influenced contemporary therapeutic care for torture survivors. It also offers insights for lay people who befriend survivors of man-made trauma. Torture destroys bodies; our own bodies can help creatively to rescue and restore others. Are our eyes, in poet Edwin Muir's phrase, sufficiently "rinsed and wrung" to notice pain, to perceive the pain in others' eyes? Are our ears attentive enough to hear others' stories, to listen to pain? Do our words create rather than destroy? Do we use them to encourage, to praise and thank, to console? Do we run toward victims of catastrophe rather than walk away from them? Do we stand *with* rather than stand by? Are our hands outstretched to offer help? Such hands, ears, words can help heal. As one torture survivor told Schlapobersky, "Yours is the hand of humanity that has reached out and saved me from drowning in my sorrow."[66]

Torture survivors and their families bear inner, human-inflicted wounds. Maimed inwardly, they may also limp or bear outward scars, but often we cannot distinguish them among the broader crowds of refugees and immigrants. Yet, remembering that they are there, wounded and still vulnerable, can make us more sensitive to all the strangers around us. A ready smile, a kindly word, an impromptu offer of help, a diplomatically inquisitive question, may have far greater significance than we might realize.

There is much that we laypersons can do to stand with and support survivors—Holocaust and torture victims included. Some readers of these words will already have bonds of friendship with Holocaust survivors, bonds that are increasingly important as the survivors age, become frail, experience bereavement, and approach death. Donating money to organizations dedicated to the relief and support of torture and Holocaust survivors is paramount, since it enables trained professionals and caring volunteers to provide skilled therapies within a healing environment. Fundraising itself, using whatever skills we have, can foster human warmth and mutual attentiveness, the very obverse of torture: coffee mornings, charity lunches, musical soirees, even holding collecting tins on main streets all build networks of friendship and are profoundly creative.

The insights of Abeles and Schlapobersky can help us as concerned people "to take responsibility for the web of relationships that fosters mental health." Abeles urges being there *for* people, never stigmatizing or labeling, being willing to learn from shared experiences of pain, and not only affirming the reality of others' suffering but also praising their achievements in having survived, in having created despite everything. Our admiration strengthens their resilience: "Making sense of what has happened, giving hearing, helps a survivor to manage."[67] The biblical verse "Be angry and sin not" is relevant here.[68] One should be fiercely angry about all forms of torture. Campaigning against the use of torture through such organizations as Amnesty International is vital. But so too is knowledge about the history of torture as well as its current geography. For, as Schlapobersky stresses, "those who apply torture know far more about it than those who oppose it."[69] To be aware that Britain used torture in Malaysia and Kenya, France in Algeria, and the United States in Iraq and elsewhere should militate against any sense of moral superiority and result in our upholding the rule of law at all costs.

Other contributors to this book ask whether my research could help "to create a moral universe in which torture becomes unthinkable." Tragically, torture will always remain thinkable, a ready tool of state dictatorships and violent extremists, a weapon of ultimate terror against individuals and the communities to which they belong. A more realizable long-term aim is bringing on the outlawing and eradication of torture by demanding accountability for its occurrence and by prosecuting perpetrators.

The Hasidic rabbi Mendl of Vorki said that three things constitute a true Jew: upright kneeling, silent screaming, motionless dance. Those three qualities are crucial to remember and emphasize when it comes to assuaging pain and providing therapeutic care for torture survivors. If we are to mend the "silent screaming" of traumatized others, an attitude of "upright kneeling"—of humble listening and service—is essential for assisting tortured survivors to find again the joy of inner "motionless dance."

NOTES

1   Jean Améry, *At the Mind's Limits: Contemplations by a Survivor on Auschwitz and Its Realities*, trans. Sidney and Stella P. Rosenfeld (Bloomington: Indiana University Press, 1980), 22, 28.
2   Ibid., 35.
3   Michael Taussig, "Culture of Terror—Space of Death: Roger Casement's Putumayo Report and the Explanation of Torture," *Comparative Studies in Society and History* 26, no. 3 (1984): 469.
4   Ariel Dorfman, "Foreword," in *Torture: A Collection*, ed. Sanford Levinson (Oxford: Oxford University Press, 2004), 16.
5   Améry, *At the Mind's Limits*, 35.
6   Helen McColl, Craig Higson-Smith, et al., "Rehabilitation of Torture Survivors in Five Countries: Common Themes and Challenges" *International Journal of Mental Health Systems* 4 (2010): 2, http://www.ncbi.nlm.nih.gov/pmc/articles/PMC2904711/?tool=pmcentrz.
7   For further information about Freedom from Torture and its history, see the organization's web site at http://www.freedomfromtorture.org/.
8   Edward Peters, *Torture* (Oxford: Basil Blackwell, 1985), 176.

9 Barbara Frey, "Documenting a Well-Founded Fear: How Medical Care-Givers Can Assist Torture Survivors in the Asylum Process," in *The Medical Documentation of Torture*, ed. Michael Peel and Vincent Iacopino (Cambridge, UK: Cambridge University Press, 2002), 48.

10 Johan Lansen, "What Does This Work Do to Us?" in *At the Side of Torture Survivors: Treating a Terrible Assault on Human Dignity*, ed. Sepp Graessner, Norbert Gurris, and Christian Pross, trans. Jeremiah Michael Riemer (Baltimore, MD: Johns Hopkins University Press, 2001), 198.

11 Dori Laub, "Introduction," in *At the Side of Torture Survivors*, xx–xxi.

12 Neil Belton, *The Good Listener: Helen Bamber, A Life against Cruelty* (New York: Pantheon, 1999), 382.

13 Medical Foundation for the Victims of Torture, *Torture: Dispelling the Myths* (Annual Review 2006–7), 8, http://www.freedomfromtorture.org/sites/default/files/documents/MF_annual_review_06-07.pdf.

14 Améry, *At the Mind's Limits*, 34.

15 Mary Raphaely, "Routes to the Unspeakable: Working with Victims of Torture," in *Bearing Witness: Psychoanalytic Work with People Traumatized by Torture and State Violence*, ed., Andrés Gautier and Anna Sabatini Scalmati (London: Karnac Books, 2010), 16.

16 Stuart Turner and Caroline Gorst-Unsworth, "Psychological Sequelae of Torture: A Descriptive Model," in *British Journal of Psychiatry* 157 (1990): 477.

17 Jeremy Woodcock, "A Systemic Approach to Trauma," Medical Foundation Series 3, https://www.researchgate.net/publication/255658978_A_Systemic_Approach_to_Trauma.

18 Interview with Helen Bamber, May 7, 2011.

19 Améry, *At the Mind's Limits*, 33.

20 Behnam Behnia, "Trust Building from the Perspective of Survivors of War and Torture," *Chicago Journal Social Service Review* 78, no. 1 (2004): 26–40, http://www.jstor.org/stable/10.1086/380768.

21 Interview with Mary Raphaely, August 18, 2011.

22 See James Welsh, "The Problem of Torture," in *The Medical Documentation of Torture*, esp. 6.

23 Interview with Bamber.

24 Sibel Agrali, "Primo Levi Association—Treatment and Support Provided by a Multiprofessional Team Working with an Interdisciplinary Approach," in *Beyond Statistics: Sharing, Learning and Developing Good Practice in the Care of the Victims of Torture*, ed. Elise Bittenbinder (Karlsruhe: Von Loeper Literaturverlag, 2012), 86–87.

25 Interview with Raphaely.

26 Interview with Bamber.

27 Interview with Elise Bittenbinder, April 19, 2011.

28 Interview with Marion Baraitser, May 9, 2011.

29 Elaine Scarry, *The Body in Pain: The Making and Unmaking of the World* (Oxford: Oxford University Press, 1985), 46.

30 Ibid.

31 Sonja Linden, "Trauma and the Writing Cure," unpublished paper, p. 3.

32 Interview with Sheila Hayman, September 12, 2011.

33 Raphaely, "Routes to the Unspeakable," 16.

34 Sonja Linden and Jenny Grut, *The Healing Fields: Working with Psychotherapy and Nature to Rebuild Shattered Lives* (London: Frances Lincoln, 2002), 41.

35 Cited in ibid., 44.

36 Naomi Stadlen, *How Mothers Love and How Relationships Are Born* (London: Piatkus, 2011), 10.

37 Shamai Davidson, "The Clinical Effects of Massive Psychic Trauma," in *Holding On to Humanity—The Message of Holocaust Survivors: The Shamai Davidson Papers*, ed. Israel W. Charny (New York: New York University Press, 1992), 30.

38 Dina Wardi, *Memorial Candles: Children of the Holocaust*, trans. Naomi Goldblum (New York: Routledge, 1992), 8–9.

39 Israel W. Charny, "Introduction: Shamai Davidson's Vision of Survivors," in *Holding On to Humanity*, xxiii.

40 Améry, *At the Mind's Limits*, 24, 30.

41 Terrence Des Pres, *The Survivor: An Anatomy of Life in the Death Camps* (New York: Oxford University Press, 1980), 51–72.

42 Shamai Davidson, "Reflections on Survival and Some Observations on Survivors in Israel, Germany, and the United States," in Charny, ed., *Holding On to Humanity*, 144.

43 Dori Laub, "Not Knowing Is an Active Process of Destruction: Why the Testimonial Procedure Is of So Much Importance," in *Trauma Research Newsletter* 1, Hamburg Institute for Social Research, July 2000.

44 See Margaret Myers Feinstein, *Holocaust Survivors in Postwar Germany, 1945–1957* (Cambridge, UK: Cambridge University Press, 2010). See also *She'erit Hapletah 1944–1948: Rehabilitation and Political Struggle* (Jerusalem: Yad Vashem, 1990).

45 Davidson, "The Clinical Effects of Massive Psychic Trauma," 35–36, 42–43.

46 Robert Krell, "Survivors and Their Families: Psychiatric Consequences of the Holocaust," in *Medical and Psychological Effects of Concentration Camps on Holocaust Survivors*, ed. Robert Krell and Marc I. Sherman, vol. 4, *Genocide: A Critical Bibliographic Review* (Jerusalem: Institute on the Holocaust and Genocide, 1997), 27.

47 Dori Laub, *Holocaust Trauma Project: Video Testimony Pilot Study of Psychiatrically Hospitalized Holocaust Survivors*, Yale University Genocide Studies Program, 2010, http://www.yale.edu/gsp/trauma_project/index.html. See also Davidson, "Reflections on Survival," 17.

48 Robert Krell, "Survivors and Their Families: Psychiatric Consequences of the Holocaust," in Krell and Sherman, eds., *Medical and Psychological Effects*, 24.

49 Elie Wiesel, "Foreword," in *Medical and Psychological Effects*, xi.

50 Laub, "Not Knowing Is an Active Process of Destruction," 1.

51 Shamai Davidson, "Recovery and Integration in the Life Cycle of the Individual and the Collective," in Charny, ed., *Holding On to Humanity*, 190.

52 Leo Eitinger, cited in Robert Krell, "'The Eitinger Bibliography': Dedication to Leo Eitinger," in Krell and Sherman, eds., *Medical and Psychological Effects*, viii.

53 Judith Hassan, *A House Next Door to Trauma: Learning from Holocaust Survivors How to Respond to Atrocity* (London: Jessica Kingsley, 2003), 78, 231.

54 Ibid., 93, 138.

55 Interview with Moshe Teller, March 2, 2012.

56 Cited in Wiesel, "Foreword," xii.

57 Scarry, *The Body in Pain*, 50.

58 Psalm 118:7 in *The Artscroll Tehillim*, trans. Rabbi Hillel Danziger (New York: Mesorah Publications, 1988), 257.

59 Scarry, *The Body in Pain*, 145.

60 Ibid., 279.

61 Ibid.

62 John Schlapobersky, "The Social World of the Forsaken Psyche," *Group Analysis* (December 2001), 1.

63 Interview with John Schlapobersky, June 28, 2013.

64 John Schlapobersky, "The Reclamation of Space and Time: Psychotherapy with Survivors of Torture and Organised Violence," unpublished manuscript.

65 Interview with Margi Abeles, June 12, 2013.

66 Schlapobersky, "The Social World of the Forsaken Psyche," 8.

67 Interview with Abeles.

68 Ephesians 4:26.

69 Interview with Schlapobersky.

9

Torture and the Totalitarian Appropriation of the Human Being

From National Socialism to Islamic Jihadism

DAVID PATTERSON

In this essay I use the word *torture* to refer to the radical imposition of pain on one person by another, with the ultimate aim of radically appropriating the body and soul of the other. Although it may be used for interrogation, punishment, or degradation, I will argue that within the Nazi totalitarian systems here considered, torture goes far beyond any utilitarian consideration. Originating from the Latin *torquere*, meaning "to twist or distort," torture is characterized by an utter distortion of the human image. I contend that torture consists of a complete undoing of the holiness of the other human being and the ethical demand that emanates from that holiness. Indeed, without the revelation of the ethical from what the contemporary philosopher Emmanuel Levinas calls "beyond being," there are no absolute grounds for objecting to torture, but only contingent grounds: it looks bad, it will anger our enemy, it does not work, and so on. Torture is an assault on the absolute "exigency of the holy,"[1] as Levinas terms it, which issues from a face naked and exposed to blows.[2] It is an assault on the absolute, divine prohibition against torture itself.

How does one undertake an assault on the absolute, divine prohibition? By crushing the other human being under the weight of sheer being, of the "there is," to borrow another term from Levinas, announcing to him that he is neither human nor a being; like the "there is," he is simply "there," neither something nor nothing, meaningless and without value. Hence, as in the infinite expanse of outer space—which may become the confines of the Nazis' torture chamber or the openness of the Taliban's stadium—no one but the torturer hears the victim scream. For the one who is tortured, the "horror," as Levinas describes the collision with the "there is," "is nowise an anxiety about death. . . . It is a participation in the *there is*, in the *there is* which returns in the heart of every negation, in the *there is* that has 'no exits.' It is, if we may say so, the impossibility of death."[3] Or perhaps better: it is the endlessness of death, where death is not the last but continuously the last. In the words of Jean Améry, torture "blots out the contradiction of death and allows us to experience it personally."[4] That's it: under torture, you cannot die. There lies the horror: the torturer encompasses even the mortality of the mortal through the imposition of a horrific immortality.

While torture has been a defining part of the assault on the holy within the human from ancient times, in the post-Holocaust era it assumes specific characteristics and has particular implications. Levinas rightly understands that the most fundamental commandment to arise from the face is the prohibition against murder.[5] Connecting this insight with the Holocaust, we recall Emil L. Fackenheim's profound realization that "the murder camp was not an accidental by-product of the Nazi empire. It was its pure essence."[6] And in the murder camp, "the Nazi state had no higher aim than to murder souls while bodies were still alive."[7] That is where torture enters into the equation: in the time of the Holocaust, Jews were not simply murdered—they were *tortured* first and then murdered, whether they were starved in the Warsaw ghetto, raped at Babi Yar, beaten in Block 11 at Auschwitz, or torn from their families in the shadow of Birkenau's chimneys. And so we come to Améry's equally profound realization: "I am convinced, beyond all personal experiences, that torture was not an accidental quality of this Third Reich, but its essence."[8] The soul is in the blood (Genesis 9:4), and in his appropriation of the soul, the torturer invades, curdles, and drains the blood of his victim. Murder is of the essence where there is an *assault* on God; torture is of the essence where there is an *appropriation* of God. Both belong to the essence of the Third Reich.

Just as the torturer spills the blood of his victim, so the essence of National Socialism has spilled into what is now one of the most pervasive post-Holocaust assaults on the holy within the human, namely Islamic jihadism. Passages from traditional Islamic texts have been selectively cited to justify jihadist murder and torture; such a selective exploitation of isolated teachings constitutes a betrayal of the very tradition that the jihadists invoke. Indeed, there are courageous Muslims who cry out against the jihadist usurpation of Islam.[9] My use of the term *Islamic jihadism*, then, is intended to single out this particular perversion, which, I contend, has resulted from the merging of elements of Islam with elements of Nazism.

Torture as the Essence of the Third Reich: The Case of Jean Améry

Jean Améry recorded one of the most penetrating reflections on torture under the Third Reich. He was arrested in July 1943 as a member of a Belgian resistance group. Before being sent to Auschwitz, where torture often—but not always—took place in the public square, he was taken to "the business room," passing "again and again . . . through heavy barred gates" before finally standing "in a windowless vault in which various iron implements lie about. From there no scream penetrated to the outside."[10] And when the scream cannot penetrate to the outside, it curls up into a never-ending nightmarish silence within the victim. "Whoever is tortured," says Améry, "stays tortured."[11] Once in Auschwitz, he could have added, you remain in Auschwitz, just as the scream remains within your soul.

The genius of Améry lies in his exposure of the Nazis' calculated destruction of the soul: because the soul is in the blood and the blood is in the body, the assault on the soul begins with a penetration of the body. We live in the world, writes Améry, with "the certainty that by reason of written or unwritten social contracts the other person will spare me—more precisely stated, that he will respect my physical, and with it also my metaphysical, being. The boundaries of my body are also the boundaries of my self. My skin surface shields me against the external world." But "the other person forces his own corporeality on me with the first blow. He is on me and thereby destroys me. It is like a rape."[12] Every bit as much as rape, torture is the radical metamorphosis of a radical relation into a radical isolation. It is "an orgy of unchecked self-expansion" of the same into the other, as Améry says.[13] In this case it is the unchecked expansion of the Aryan into the Jew, the ultimate Aryanization of the Jew.

When considering the Nazis' (and, as we will see, the jihadists') use of torture, the Jew hatred that defines their ideology must be kept in mind. As

Fackenheim correctly understood, the Nazis were not antisemitic because they were racists. It is just the reverse: they were racists because they were antisemitic.[14] To arrive at a racist, dehumanizing view of the other human being that would dictate the use of torture, one must first determine a view that runs counter to the millennia-old Jewish teaching concerning the inherent sanctity of the other human being. Therefore, in Améry's words, the Nazis "hated the word 'humanity' like the pious man hates sin."[15] They hated the word *humanity* because they hated the absolute demand of the holy revealed through the face of the human being. As often happens, what befalls humanity befalls the Jews first. The object of the Nazis' systematic program of torture was first of all the Jew. Jews, not Poles, had their beards torn out. Jews, not Lithuanians, were forced to desecrate their places of worship and study. Jews, not Ukrainians, were stripped naked in freezing cold before they were shot into mass graves. Once the body and soul of the Jew thus become the object of the torturer's invasion, any human being is subject to such an assault. And making the other human being subject to such an assault is central to the totalitarian aspiration to be as God.

This last point eludes Améry, but one of his most profound insights illuminates it. "It was precisely in torture that the Third Reich materialized in all the density of its being," he writes. For Amery, "torture was no invention of National Socialism. But it was its apotheosis. The Hitler vassal did not yet achieve his full identity if he was merely as quick as a weasel, tough as leather, hard as Krupp steel. No Golden Party Badge made of him a fully valid representative of the Führer and his ideology, nor did any Blood Order or Iron Cross. He had to *torture*, destroy."[16] And he had to lay claim to the victim's being by drawing it into his own being, like a single-cell creature surrounding and swallowing another creature into itself. Torture entails what Améry calls "existential psychology, in which it appears as the radical negation of the other."[17] It is a negation of the other expressed most radically in a radical appropriation of the other, as a matter of *absolute fidelity* to the totalitarian ideological premise. As an *absolute* appropriation of the absolute within the other, torture is absolute "dominion over spirit and flesh."[18] This is how we are to make sense of Améry's statement that the Nazis tortured, not just to get information, but "with the good conscience of depravity. . . . They placed torture in their service. But even more fervently they were its servants."[19] To become such a servant is to devote oneself, body and soul, to the appropriation of the body and soul of another. They were the servants of torture as one is a servant to an idol, just as a jihadist is a servant to his own false god, who demands the use of torture. Indeed, the Nazis' example did not pass away with their passing, for it lives on in the sacralization of torture in the form of Islamic jihadism.

From National Socialism to Islamic Jihadism

Bernard Lewis has demonstrated that "the close and at times active relationship that developed between Nazi Germany and sections of the Arab leadership, in the years from 1933 to 1945, was due not to a German attempt to win over the Arabs but rather to a series of Arab approaches to the Germans."[20] The most direct link between National Socialism and Islamic jihadism existed in the person of Haj Amin al-Husseini, the fugitive mufti of Jerusalem who did Arabic-language Nazi propaganda radio broadcasts from Berlin and organized the infamous 13th Handschar Division, an SS killing unit of 21,065 Bosnian Muslims. Following his meeting with Hitler on November 28, 1941, the mufti recorded in his diary the Führer's avowal that the Nazis and the Arabs were engaged in the same struggle, namely, to exterminate the Jews.[21] Having been in contact with the Muslim Brotherhood since 1935,[22] al-Husseini turned up in Egypt on June 20, 1946, whereupon the Brotherhood's newspaper *Al Ikhwan Al Muslimin* declared this Nazi war criminal to be "the Arab hero and symbol of Al Jihad and patience and struggle."[23] Within a week of his arrival, he had his first meeting with the Brotherhood's ideologue Sayyid Qutb and its founder Hasan al-Banna, who showered Hitler's *Grossmufti* with praise, saying, "The Mufti is worth the people of a whole nation put together."[24] The National Socialism that had so deeply influenced al-Husseini now had its impact on the Muslim Brotherhood's jihadist thinking. To be sure, al-Banna had long since been a great admirer of Hitler.[25]

There are other points of contact between National Socialism and Islamic jihadism. Laurent Murawiec notes that "just as the Young Egypt movement borrowed from the Nationalsozialistische Deutsche Arbeiterpartei (NSDAP), so did the radical Islamist movement as a whole [borrow] its racism and anti-Semitism.... [Thus] Islamic extremists acquired the perverse modern form of racism, biological racism and racial theory."[26] For both the Nazi and the jihadist, race is not just a biological classification but also a metaphysical category. According to Nazi ideologue Alfred Rosenberg, for example, the Aryan race "has been poisoned by Judaism," and not merely by Jewish blood, because the -ism was *in* the blood.[27] Therefore, he insisted, all Jews are prone to think talmudically, "whether they are atheistic Bourse-speculators, religious fanatics, or Talmudic Jews of the cloth."[28] Similarly, Qutb maintained that "Jews as Jews were *by nature* determined to fight Allah's Truth and sow corruption and confusion."[29] Like the Nazis, the jihadists' aim, as the late Robert Wistrich correctly pointed out, "is not simply to morally delegitimize Israel as a Jewish State and a national entity in the Middle East, but to dehumanize Judaism and the Jewish people as such."[30] Once dehumanized, the Jew is easily demonized. Once demonized, the Jew cannot be accorded the same possibility of conversion that is open to the rest of humanity.

Among the most fervent admirers of Qutb and the Muslim Brotherhood was Ruhullah Khomeini, supreme guide of the first jihadist state, the Islamic Republic of Iran, founded in 1979. In a speech delivered on December 12, 1984, Khomeini cried out, "Those who follow the rules of the Qur'an are aware that we have to apply the laws of Qissas [retribution] and that we have to kill. . . . It is Allah himself who commands men to wage war and to kill."[31] These lines echo what Khomeini learned from his teacher Muhammed Navab-Safavi, the cleric who drew the Ayatollah into the fold of the Muslim Brotherhood: "Killing is tantamount to saying a prayer."[32] Hence, Ayatollah Sadeq Khalkhali, a member of Khomeini's inner circle, once declared, "Those who are against killing have no place in Islam,"[33] beginning with killing the Jews. This is the meaning of the phrase from the Brotherhood's slogan: "Jihad is our way."

Ahmed Yassin, one more post-Holocaust enemy of the Jews spawned by the Brotherhood, is worth a brief note, since in 1987 he founded Hamas, an organization that, like Iran, has at times called for the extermination of Jews; in its founding charter, Hamas called explicitly for the destruction of the Jewish state. Operating in Gaza from 1973 onward, Yassin was instrumental in establishing the University of Gaza, whose former rector and now member of the Palestinian Authority's Fatwa Council, Dr. Ahmad Abu Halabiya, is known for publicly calling for the massacre of Jews everywhere. In a Palestinian television broadcast from 2000, for example, he ranted, "None of the Jews refrain from committing any possible evil. . . . They are the ones who must be butchered and killed, as Allah the Almighty said: 'Fight them: Allah will torture them at your hands, and will humiliate them and will help you to overcome them.'"[34] Yes, Allah himself will torture them, but with your hands: your hands are the hands of Allah.

Torture and the Jihadist Appropriation of God

Few people are surprised by reports that Hamas and Fatah,[35] Hezbollah,[36] al-Qaeda,[37] the Sudanese National Islamic Front,[38] and Islamic Jihad[39]—all of whom can be ideologically traced to the Muslim Brotherhood—torture people. To be sure, the former president of an Islamic jihadist state, Mahmoud Ahmadinejad, has been identified as a torturer by one of his victims.[40] Few heads of state have personally served their country in the torture chamber. Other regimes sympathetic to Islamic jihadism, such as Libya, Syria, and Saudi Arabia, are notorious not just for their totalitarianism but also for their use of torture. Again, no one is surprised. But why is no one surprised? Is it the racist view that would suggest, "Well, that's how those people are," and thus give the torturers a pass? Or does it run deeper than mere racism?

The ideological founder of modern totalitarian Islamic jihadism was Abdul Al'a Maududi, who declared that National Socialism could have been created only "by the theories of leaders" such as "Nietzsche and . . . Hitler. Exactly in the same way the Islamic revolution can be brought about only when a mass movement is initiated based on the theories and conceptions of the Quran and the example and practice of Muhammad."[41] The totalitarian nature of his ideology is evident in his insistence that "Islam is a revolutionary ideology and program which seeks to alter the social order of the whole world and rebuild it in conformity with its own tenets and ideals. . . . Islam wishes to destroy all states and governments on the face of the earth which are opposed to the ideology and program of Islam."[42] Echoing Alfred Rosenberg's call for the "universality of an all-embracing spirit, a *universal* striving,"[43] Maududi insists that "the Islamic movement is universal in nature."[44] Sharing with National Socialism a contempt for Western democratic systems of government, he once asserted that the "the ungodly democracy of the West . . . is the antithesis of Islam."[45] Significantly, Maududi, as well as Hasan al-Banna, deeply influenced Sayyid Qutb's thinking, as Qutb himself affirmed.[46] The totalitarian thinking of these key figures has had an impact on nearly every modern jihadist movement, from the National Islamic Front in the Sudan to the Islamic Revolution in Iran, from Hamas to Hezbollah, from al-Qaeda to the al-Aqsa Martyrs and the Islamic State of Iraq and Syria (ISIS).

In contrast to the Nazis, the totalitarian reach of Islamic jihadism extends not only throughout this world but also into the next. "Islam," says al-Banna, "is an all-embracing concept which regulates . . . the affairs of men in this world and the next."[47] Thus al-Banna announces the tyranny of jihadism over time and eternity. Similarly, Hezbollah is not just another revolutionary or religious movement; no, it is the "Party of Allah," and the Party of Allah "is a way of life, an 'army of civilians,' a semi-secret fraternity, and, last but not least, a 'clearinghouse for mankind,' where those who will be admitted into paradise are separated from those destined for hell."[48] Whereas Allah had once been the one to decide who would be redeemed and who would be damned, that prerogative now falls to Hezbollah: Allah and Hezbollah are one and the same. Similarly, the Hamas charter is called the Charter of Allah, so that the words of Hamas are the words of Allah. This appropriation of God entails the appropriation of the soul, in this world and the next, in life and in death. And the appropriation of the soul requires torture. Torture, therefore, is a defining feature of Islamic jihadism, sanctioned in the name of Allah, which is in fact a usurpation of Allah.

The invasion of body and soul that characterizes Islamic jihadism underlies what Murawiec calls "bloodlust": "The lust for blood and killing expresses an infinite lust for power, control, and domination. Is there a greater (if pathological), more intoxicating sense of power than that in which a man tortures, invades, torments, maims the body, severs the limbs and more of another one? *Wille zur Macht*, the will to power, the exacerbated desire for overpowering and controlling, expresses itself *in fine* as bloodlust."[49] Contrary to what Murawiec suggests, however, this lust is not a passion run amok; no, it is part of a systematic, all-encompassing ideology. The lust for blood that defines the jihadist lust for torture is a lust for the soul that is in the blood. Hence the photographs of kindergarten children, hands raised and painted blood-red, imitating the gesture of the blood-covered murderers who butchered Yossi Avrahami and Vadim Norjitz in Ramallah on October 13, 2000.[50] Hence the jihadist conviction that "Allah wants blood, needs blood, that blood pleases Allah, whether the blood is that of His martyrs or that of His enemies. Allah demands blood as evidence of worship."[51] Perhaps the ultimate appropriation of the blood of the other can be found in a report on the assassination of Jordan's prime minister Wasfi al-Tal by jihadists on November 28, 1971: as al-Tal lay bleeding to death in front of Cairo's Sheraton Hotel, one of his assassins came over and licked his blood.[52] "We drink the blood of the enemy," boasts British-born jihadist Abu Izzadeen. "That is Islam and that is jihad."[53] While this appropriation of the soul of the other through the appropriation of his blood may not be Islam, it is ideologically consistent with Islamic jihadism.

The jihadist fixation on blood is a key to the defining role of torture in the jihadist appropriation of God through the consumption of the soul, the spilling out of the soul, and the dominion over the soul. One manifestation of this appropriation of God can be found in the jihadist invocation of Sharia as the divine law that must rule over all, in this world and in the next, and that sanctifies the radical invasion of the body and the blood. In keeping with Sharia, for example, al-Banna called for lashes, stoning, amputation, and other forms of torture to be routinely applied as forms of punishment.[54] Similarly, Khomeini insisted that a key to Islamic government is "implementing the penal law of Islam and the sanctions it provides" as prescribed in the Quran: for example, lashes for adulterer and adulteress (24:2–3); for "waging war against Allah," it is "execution in an exemplary [i.e. public] way," by crucifixion, beheading, amputation of hands and feet on opposite sides of the body (5:33–34); amputation of hands for theft (5:38–39).[55] This is the law that, according to Qutb, "governs the entire universe."[56] When one is being tortured under such a divine law, one's body *is* the entire universe.

Here we come to a realization that lies at the heart both of the Nazi and of the jihadist insistence upon the need to torture: the need to torture is a need to negate the flesh-and-blood being of the victim, and *pain* is the most primal manifestation of that negation. Such a negation is necessary to the radical imposition upon the victim either of the being or of the belief of the torturer. In fact, according to Osama bin Laden, the aim of Sharia law is the imposition of belief upon the nonbeliever.[57] Recall Améry's remark that "my skin surface shields me against the external world." Penetrating the skin, the torturer collapses the boundary between inside and outside by inflicting unthinkable pain upon the other, a pain that erupts involuntarily in a scream, which takes on an existence of its own to tear itself from the throat of the one tortured, an existence that negates the existence of the one who screams in such a way that his existence is swallowed up by the existence of the torturer.

Thus pain destroys language, as Elaine Scarry has said,[58] by collapsing the word into a scream, as the torturer elicits the scream from the one tortured. That is what the torturer, whether Nazi or jihadist, demands: the scream. Neither information nor confession, neither expiation nor compensation. Just the scream. For the scream announces the demise of the

soul of the mortal victim, as it is appropriated absolutely by the divine torturer. Any confession that may come at the end of the scream is the word
not of the victim but of the torturer, who, like God, is the word that was in
the beginning. As Hamas is Allah, the torturer is God and, in Scarry's
insightful words, "claims pain's attributes as his own,"[59] in a totalitarian
eclipse of the attributes of the other, of the Holy One within the human,
which is the complete appropriation of soul that defines Islamic jihadism.
And, as in the case of National Socialism, it defines the Jew hatred that
drives the torturer. Both the Nazi and the jihadist torturer must hate the Jew,
for the Jew most fundamentally undermines everything they represent.

Torture and Jew Hatred: A Concluding Thought

The torture so central to the totalitarian appropriation of the human
being, from National Socialism to Islamic jihadism, is linked to the Jew
hatred that also defines the two ideologies. For the metaphysical ground
for objecting to the torture lies in a specifically Jewish teaching and tradition concerning the sacred tie and infinite responsibility that bind each
human being to the other. For the totalitarian ideology to proceed, it
must eliminate the metaphysical, and not just the political or cultural,
grounds for objecting to torture. Inasmuch as these ideologies are defined
by murder and torture, they must get rid of Judaism, a point that both
Nazis and jihadists understand very well. Recall the assertion of Nazi ideologue Alfred Rosenberg that the Aryan *Geist*, which is mind or spirit, "has
been poisoned by Judaism," and not merely by Jewish blood, for the -ism
is *in* the blood.[60] Recall, too, Article 28 of the Hamas Charter of Allah,
which identifies "Israel, Judaism, and the Jews" as the evil and the enemy of
humankind. The very breath of a single Jew is a testimony against National
Socialism, against Islamic jihadism, and against the torture that defines
both. And the ideologues of both know it. The totalitarian torturer is an
antisemite not because he tortures; rather, he tortures because he is an
antisemite. Here lies the post-Holocaust insight into the phenomenon of
torture. For if the Holocaust is defined by anything, it is defined by Jew
hatred.

Améry states that, while communism may be able to de-Stalinize itself,
National Socialism can never de-Hitlerize itself.[61] Just so, Islamic jihadism
can never de-Qutbize itself. The question remains as to whether Islam can
de-Sharia itself, as least with regard to the Islamic jihadist reading of Sharia:

is it possible for a jihadist to object to the torture prescribed by Sharia? If not, then it is impossible for a jihadist to oppose either Jew hatred or torture. One goes with the other. Muslims who object to the Jew hatred, torture, and murder perpetrated by Islamic jihadists must find a way to oppose the fanatic jihadist reading of Sharia and remain good, observant Muslims. They must oppose both torture and Jew hatred. Until that happens, National Socialism will prevail in its reach into modern Islamic jihadism, which threatens the soul of Islam itself.

CONTRIBUTORS' QUESTIONS FOR DAVID PATTERSON

1. You argue that torture is endemic to Islamic jihadism. Is it not the case, however, that torture, which you identify as an assault on the sanctity of the other's personhood, defines *all* ideologically driven movements that gain power? While we can uncover the influence of Nazism on jihadism, it is nonetheless the case, according to your own argument, that *any* "totalizing"—and thus totalitarian—movement must engage in an "appropriation of the soul" that contradicts Jewish teachings. Do not all such movements—state sponsored or not—employ torture not only to serve utilitarian purposes but also to dehumanize the other? Does a movement's or regime's reluctance to torture mean that "blood lust" or aims for world domination are less present than they may be among jihadists? Jihadism is certainly guilty of overt anti-Jewish and, more pointedly, anti-Israel rhetoric. However, might focusing on one (currently headlined) extremist ideology distract us from being alert to the "appropriation of the soul" inherent in *all* such ideologically driven, totalizing strains—including support for torture, covert or otherwise, in our own political circumstances? What is the moral difference, if any, between torture inflicted in recent times by jihadists or by American and Israeli administrations?

2. You agree with Jean Améry and Emil Fackenheim that torture was not accidental but essential to the Third Reich. Why is it so important to them—and to you—to maintain this point? Although many, if not most, Jews were tortured before they died—especially if we use a broad definition of *torture*—can it be claimed that *all* Jews were tortured in the sense that you understand the term *torture*? Given your understanding, if torture of that kind had been inflicted on the Jews before they were murdered, arguably the Nazis would not have been able to

kill as many Jews as they did under the cover of World War II. The "Final Solution" was implemented with the greatest efficiency and effectiveness only when murder was impersonally industrialized. How does the reality of an impersonal, streamlined mode of mass killing square with the claim that torture was of the essence of the Nazi genocide against the Jews? What, ultimately, is at stake with regard to your responses to this question?

RESPONSE BY DAVID PATTERSON

Some of the issues raised in the first set of questions simply reaffirm one of my basic points: namely, that all totalizing ideologies and totalitarian movements set out on a path that has torture as its defining end, not only to serve utilitarian purposes but also to dehumanize the other. The key words here, of course, are *totalizing* and *totalitarian*. Not every political movement seeking the acquisition of power is necessarily totalitarian; indeed, anyone who seeks political advantage seeks power on some level. The critical question concerns the ideological stance toward the other human being: does ideological hegemony take precedence over human sanctity? And is the regard for the other human being rooted in an absolute, transcendent commandment, as it is in Judaism, or does it lie in some ontological contingency, such as social convention?

My focus on jihadism, to respond to another question, derives from the post-Holocaust context of the investigations that have gone into this volume. While other regimes rooted in a totalitarian ideology—such as the current North Korean regime, the Chinese government, or any number of African states—routinely use torture, in Islamic jihadism we find both influences from and parallels to National Socialism. This makes Islamic jihadism a specifically post-Holocaust concern; as in National Socialism, antisemitism is a defining feature of the jihadists' *Weltanschauung*, and its antisemitic essence underlies not only its use but its affirmation of torture. Further, unlike strictly political forms of totalitarianism, the jihadist totalitarian appropriation of the soul of the other aspires to dominate every aspect of the life of the soul not only in this world but also in the next, as noted in my essay.

The question concerning the moral difference between torture inflicted by jihadists and the "enhanced interrogation" methods used by Americans and Israelis can be answered by pointing out the obvious:

- Torture perpetrated by the Americans and Israelis is scandalous precisely because they espouse principles concerning the sanctity of the other person that would preclude the use of torture. In the case of Islamic jihadists, there is no embrace of any such principle with regard to the nonbeliever, nor is the use of torture scandalous to their thinking.
- Whereas the Sharia promulgated by Islamic jihadism prescribes various tortures as a form of punishment, American and Israeli codes of law prohibit such a use of torture.
- In American and Israeli societies, the use of torture must be justified (if, indeed, it is ever justifiable) as a means to a higher end, such as saving lives; among the jihadists, it requires no justification because torture is its own justification: it is an end unto itself.
- In American and Israeli societies, the use of torture is exceptional; in jihadist culture, it is routine. Most people arrested by the police in Dallas can safely assume that they will not be subjected to torture; most people arrested by the police in Gaza can assume that they will certainly be tortured.
- American and Israeli cultures preach tolerance for the lifestyles and the ideas of people whose preferences and thinking run against the grain of social norms; women who dress in a sexually provocative manner, avowed homosexuals, and critics of the government live without fear of imprisonment and torture. In jihadist culture, such individuals live in constant fear of imprisonment and torture.

These differences strike me as profoundly significant; to suggest a similarity between Americans and jihadists with regard to the use of torture would require demonstrating that these and other differences are insignificant and incidental.

The second set of questions runs much deeper than the first. Here I may have to concede to a broadening of the notion of torture if I wish to maintain that all Jews were tortured before they were murdered. To begin with, the appropriation of the other would include both the invasion of the body and the obliteration of the soul; I do not think this inclusion of the assault on the soul undermines the notion of torture that I have set forth. If we speak not only of torture but also of the ideological path to torture, it may be argued that the Nazis' first step down the path to the torture of the Jews was taken on April 7, 1933, with the passing of the first of hundreds of anti-

Jewish laws in Germany, laws aimed at legislating the Jews out of society and then out of existence. This law limiting the Jews' ability to earn a livelihood was followed by a law limiting their ability to serve God: as of April 21, 1933, German legislation prohibited ritual slaughter.

As the hour of extermination grew near, most Jews may not have been tortured as Améry was tortured, but they were certainly and systematically subjected to torturous conditions. Jews placed in ghettos and sent to forced labor camps were invariably subjected to starvation, brutality, dehumanization, exposure, and disease. Indeed, not only were they tortured in this sense, but they were tortured to death, as Yitzhak Katznelson indicates in an entry from his *Vittel Diary*: "Throughout the era of Hitler, the agent of the whole non-Jewish world, not a single Jew died, they were just murdered, murdered."[62] They saw their synagogues and holy books burned and desecrated and had their beards torn out. They were forbidden to pray, to use the ritual bath, and to observe holy days; the Nazis, in fact, planned their actions against the Jews according to the Hebrew holy calendar. The conditions that Jews endured on most of the trains arriving at the camps were so severe that as many as 30 percent of the transport were dead on arrival.[63] Children were torn from their families, and fathers and mothers were torn from their children. Almost everywhere in Nazi-controlled Europe, every Jew was homeless, living in a camp, in a ghetto, or in hiding.

This torturous treatment of the Jews went into the systematic creation of the *Muselmann*, the one whom Primo Levi describes as the "backbone of the camp"[64] and Emil Fackenheim deems the Nazis' "most characteristic, most original product."[65] Far more than the victim of starvation, exposure, and brutality, the *Muselmann* is *the tortured Jew* whose very existence was deemed criminal and whose prayers were regarded as an act of sedition. He is *the tortured Jew* for whom marriage and childbirth were forbidden and for whom there was no protection under the law. He is *the tortured Jew*, both widowed and orphaned, rendered "ferociously alone"[66] before being rendered ferociously faceless.

As for the hundreds of thousands who were shot into mass graves by the Einsatzgruppen, they were certainly subjected to paralyzing terror if not torture before they were shot naked into the cold earth, with bodies piled upon bodies as others stood in line waiting to be murdered. When I was working on an English translation of *The Complete Black Book of Russian Jewry*, plowing through account after eyewitness account of the Nazis' murderous savagery, I came to a realization: the Nazis' torturous treatment of the Jews was not unimaginable—on the contrary, the imagination was the only limit to what they perpetrated. For they had no other limiting principle to curb their actions against humanity: any cruelty they could imagine they imposed. The one principle they consistently followed was the principle of mental, spiritual, and physical torture with the aim of a total appropriation of the Jew, body and soul, ending in the total obliteration of the Jew.

On the matter of impersonalized murder, the fact that it was systematically depersonalized makes it deeply personal in a dialectical sense. The depersonalization lies in the mutation of the Jew into an abstract, metaphysical category as the source of all evil; this is something the Nazis have in common with the jihadists. Only the knowledge that the Jews were human, however suppressed, can explain the fanatic measures taken to dehumanize them.

The stake in the claim that torture was of the essence in the Nazis' assault on the body and soul of Israel lies in arriving at a better understanding of what exactly defines the Holocaust and the systematic extermination of the Jews. It lies in understanding what it means to assert that the Nazis set out to murder the souls of the Jews before they murdered their bodies. It lies in understanding the singular horror of the Holocaust as an assault on the very holiness of the other human being, which is what makes other human catastrophes horrific. For the Jewish people represent, by their very presence in the world, the millennial testimony to the holiness of the other.

NOTES

1   Emmanuel Levinas, *Ethics and Infinity*, trans. Richard A. Cohen (Pittsburgh, PA: Duquesne University Press, 1985), 105.

2   See Emmanuel Levinas, *Difficult Freedom: Essays on Judaism*, trans. Sean Hand (Baltimore, MD: Johns Hopkins University Press, 1990), 8.

3   Emmanuel Levinas, *Existence and Existents*, trans. Alphonso Lingis (The Hague: Martinus Nijhoff, 1978), 61.

4   Jean Améry, *At the Mind's Limits: Contemplations by a Survivor on Auschwitz and Its Realities*, trans. Sidney Rosenfeld and Stella P. Rosenfeld (Bloomington: Indiana University Press, 1980), 34.

5   Levinas, *Ethics and Infinity*, 86.

6   Emil L. Fackenheim, *The Jewish Return into History* (New York: Schocken Books, 1978), 246.

7   Emil L. Fackenheim, *To Mend the World: Foundations of Post-Holocaust Jewish Thought* (New York: Schocken Books, 1989), 100.

8   Améry, *At the Mind's Limits*, 24.

9   See, for example, the contributions of Riffat Hassan, Zayn Kassam, Khaleel Mohammed, Bülent Şenay, Sana Tayyen, and Bassam Tibi in *Encountering the Stranger: A Jewish-Christian-Muslim Trialogue*, ed. Leonard Grob and John K. Roth (Seattle: University of Washington Press, 2012).

10 Améry, *At the Mind's Limits*, 22.

11 Ibid., 34.

12 Ibid., 28.

13 Ibid., 36.

14 See Emil L. Fackenheim, "The Holocaust and the State of Israel," in *A Holocaust Reader: Responses to the Nazi Extermination*, ed. Michael L. Morgan (New York: Oxford University Press, 2001), 132.

15 Améry, *At the Mind's Limits*, 31.

16 Ibid., 30.

17 Ibid., 35.

18 Ibid., 36.

19 Ibid., 31.

20 Bernard Lewis, *Semites and Anti-Semites: An Inquiry into Conflict and Prejudice* (New York: W. W. Norton, 1999), 140.

21 Joseph B. Schechtman, *The Mufti and the Fuehrer: The Rise and Fall of Haj Amin el-Husseini* (New York: Thomas Yoseloff, 1965), 306.

22 See Lukasz Hirszowicz, *The Third Reich and the Arab East* (London: Routledge and Kegan Paul, 1966), 13.

23 Jeffrey Herf, *Nazi Propaganda for the Arab World* (New Haven, CT: Yale University Press, 2009), 242.

24 Quoted in ibid., 244.

25 See, for example, Hasan al-Banna, *Five Tracts of Hasan al-Banna: A Selection from the Majmuat Rasail al-Imam al-Shahid Hasan al-Banna*, trans. Charles Wendell (Berkeley: University of California Press, 1978), 97.

26 Laurent Murawiec, *The Mind of Jihad* (Cambridge, UK: Cambridge University Press, 2008), 255.

27 Alfred Rosenberg, *Race and Race History and Other Essays*, ed. Robert Pais (New York: Harper and Row, 1974), 131–32.

28 Ibid., 181.

29 Quoted in Ronald L. Nettler, *Past Trials and Present Tribulations: A Muslim Fundamentalist's View of the Jews* (Oxford: Pergamon, 1987), 35; emphasis added.

30 Robert Wistrich, *Muslim Anti-Semitism: A Clear and Present Danger* (New York: American Jewish Committee, 2002), 4.

31 Quoted in Lawrence Wright, *The Looming Tower: Al-Qaeda and the Road to 9/11* (New York: Alfred A. Knopf, 2006), 123–24.

32 Ibid., 32.

33 Quoted in Amir Taheri, *Holy Terror: Inside the World of Islamic Terrorism* (Bethesda, MD: Adler and Adler, 1987), 44.

34 "PA TV Broadcasts Call for Killing Jews and Americans," MEMRI, October 13, 2000, http://www.memri.org/bin/articles.cgi?Area=sd&ID=SP13800.

35 Donald Macintyre, "Hamas and Fatah Both Accused of Torturing Their Opponents," *Independent*, October 24, 2007, http://www.independent.co.uk/news/world/middle-east/hamas-and-fatah-both-accused-of-torturing-their-opponents-395236.html.

36 Bradley Burston, "The Pleasure That Hezbollah Takes in Torture," *Haaretz Online*, July 15, 2008, http://www.haaretz.com/hasen/spages/1002317.html.

37 Excerpts from "Al Qaeda—Al Qaeda Training Manuel," in "Inside The Terror Network," *Frontline*, http://www.pbs.org/wgbh/pages/frontline/shows/network/alqaeda/manual.html.

38 Carolyn Fluehr-Lobban and Richard Lobban, "The Sudan since 1989: National Islamic Front Rule," *Arab Studies Quarterly* 23, no. 2 (Spring 2001), http://www.jstor.org/discover/10.2307/41858370?sid=21105753037313&uid=2&uid=3739256&uid=4.

39 Reuters, "Rights Group: Islamic Jihad Torturing Collaborators," *Israel News*, May 31, 2008, http://www.ynetnews.com/articles/0,7340,L-3550122,00.html.

40 Iranian Action Committee, "Former US Hostages and Victims of Torture Point Finger at Visiting Iranian President," Iranian Action Committee, September 14, 2005, http://www.prnewswire.com/news-releases/former-us-hostages-and-victims-of-torture-point-finger-at-visiting-iranian-president-67401217.html.

41 Sayyed Abulala Maududi, *The Process of Islamic Revolution*, 2nd ed. (Lahore: Urdu Type Press, 1955), 25.

42 Abdul Al'a Maududi, *Jihad in Islam* (Lahore: Islamic Publications, 2001), 8–10.

43 Rosenberg, *Race and Race History and Other Essays*, 134.

44 Abdul Al'a Maududi, *Selected Speeches and Writings*, trans. S. Zakir Aijaz (Karachi: International Islamic Publishers, 1981), 1:5.

45 Ibid., 2:209.

46 See, for example, Sayyid Qutb, *In the Shade of the Quran*, trans. M. A. Salahi and A. A. Shamis (Alexandria, VA: Al Saadawi Publications, 1997), 91–92.

47 Al-Banna, *Five Tracts of Hasan al-Banna*, 46–47.

48 Taheri, *Holy Terror*, 87.

49 Murawiec, *The Mind of Jihad*, 8.

50 For relevant images, see, "The Ramallah Lynching," www.think-israel.org/freerepublic.octoberramallahlynch.html.

51 Murawiec, *The Mind of Jihad*, 59–60.

52 See Barry Rubin, *Revolution until Victory? The Politics and History of the PLO* (Cambridge, MA: Harvard University Press, 1994), 37–38.

53 See Robert Spencer, "We Are the Muslims," *Jihad Watch*, January 18, 2007, https://www.jihadwatch.org/2007/01/we-are-the-muslims-we-drink-the-blood-of-the-enemythat-is-islam-and-that-is-jihad.

54 Christina Phelps Harris, *Nationalism and Revolution in Egypt: The Role of the Muslim Brotherhood* (The Hague: Mouton, 1964), 163.

55 Ruhullah Khomeini, *Islam and Revolution: Writings and Declarations of Imam Khomeini*, trans. Hamid Algar (Berkeley, CA: Mizan Press, 1981), 74.

56 Sayyid Qutb, *Maalim fi al-Tariq* [Milestones] (Damascus: Dar Al-Ilm, 2006), 88.

57 See Raymond Ibrahim, ed., *The Al Qaeda Reader*, trans. Raymond Ibrahim (New York: Doubleday, 2007), 51.

58 Elaine Scarry, "Pain and the Self," in *The Phenomenon of Torture*, ed. William F. Schultz (Philadelphia: University of Pennsylvania Press, 2007), 173.

59 Ibid., 175.

60 Rosenberg, *Race and Race History and Other Essays*, 131–32.

61 Améry, *At the Mind's Limits*, 31.

62 Yitzhak Katznelson, *Vittel Diary*, trans. Myer Cohn, 2nd ed. (Tel-Aviv: Hakibbutz Hameuchad, 1972), 228.

63 See Yehuda Bauer, *History of the Holocaust*, rev. ed. (New York: Franklin Watts, 2001), 254.

64 Primo Levi, *Survival in Auschwitz: The Nazi Assault on Humanity*, trans. Stuart Woolf (New York: Simon and Schuster, 1996), 90.

65 Fackenheim, *To Mend the World*, 100.

66 Ibid., 88.

10

Crying Out

Rape as Torture and the Responsibility to Protect

JOHN K. ROTH

> Somewhere, someone is crying out under torture. Perhaps in
> this hour, this second.
>> —Jean Améry, "Torture"

As the second decade of the twenty-first century continues, so do the mass
atrocities perpetrated on Syrian people by Bashar al-Assad, Syria's dictator-
president, and by the so-called Islamic State in Iraq and Syria (ISIS).[1] From
time to time during this disaster, I have put the phrase *rape and torture
in Syria* into my computer's Google search engine. Instantly, an astonish-
ing number of "hits" arrives.[2] They provide telling reminders of the grim
accuracy of the 1966 statement by Jean Améry, Jewish philosopher and
Holocaust survivor, quoted in the epigraph above.[3] As in other places where
rape and torture become state policy, many of the victims of those acts in
Syria have been "done to death."[4]

Adopted by the United Nations General Assembly on December 10, 1984,
the Convention against Torture and Other Cruel, Inhuman or Degrading
Treatment or Punishment came into force on June 26, 1987, following ratifi-
cation by the twentieth state party. The convention defines torture to include

any act by which severe pain or suffering, whether physical or mental, is intentionally inflicted on a person for such purposes as obtaining from him or a third person information or a confession, punishing him for an act he or a third person has committed or is suspected of having committed, or intimidating or coercing him or a third person, or for any reason based on discrimination of any kind, when such pain or suffering is inflicted by or at the instigation of or with the consent or acquiescence of a public official or other person acting in an official capacity.[5]

About a decade after the Convention against Torture came into force, another defining moment in international law took place in the 1996–98 case brought by the International Criminal Tribunal for Rwanda (ICTR) against Jean-Paul Akayesu, the Hutu mayor of the Taba commune in Gitarama prefecture. The 1998 judgment against Akayesu, who was found guilty of committing genocide—and using rape to do so—"provided for the first time in legal history a definition of rape as a crime under international law."[6] The ICTR ruled as follows:

The Chamber must define rape, as there is no commonly accepted definition of this term in international law. While rape has been defined in certain national jurisdictions as non-consensual intercourse, variations on the act of rape may include acts which involve the insertion of objects and/ or the use of bodily orifices not considered to be intrinsically sexual. . . . The Chamber defines rape as a physical invasion of a sexual nature, committed on a person under circumstances which are coercive. Sexual violence which includes rape, is considered to be any act of a sexual nature which is committed on a person under circumstances which are coercive.[7]

Subsequent to the Akayesu case, definitions of rape pertaining to crimes against humanity and genocide have been elaborated and amplified. In particular, some prosecutions carried out after the Akayesu case by the International Criminal Tribunal for the former Yugoslavia (ICTY) differed from the ICTR in their detailed attention to the ways in which penetration, coercion, and lack of consent should be understood. Efforts have also been made to ensure that definitions of conflict-related rape are gender neutral. That atrocity can be inflicted on boys and men as well as on girls and women. As for those who inflict rape in war and genocide, the perpetrators are primarily male, but sometimes women are implicated in that atrocity as well.[8]

Importantly, the ICTR prefaced its definition of rape in ways that link that atrocity to torture. "Like torture," the tribunal stated, "rape is used for such purposes as intimidation, degradation, humiliation, discrimination, punishment, control or destruction of a person. Like torture, rape is a violation of personal dignity, and rape in fact constitutes torture when inflicted by or at the instigation of or with the consent or acquiescence of a public official or other person acting in an official capacity."[9]

Torture denotes more than rape, but those atrocities are closely related and intertwined. As Manfred Nowak, special rapporteur on torture for the United Nations Commission on Human Rights, has pointed out, "It is widely recognized, including by former Special Rapporteurs on torture and by regional jurisprudence, that rape constitutes torture when it is carried out by or at the instigation of or with the consent or acquiescence of public officials."[10] In international law, moreover, both torture and rape can be crimes against humanity and acts of genocide.

Prior to his deportation to Auschwitz, Jean Améry was interrogated and tortured in Belgium by his German captors. Torture left marks that went deep down. Likening its first blows to "rape, a sexual act without the consent of one of the two partners," Améry depicted how "he is on me and thereby destroys me," not necessarily by killing but definitely by demolishing what Améry called "trust in the world."[11] It was with similar effects in mind that the ICTR likened rape to torture and stated that, under certain circumstances, rape constitutes torture.

Améry noted that "trust in the world" is grounded in the conviction that "by reason of written or unwritten social contracts the other person will spare me—more precisely stated, that he will respect my physical, and with it also my metaphysical, being." Trust in the world, he affirmed, is also rooted in "the expectation of help, the certainty of help, [which] is indeed one of the fundamental experiences of human beings." Améry added his belief that "the boundaries of my body are also the boundaries of my self. My skin surface shields me against the external world. If I am to have trust, I must feel on it only what I *want* to feel." Thus the first blows of torture and rape are likely to dash those precious convictions and expectations. Once such violence strikes, as Améry put it, "a part of our life ends and it can never again be revived."[12]

No book on torture can pass muster if it fails to concentrate on rape or on what might better be identified as *rape/torture* and, in particular, on what I call *rape/torture-as-policy*—intentional and systematic uses of rape/ torture as a weapon of war and genocide.[13] So this essay takes up those considerations. Rape/torture-as-policy, especially in its genocidal forms, involves gender, sex, and torturous violence but so much more because its wreckage extends beyond the meaning of such terms and the reach of those realities. As the ICTR stated, "The crime of rape cannot be captured in a mechanical description of objects and body parts." In Rwanda, the ICTR went on to say, the genocidal forms of rape-as-policy produced "physical and psychological destruction of Tutsi women, their families and their communities. Sexual violence was an integral part of the process of destruction, specifically targeting Tutsi women and specifically contribut-ing to their destruction and to the destruction of the Tutsi group as a whole."[14] Such acts and outcomes are torture or nothing could be. Sadly, moreover, Tutsi is but one of many group names that could be linked to the ICTR's description of the disastrous toll taken by the torture inflicted and encompassed by rape-as-policy.

New Words

The *New York Times* op-ed writer Nicholas D. Kristof uses his influence and leverage to call attention eloquently and persistently to human rights abuses that affect women and girls.[15] On February 11, 2010, for instance, Kristof published an essay called "The Grotesque Vocabulary in Congo."[16] Beginning with the observation that he had "learned some new words" while in the Democratic Republic of Congo (DRC), Kristof continued his editorial as follows: "One is 'autocannibalism,' coined in French but equally appropriate in English. It describes what happens when a militia here in eastern Congo's endless war cuts flesh from living victims and forces them to eat it. Another is 're-rape.' The need for that term arose because doctors were seeing women and girls raped, re-raped and re-raped again, here in the world capital of murder, rape, mutilation."

Arguably, when Kristof identified the DRC as "the world capital of mur-der, rape, mutilation," he did not at the time exaggerate. "The brutal war here in eastern Congo has not only lasted longer than the Holocaust," Kristof underscored in a *New York Times* editorial dated February 7, 2010, "but also appears to have claimed more lives. A peer-reviewed study put the Congo's war death toll at 5.4 million as of April 2007 and rising at 45,000 a month. That would leave the total today, after a dozen years, at 6.9 million."[17] Although the precise numbers cannot be known, rape, *re-rape*, and the torture they involve have contributed significantly to those millions of deaths.

The new words that Kristof learned relate to paragraphs 138 and 139 from the Outcome Document of the United Nations World Summit, which took place in 2005. Those paragraphs state the following commitments:

> 138. Each individual State has the responsibility to protect its populations from genocide, war crimes, ethnic cleansing and crimes against humanity. This responsibility entails the prevention of such crimes, including their incitement, through appropriate and necessary means. We accept that responsibility and will act in accordance with it. The international community should, as appropriate, encourage and help States to exercise this responsibility and support the United Nations in establishing an early warning capability.
>
> 139. The international community, through the United Nations, also has the responsibility to use appropriate diplomatic, humanitarian and other peaceful means, in accordance with Chapters VI and VIII of the Charter, to help to protect populations from genocide, war crimes, ethnic cleansing and crimes against humanity. In this context, we are prepared to take collective action, in a timely and decisive manner, through the Security Council, in accordance with the Charter, including Chapter VII, on a case-by-case basis and in cooperation with relevant regional organizations as appropriate, should peaceful means be inadequate and national authorities are manifestly failing to protect their populations from genocide, war crimes, ethnic cleansing and crimes against humanity. We stress the need for the General Assembly to continue consideration of the responsibility to protect populations from genocide, war crimes, ethnic cleansing and crimes against humanity and its implications, bearing in mind the principles of the Charter and international law. We also intend to commit ourselves, as necessary and appropriate, to helping States build capacity to protect their populations from genocide, war crimes, ethnic cleansing and crimes against humanity and to assisting those which are under stress before crises and conflicts break out.[18]

The 2005 United Nations World Summit commemorated the organization's founding sixty years earlier. In the wake of World War II, the United

Nations came into existence when its charter was signed in San Francisco on June 26, 1945, and came into force on October 24 of that same year. The charter's preamble affirms that the peoples of the United Nations are determined "to save succeeding generations from the scourge of war, . . . to reaffirm faith in fundamental human rights, in the dignity and worth of the human person, in the equal rights of men and women and of nations large and small, and . . . to promote social progress and better standards of life in larger freedom."[19] At the same time, the charter stressed that, with the exception of acts of international aggression or actions that threaten or breach international peace, the United Nations is not authorized "to intervene in matters which are essentially within the domestic jurisdiction of any state."[20]

As the latter provisions imply, the United Nations in many ways privileged national sovereignty over human rights, for under the UN charter, massive human rights abuses and even crimes against humanity could take place within a state without those conditions being construed as threats to or breaches of international peace, let alone as acts of international aggression. But if paragraphs 138 and 139 of the Outcome Document of the 2005 United Nations World Summit are honored, then for the following reasons national sovereignty does not trump human rights, at least not as much as it could and did before.

First, paragraph 138 affirms that each individual state has the primary responsibility to *protect* its populations from genocide, war crimes, crimes against humanity, and ethnic cleansing. That responsibility also entails that individual states are obliged to *prevent* those crimes from happening to their populations. Second, paragraph 139 indicates that the international community has the responsibility to help populations threatened by genocide, war crimes, crimes against humanity, and ethnic cleansing. Furthermore, if an individual state is unable or unwilling to protect its populations from these mass atrocity crimes, which definitely include torture and rape used as weapons of war and genocide, then the international community has the responsibility to take "collective action, in a timely and decisive manner." If peaceful means are inadequate to provide the needed protection, the international community must take stronger measures, including collective use of force authorized by the Security Council under Chapter VII of the United Nations charter.

A New Norm

Gareth Evans, chancellor of the Australian National University, formerly Australia's foreign minister, and from 2000 to 2009 president and chief executive officer of the International Crisis Group, coined the term *responsibility to protect* during his 2000–2001 tenure as co-chair of the International Commission on Intervention and State Sovereignty. The responsibility to protect (R2P, as it is sometimes abbreviated) became more than an idealistic concept in September 2005, when heads of state and government agreed to paragraphs 138 and 139 in the Outcome Document of the United Nations World Summit, an action that gave R2P a foothold in international law.[21]

The political scientist Thomas Weiss has argued that "with the possible exception of the prevention of genocide after World War II, no idea has moved faster or farther in the international normative arena."[22] Nevertheless, the potency and status of this new norm are still very much works in progress. The reasons for that uncertainty are multiple and complex. Crucial among them are factors that remain critical more than a decade after the appearance of *The Responsibility to Protect*, the 2001 report of the International Commission on Intervention and State Sovereignty (ICISS), and its sixth chapter in particular. This report, which was a crucial driving force behind the United Nations' eventual support for paragraphs 138 and 139 in the 2005 Outcome Document, referred to "conscience-shocking situations crying out for action" (6.36–40, an important section titled "The Implications of Inaction").[23]

The ICISS report refers repeatedly to rape, including systematic rape, as among those "conscience-shocking situations crying out for action," especially insofar as rape is part of ethnic cleansing and, by implication, genocide. Speaking about "large scale" loss of life and ethnic cleansing, the ICISS report highlights "acts of terror and rape," as indicated in the following propositions:

> military intervention for human protection purposes is justified in two broad sets of circumstances, namely in order to halt or avert:
>
> - *large scale loss of life, actual or apprehended, with genocidal intent or not, which is the product either of deliberate state action, or state neglect or inability to act, or a failed state situation; or*

- *large scale "ethnic cleansing," actual or apprehended, whether carried out by killing, forced expulsion, acts of terror or rape.*

If either or both of these conditions are satisfied, it is our view that the "just cause" component of the decision to intervene is amply satisfied. (4.19)

As an international norm, R2P is in its infancy. Arguably, if it had existed robustly in, say, 1990, "rape camps" and the torture they involved might not have existed in the former Yugoslavia because there would have been forceful international intervention against ethnic cleansing there, and countless Tutsi women might not have been raped and *re-raped* because there would have been forceful international intervention against genocide in Rwanda. More recently, if R2P had existed robustly in, say, 2000, Nicholas Kristof might not have had to learn new words—*autocannibalism* and *re-rape*—because there would have been forceful international intervention to protect Congolese women and girls. Unfortunately, R2P neither existed robustly then nor does it now, and circumstances, events, and weakness of political will may doom it to be an idea whose time has *not* come or worse—like the slogan "Never Again"—a banal cliché.

Winning the support that R2P needs to be effective may well be a forlorn cause. But if R2P is to gain traction that can curb if not eliminate rape/torture as a weapon of war and genocide, work in that direction will have to include what the eighth chapter of the ICISS report urges: namely, attention to moral appeals that might prevent, avert, and halt such devastation. Importantly, the report aptly notes that "getting a moral motive to bite means . . . being able to convey a sense of urgency and reality about the threat to human life in a particular situation" (8.13).

Do the Dead Cry Out for Action?

Where rape-as-policy and the torture it entails are concerned, how can "a sense of urgency and reality" about that devastation be bolstered? Could such prospects be enhanced, at least in some significant ways, by remembering the women and girls, and the men and boys, who have been killed after or as a result of being raped/tortured, if not "done to death" directly and immediately by such atrocities?

Reflection on those questions invites consideration of others: Can the dead themselves, specifically those whose lives have been taken by rape/torture, especially in circumstances of rape/torture-as-policy, prompt "a sense of urgency and reality" about the importance of protection and resistance against the sexual torture that stole life from them? Can those dead "cry out for action" in ways that the living never can? Could listening to the dead, those "done to death" by rape/torture-as-policy in war and genocide, improve the odds that moral motives will bite in the ways we need them to do?

Lest my intentions be misunderstood, some explanation is needed before proceeding further. When I speak of "the dead," doing so with specific reference to those whose lives were lost when rape/torture became a weapon of war and genocide, my aim is not to lump individuals together in an anonymous, faceless, genderless, and ultimately disrespectful way. To the contrary, as I think of "the dead," the point is to underscore that *individual* girls and women, boys and men, have been "done to death" by rape/torture-as-policy. If "the dead" can be said to "speak," their "word" comes from individuals who compel respect from us, the living, and also from their "chorus," for every individual who has suffered and died through rape/torture-as-policy is one of many. In both forms—as one and as many—the voices of the dead reverberate in awesome ways if we allow them to do so. Listening, trying to hear what these voices—individual and collective—might say to us as they reach a silent but deeply moving crescendo constitutes one of the most respectful and instructive actions we can take.

No One's Death Should Come That Way

If those "done to death" by rape/torture, especially in circumstances of rape-as-policy, can and do speak in and through their silence, what do they say? Here, I believe, a combination of cautious restraint and bold statement must remain in respectful tension. Restraint is needed because the bold responses that are right and good are also likely to sound like clichés if they are articulated. Silence followed by action that resists death's waste may be the wisest course. But silence, even when accompanied by action that resists death-dealing rape/torture, may be insufficient and irresponsible.

Those "done to death" by rape/torture, especially through rape-as-policy in war and genocide, can and do cry out for action. Perhaps one way to interpret their cry is to say not so simply: Yes, we all are dying and will soon be dead, but no one's death should come *that way*. What *that way* was and means is partly knowable because we have testimony, memoirs, trial records, historical research, and even new words such as *autocannibalism* and *re-rape* that state and document the butchery. What *that way* was and means is also unutterable, for one cannot interview the dead. But because the latter realization persists, revealing as it does that, in David Boder's words, "the grimmest stories" are not the ones that are told, responses in word and deed that join with the dead to "see through the gloom" may still be found.[24] Such seeing would not dispel the gloom of atrocity. Nothing, not even a robustly normative responsibility to protect, can do so, at least not completely. But *seeing through* might suggest a much-needed combination: namely, a linking of *seeing through* as refusing to forsake those "done to death," however disconsolate that commitment may be, with a *seeing through* that entails doing as much as one/we can to find ways to keep the gloom from overwhelming us. If the responsibility to protect is not one of those ways, nothing could be. It emanates from atrocity's dead, and fulfilling that responsibility, even imperfectly, is arguably one of our best ways to hear and respect them.

Concluding his important book, *The Dominion of the Dead*, Robert Pogue Harrison observes that the dead may be "our guardians. We give them a future so that they may give us a past. We help them live on so that they may help us go forward."[25] That description can fit those "done to death" by rape/torture and our relationship to them. By remembering them, by allowing them to indwell our worlds, by allowing them to speak to and through us, we may yet find ways, including R2P, to curb at least some of the conditions that destroyed them. Such action would not bring back those "done to death" by rape/torture-as-policy, but it would create a present and a future—and even a past—more worth having.

CONTRIBUTORS' QUESTIONS FOR JOHN K. ROTH

1. You reference torture-related policies adopted by the United Nations and other international bodies since the 1980s. In a volume in which Holocaust scholars reflect on torture, questions such as the following come to mind: Why should we who study the Holocaust think about or study contemporary cases of rape/torture-as-policy? What might be some parallels between rape/torture-as-policy in the cases you have mentioned—Syria and the Democratic Republic of Congo today, Rwanda

in the 1990s—and Nazi practices during World War II? Did the Holocaust and postwar Holocaust survivors influence the eventual international recognition of torture and rape as war crimes, crimes against humanity, and acts of genocide?

2. You urge action by the international community against rape-as-policy and other forms of torture so prevalent throughout the ages. You rightly support appropriate military action at the international level based on recent UN backing for the "responsibility to protect." However, might we also cry out for an international reform of education so that honoring the personhood of the other becomes a central theme across the curriculum? If such reform fails to be enacted in schools throughout the world, how can we expect troops to refrain from committing the very atrocities—including rape-torture—that they are empowered internationally to curtail or prevent? Might we who respond to your appeal to "listen to the dead" hear from them not only a call to arms to protect those vulnerable to torture but also a summons to parent our children and teach our students in radically new ways that will help to foster moral agency?

RESPONSE BY JOHN K. ROTH

On March 14, 2013, Ban Ki-moon, the secretary-general of the United Nations, released his report "Sexual Violence in Conflict."[26] Focusing on data from December 2011 to December 2012, it interpreted sexual violence to include "rape, sexual slavery, forced prostitution, forced pregnancy, enforced sterilization and any other form of sexual violence of comparable gravity perpetrated against women, men or children with a direct or indirect (temporal, geographical or causal) link to a conflict." Implicitly acknowledging the reality of rape/torture as policy, the secretary-general's account stressed that "sexual violence is almost universally underreported, for multiple reasons, including the risks faced by survivors, witnesses, humanitarian workers and journalists who come forward, including the risk of reprisal." Then the report documented the devastation that sexual violence in conflict has wreaked in nineteen countries, among them Afghanistan, Bosnia-Herzegovina, Colombia, the Democratic Republic of Congo (DRC), Sierra Leone, Sudan (Darfur), and the Syrian Arab Republic.

Neither the countries identified in Ban Ki-moon's report nor even the sexual violence unleashed within them evokes the Holocaust, at least not immediately or primarily. So why should the United Nations report "Sexual Violence in Conflict" particularly distress Holocaust scholars—a person like me, for instance—and challenge us to deal with rape/torture as policy? One answer might be that direct connections exist between these post-Holocaust atrocities and rape/torture as policy during the Holocaust. Such connections, however, are tenuous. At least two factors support that judgment. First, until a few years ago, sexual violence during the Holocaust, including rape/torture as policy, was little discussed. As Jean Améry's reflections illustrate, survivors did speak about torture, but scarcely any survivors or perpetrators spoke explicitly and openly about rape as torture.[27] Postwar trials turned attention elsewhere; only a few scholars argued that such violence was widespread. With many taking the opposite position, research about Holocaust-related sexual violence was sidelined, partly because for many years Holocaust studies failed to pay sufficient attention to gender and, in particular, to the sexually specific ways in which Jewish women and girls came under attack by the Germans and their collaborators.[28] Second, attention to rape/torture as policy came to the fore mainly as knowledge grew about the calculated and systematic use of sexual violence in genocidal campaigns in the former Yugoslavia and Rwanda in the mid-1990s and then, more recently, in places such as Darfur and the DRC. Among other things, this attention led to legal proceedings in which torture was defined to include rape and rape was defined in ways that could make it a crime against humanity and an act of genocide. As far as attention to rape/torture as policy is concerned, the lines of connection did not run from the Holocaust to more recent events but rather the other way around. Recent awareness and concern about rape/torture as policy, in fact, did a great deal to crack open the barriers and demystify the taboos that blocked inquiry and even testimony about Holocaust-related sexual violence.

Jean Améry believed that "torture was the essence of National Socialism."[29] Without contradicting that judgment, current research indicates that during the Holocaust the infliction of rape/torture was not an officially implemented policy embedded in the Third Reich's genocide against the Jewish people. That same research, however, underscores that rape/torture of Jewish women and girls was nevertheless widespread, laws and sanctions against *Rassenschande* (race defilement) notwithstanding. A key point that emerges from study of what Ban Ki-moon's report calls "sexual violence in conflict" is that wherever genocidal acts are perpe-trated, rape/torture—as official policy or not—will likely be among them. Améry's quintessential essay on torture is sufficient to enlist Holocaust scholars—indeed anyone who reads it—in resisting that atrocity. But that realization remains incomplete unless it includes awareness of and resis-tance to rape/torture in particular.

As the questions asked of me suggest, resisting rape/torture, especially in cases where rape/torture is policy, is easier said than done. I have argued that the emerging norm called the "responsibility to protect," which includes provisions for humanitarian and even military intervention, offers hope that deserves international support. That support, I have also suggested, could be enhanced if we learned better to hear those who have had life stolen from them by rape/torture and to listen to the murdered dead, espe-cially those violated by rape/torture. Such hearing and listening have to be part of an educational process, one focused not exclusively but signifi-cantly on boys and men. Sexual violence in conflict and rape/torture in par-ticular are perpetrated primarily by males. Men have to be in the vanguard of resistance to these atrocities. Otherwise the chances to curb such acts are greatly reduced.

On June 24, 2013, not long after Ban Ki-moon released "Sexual Violence in Conflict," the United Nations Security Council unanimously adopted Resolution 2016 (2013).[30] It identifies many of the steps that need to be taken to curb, if not to eliminate, sexual violence during armed conflict. "Affirming that women's political, social and economic empowerment, gender equality and the enlistment of men and boys in the effort to combat all forms of violence against women are central to long-term efforts to prevent sexual violence in armed conflict and post-conflict situations," Resolution 2016 (2013) identifies actions that depend on education. The needed education must be advanced not only for the young in schools, colleges, and univer-sities but also for adults in government, police forces, and military units, including United Nations peacekeeping forces. Especially important, the resolution notes, is the necessity to combat a culture of impunity that takes sexual violence in conflict to be unavoidable, inevitable, and unprevent-able. Much more needs to be said than I can offer in this brief response, but my commentators are on target when they emphasize that the education entailed by Resolution 2016 (2013) must "help to foster moral agency" and "honor the personhood of the other."

Everyone who reads such words can and should ask, "What can I do to advance those ethical goals?" Good responses to that question are so numerous that they can be unending, a prospect that kindles hope even as it confers responsibility. When I think about conferring responsibility in regard to fostering moral agency and honoring personhood, I do not think only or even primarily about ethical injunctions, philosophical principles, or religious imperatives that emphasize such moral responsibility. Increasingly, my attention is directed to and governed by people whose deeds and words have moved me and challenged me to leverage my best chances to make a contribution, small though it might be, in the battle against torture and rape/torture in particular. Some of these people are known to me only through their writings. Jean Améry is one example. After I first read "Torture," I studied it every year with my students. That work affected my priorities as a teacher and a scholar. Among other things, that path led to my contributing to this book.

I think too of the courageous journalist Nicholas Kristof, whose *New York Times* columns often document and powerfully protest against torture and sexual violence. Emphasizing testimony he has heard, Kristof frequently gives voice to those—including sometimes the dead—who have had life stolen from them by rape/torture. On July 24, 2013, for example, Kristof published "A Policy of Rape Continues," which documents how ten years after genocide began in Darfur, rape/torture continues to be a devastating weapon in the Sudanese government's genocidal policies.[31] His article ends with the testimony of a seventeen-year-old Salamat girl named Jawahir, raped repeatedly by three men in military uniforms during an eleven-hour ordeal.[32] Courageously speaking about her rape/torture and the implications of the cultural dishonor that sexual violation has brought upon her, Jawahir told Kristof, "This is something that happened. So people should know. I want to the world to know." Hearing and heeding her voice are immensely important for implementing the education entailed by Resolution 2016 (2013).

Jean Améry, Nicholas Kristof, a young Salamat woman named Jawahir—such people, their testimonies and examples, insist that each of us can do something, can do more, to promote education that helps to foster moral agency and to honor the personhood of the other. To that list, I can add many other names, including, prominently, the contributors to this book, who each and all have challenged me and everyone who reads their words to take up the education/resistance that torture enjoins us to pursue.

NOTES

1 See, for instance, *Report of the Independent International Commission of Inquiry on the Syrian Arab Republic,* submitted to the United Nations Human Rights Council, February 5, 2015, http://www.ohchr.org/EN/HRBodies/HRC/IICISyria /Pages/Documentation.aspx. United Nations documentation of atrocities committed by ISIS, including that regime's use of sexual violence as "a deliberate tactic of war," can be found in *Report on the Protection of Civilians in the Armed Conflict in Iraq: 11 December 2014–30 April 2015,* http://www.ohchr.org/Documents /Countries/IQ/UNAMI_OHCHR_4th_POCReport-11Dec2014-30April2015 .pdf?ct=t(RtoP_Weekly_1_5_June_20156_1_2015). Also significant is "Evidence of Atrocities in Syria," the United States Holocaust Memorial Museum's exhibit of some of the 55,000 photos smuggled out of Syria in July 2014 by a former Syrian military photographer, code-named Caesar to protect him and his family. Before he defected, his task was to photograph the corpses of those who died at the hands of the Syrian government. Examples of these often graphic images are accessible at http://www.ushmm.org/confront-genocide/cases/syria/syria-photo-galleries/evi dence. For more information about the photographs and what they reveal about torture in Syria, see Stan Ziv, "Syria Torture Photos 'Depict Real People and Events': FBI Report," *Newsweek,* July 22, 2015, http://www.newsweek.com/syria-torture-photos -depict-real-people-and-events-fbi-report-356057.

2 See, for example, the United Nations Human Rights Council's "Report of the Independent International Commission of Inquiry on the Syrian Arab Republic" (February 22, 2012), especially paragraphs 58–70, which include discussion of torture and other human rights abuses. The document is available at http://www.nytimes .com/interactive/2012/02/23/world/middleeast/24syria-document.html?ref=warcr imesgenocideandcrimesagainsthumanity. See also "Syria Forces Reportedly Using Rape, Sexual Torture in Fight against Opposition," *CBS News,* July 12, 2012, http:// www.cbsnews.com/8301-503543_162-57470955-503543/syria-forces-reportedly-using -rape-sexual-torture-in-fight-against-opposition/. In addition, see Lauren Wolfe, "The Ultimate Assault: Charting Syria's Use of Rape to Terrorize Its People, *Atlantic,* July 11, 2012, http://www.theatlantic.com/international/archive/2012/07/the-ulti mate-assault-charting-syrias-use-of-rape-to-terrorize-its-people/259669/. Wolfe directs Women under Siege, an initiative of the Women's Media Center. Documenting how rape and other forms of sexualized violence are used as weapons of war and genocide, Women under Siege has recently devoted much of its attention to atrocities in Syria. See the project's web site, http://www.womenundersiegeproject.org/.

3 See Jean Améry's chapter entitled "Torture" in his *At the Mind's Limits: Contemplations by a Survivor on Auschwitz and Its Realities,* trans. Sidney Rosenfeld and Stella P. Rosenfeld (Bloomington: Indiana University Press, 1980), 21–40, esp. 24. Parts of this essay are adapted from my contributions to *Rape: Weapon of War and Genocide,* ed. Carol Rittner and John K. Roth (St. Paul, MN: Paragon House, 2012) and from my book *The Failures of Ethics: Confronting the Holocaust, Genocide, and*

Other Mass Atrocities (Oxford: Oxford University Press, 2015). See also Carol Rittner and John K. Roth, eds., *Teaching about Rape in War and Genocide* (New York: Palgrave Macmillan, 2015).

4   The phrase *done to death* is George Steiner's. See his *Language and Silence: Essays on Language, Literature, and the Inhuman* (New York: Atheneum, 1967), 157. I am indebted to Paul C. Santilli for this reference. Santilli's thought about the importance of encountering the dead, especially the murdered dead, has influenced mine. See especially Paul C. Santilli, "Philosophy's Obligation to the Human Being in the Aftermath of Genocide," in *Genocide and Human Rights: A Philosophical Guide*, ed. John K. Roth (New York: Palgrave Macmillan, 2005), 220–32.

5   Part I of the Convention, Article 1.1. The text is available at http://www.hrweb.org /legal/cat.html.

6   Kingsley Moghalu, *Rwanda's Genocide: The Politics of Global Justice* (New York: Palgrave Macmillan, 2005), 82. See also Maria Eriksson, *Defining Rape: Emerging Obligations for States under International Law?* (Örebro, Sweden: Örebro University, 2010), esp. 413–19, accessible at http://www.diva-portal.org/smash/get/diva2:317541 /FULLTEXT02.pdf.

7   *Prosecutor v. Akayesu*, Judgment (paragraphs 596–98), International Criminal Tribunal for Rwanda, Case No. ICTR-96-4-T (1998). The entire judgment is accessible at http://unictr.unmict.org/sites/unictr.org/files/case-documents/ictr-96-4/trial-judge ments/en/980902.pdf.

8   On this point, as well as the preceding one about men and boys as victims of rape in war and genocide, see Dara Kay Cohen, Angelia Hoover Green, and Elisabeth Jean Wood, "Wartime Sexual Violence: Misconceptions, Implications, and Ways Forward," Special Report 323, United States Institute of Peace, Washington, DC, February 2003, 4–5, http://www.usip.org/sites/default/files/resources/SR323.pdf.

9   *Prosecutor v. Akayesu*, Judgment (paragraphs 597 and 598).

10 Quoted in *Interpretation of Torture in the Light of the Practice and Jurisprudence of International Bodies*, 18. This 2011 document guides the deliberations, policies, and practices of the United Nations Voluntary Fund for Victims of Torture (UNVFVT), which the General Assembly of the United Nations established in 1981. The document is accessible at www.ohchr.org/Documents/Issues/Torture/UNVFVT/Inter pretation_torture_2011_EN.pdf. For more detail on rape as torture, see also Eriksson, *Defining Rape*, esp. 301–34. Debate continues to focus on issues about the applicability of international law, including its interpretations of rape-as-torture, to non-state actors—organizations that have significant political influence and control, often by means of violence, but are not officially allied to any particular country or state. Helpful analysis can be found in "Torture by Non-State Actors: A Primer," a report by the Redress Trust as part of the Prevention through Documentation Project, an initiative of the International Rehabilitation Council for Torture Victims (IRCT), the World Medical Association (WMA), the Human Rights Foundation of Turkey (HRFT), and Physicians for Human Rights USA (PHR USA). The document is accessible at www.irct.org/Files/Filer/IPIP/training/Torture

_by_Non-State_Actors-Primer.pdf. The trend is to ensure that non-state actors are held accountable when their aims include the use of rape-as-torture.

11 Améry, *At the Mind's Limits*, 28.

12 Ibid., 28–29.

13 In this essay, the terms *rape* and *rape/torture* will typically be used in synonymous ways. The same holds for the terms *rape-as-policy* and *rape/torture-as-policy*.

14 *Prosecutor v. Akayesu,* Judgment (paragraphs 597 and 731).

15 In addition to Kristof's many *New York Times* editorials on these topics, see Nicholas D. Kristof and Sheryl WuDunn, *Half the Sky: Turning Oppression into Opportunity for Women Worldwide* (New York: Alfred A. Knopf, 2009).

16 Nicholas Kristof, "The Grotesque Vocabulary in Congo," *New York Times*, February 11, 2010, http://www.nytimes.com/2010/02/11/opinion/11kristof.html.

17 Nicholas Kristof, "The World Capital of Killing," *New York Times*, February 7, 2010, http://www.nytimes.com/2010/02/07/opinion/07kristof.html. The peer-reviewed study cited by Kristof is "Mortality in the Democratic Republic of Congo: An Ongoing Crisis," which is a special report by the highly respected International Rescue Committee. The report is available at http://www.rescue.org/sites/default /files/migrated/resources/2007/2006-7_congomortalitysurvey.pdf.

18 These paragraphs are from General Assembly of the United Nations, "2005 World Summit Outcome," October 24, 2005, http://www.un.org/en/ga/search/view_doc .asp?symbol=A/RES/60/1. See in particular p. 30.

19 The Charter of the United Nations is available at the UN web site, http://www.un.org /en/charter-united-nations/.

20 Chapter I, Article 2, Paragraph 7. The qualifications pertain to the conditions enumerated in Chapter VII.

21 A good source for further information about these developments is the web site for the International Coalition for the Responsibility to Protect, http://www.responsi bilitytoprotect.org/index.php/about-rtop.

22 See Thomas G. Weiss, "R2P after 9/11 and the World Summit," *Wisconsin International Law Journal* 24, no. 3 (2006): 741.

23 See *The Responsibility to Protect: Report of the International Commission on Intervention and State Sovereignty* (Ottawa: International Development Research Centre, 2001). Citations refer to the report's internal enumeration of sections and paragraphs. The report can be found at http://responsibilitytoprotect.org/ICISS%20 Report.pdf. See also Gareth Evans, *The Responsibility to Protect: Ending Mass Atrocity Crimes Once and for All* (Washington, DC: Brookings Institution Press, 2008).

24 Boder, an American psychologist, was among the first to interview survivors of the Holocaust and other Nazi crimes after World War II. Eight of these interviews were published by the University of Illinois Press in 1949. Boder ended the introduction to his book with these words: "The verbatim records presented in this book make uneasy reading. And yet they are not the grimmest stories that could be told—I did not interview the dead." That last thought-provoking phrase—"I did

not interview the dead"—became his book's title. See David P. Boder, *I Did Not Interview the Dead* (Urbana: University of Illinois Press, 1949), xix. For a significant study of Boder and his work, see Alan Rosen, *The Wonder of Their Voices: The 1946 Holocaust Interviews of David Boder* (New York: Oxford University Press, 2010). The phrase *see through the gloom* comes from Robert Pogue Harrison, *The Dominion of the Dead* (Chicago: University of Chicago Press, 2003), 159.

25 Harrison, *The Dominion of the Dead*, 158.

26 Identified as United Nations document A/67/792-S/2013/149, the report is available online at http://www.un.org/sexualviolenceinconflict/key-documents/reports/.

27 Although Améry did not say that rape was a method of torture inflicted on him by his German captors, he likened his torture to rape.

28 Fortunately, scholarship is beginning to make up for lost time in this area. For recent examples, see Myrna Goldenberg and Amy H. Shapiro, eds., *Different Horrors, Same Hell: Gender and the Holocaust* (Seattle: University of Washington Press, 2013); Sonja M. Hedgepeth and Rochelle G. Saidel, eds., *Sexual Violence against Jewish Women during the Holocaust* (Waltham, MA: Brandeis University Press, 2010); and Carol Rittner and John K. Roth, eds., *Rape: Weapon of War and Genocide* (St. Paul, MN: Paragon House, 2012). Also relevant is Lenore J. Weitzman, "Women," in *The Oxford Handbook of Holocaust Studies*, ed. Peter Hayes and John K. Roth (Oxford: Oxford University Press, 2010), 203–17. In addition, see the highly significant work of Father Patrick Desbois, whose literally groundbreaking explorations in Ukraine, Belarus, Russia, and other parts of Nazi-occupied eastern Europe show that sexual assaults against Jewish women and girls were commonplace before the mass shootings that murdered 1.5 million Jews in what Desbois calls "the Holocaust by bullets." For articles and reports about Desbois's work, see http://www.yahadinunum.org/fieldwork/articles-and-reports/?lang=en.

29 Améry, *At the Mind's Limits*, 30.

30 The text of this resolution, plus discussion that led to its passage, is accessible online at http://www.un.org/News/Press/docs/2013/sc11043.doc.htm.

31 Nicholas Kristof, "A Policy of Rape Continues," *New York Times*, July 24, 2013, http://www.nytimes.com/2013/07/25/opinion/kristof-a-policy-of-rape-continues.html?ref=nicholasdkristof&_r=0.

32 In 2013, the Salamat were in the middle of intertribal and interethnic fighting, especially with their rivals, the Misseriya. Government-linked militia and paramilitary groups have compounded the plight of the Salamat.

Epilogue

Again, the Questions of Torture

LEONARD GROB AND JOHN K. ROTH

> Imagine that you are creating a fabric of human destiny
> with the object of making men happy in the end . . . but that
> it was essential and inevitable to torture to death only one
> tiny creature. . . . Would you consent to be the architect on
> those conditions?
>
> —Fyodor Dostoevsky, *The Brothers Karamazov*

The challenge posed by Dostoevsky's Ivan Karamazov to his brother
Alyosha—"Would you consent to be the architect on those conditions?"—
resounds in this book's ethical inquiry. The contributors hope that you,
the reader, have been moved to wrestle with the many questions raised in
this book's pages. They include: Is a prohibition against torture absolute,
admitting of no exceptions? What constitutes responsible witnessing to
testimony—written or oral—about torture? What kinds of ethical concerns
justify relating torture to genocide and to the Holocaust in particular?
What is responsible conduct toward victims of torture? Where should one
stand in debates about torture and public policy? What steps must I—and
we—take to come closer to a society in which torture is unthinkable?

No book can answer such questions finally and completely, but the contributors to this volume have shown how torture shakes the very foundations of society. As Jean Améry so tellingly understood, the allegedly tightly

woven fabric of society—secured by means of written or unwritten contracts promising that "the other person will spare me"—can easily unravel, especially when torturers are allowed to do their grisly work.[1] The presence of torture across cultures and centuries shows how trust in the world can be rapidly and completely eroded. Following Améry's insights, one of this book's major themes has been that while society may permit us to live with dignity, resolute vigilance is required lest that trust be betrayed. Torture, which also, unfortunately, is a social reality, does just that and therefore must be combatted whenever it appears.

The events of 1939–45 put the fragility of trust in society, let alone the world, into bold relief. Again, taking seriously Améry's lead when he insisted that "torture was not an accidental quality of this Third Reich, but its essence," the Holocaust scholars included here felt compelled to create this volume on torture.[2] If we do not agree completely about the relationships between genocide and torture, we hold that societies in which torture prevails are likely to be genocidal and that genocides do not exist without torture. While torture is neither a necessary nor a sufficient condition for genocide, torture aids and abets genocidal inclinations, and torture is often one of genocide's most destructive accomplices. In a post-Holocaust world, where torture is rife and the threats of genocide persist, questions about torture loom large, again and again.

Raised because torture persists so stubbornly, the questions of torture may sometimes seem to produce hopelessness and despair more than anything else. Even this book's title, *Losing Trust in the World,* might seem to head in that direction. To the contrary, however, Jean Améry's theme rallied us to stand in solidarity with him and with every torture victim to encourage resistance in spite of despair and to affirm that steps can be taken to keep torture at bay, if not to eliminate it altogether. So it is fitting that *Losing Trust in the World* concludes with thoughts about ways in which we—not only this book's authors and readers but all who call this planet home—can contribute to creating a world without torture.

We have little time to waste. Theologian George Hunsinger, founder of the National Religious Campaign against Torture, warns that we face a crisis which calls for immediate action. Far from being an apt response to so-called ticking time bombs, torture itself, insists Hunsinger, "is the ticking time bomb."[3] Averting one's eyes from acts of torture—with the excuse that "there is nothing I can do about it"—smacks of the bystander behavior so familiar to students of the Holocaust. Human rights activist and former torture victim Juan E. Méndez sounds the call to action: "Torture will be abolished when all of us make ourselves responsible for it; for abolishing it and for enforcing its prohibition. Especially if cruelty is inflicted on others in our name and for our sake, we are guilty of it unless we take responsibility for rejecting it and for campaigning to abolish it."[4]

As individuals and as members of grassroots organizations, we have work to do. As torture researcher Darius Rejali contends, "When we watch, torturers care. Torturers actually care about what your church group, or your newspaper, or anybody says. Public monitoring really works."[5] Examples of activities an individual may undertake include organizing community vigils, teach-ins, demonstrations to educate community members and to register protest about torture issues; unmasking, in letters and oral presentations, euphemisms such as "enhanced interrogation," employed to dismiss the cruel reality of torture; centering local campaigns against torture on religious teachings; and using the arts—music, drama, visual art, poetry, fiction, essays—to bring this issue to the forefront of individual and community consciousness. Sustained awareness of torture for what it is, combined with a commitment to act, will help move our world closer to curbing this atrocity.

Difficult as it for individuals to avoid bystander behavior and to take actions such as those identified above, "the harder thing," Rejali claims, "is to persuade governments to stop creating the conditions that produce torture."[6] In the face of danger to the nation-state, governments are tempted to argue for exceptionalism, to claim that bad times call for measures that would be morally reprehensible under ordinary circumstances. The United States sometimes operated that way after 9/11. Other nations have done likewise in the twenty-first century when facing perceived threats to their security. Méndez challenges this posture and the policy that emerges from it, arguing that a great society does not depart from its moral norms in the face of such challenges.[7]

What can governments themselves do to limit the conditions that produce torture? An important response to that question comes from Amnesty International, which offers a "12-Point Program for the Prevention of Torture."[8] This program emphasizes imperatives to *condemn* torture whenever or wherever it appears; to *ensure* that legal and judicial authorities have access to prisoners; to *make certain* that detention sites are never kept secret; to *safeguard* the rights of prisoners during periods of detention and interrogation by means of inspections by independent parties; to *prohibit* all forms of torture by passing laws consistent with the UN Convention against Torture; to *employ* independent agencies to investigate all reports of torture; to *prosecute* those responsible for torture, including, if called for, surrendering suspected torturers to an international criminal court; to *ensure* that no statements obtained through torture be cited in any legal proceeding; to *educate* officials involved in prisoner interrogation to understand that torture is a criminal act; to *provide* state-sponsored reparations, including rehabilitation, to victims of torture; to *ratify* all international treaties that protect citizens against torture; and to *intercede* with the governments of states in which torture is reported.

Formulating a twelve-point program to help eradicate torture is masterful. Whether governments will put such a program into practice is another matter. Here we return to the issue of individual responsibility: *citizens must prompt, prod, rouse their governments to act according to imperatives such as those proposed by Amnesty International.* Bearing witness to the inviolability of our fellow humans is a pathway to eliminating torture and, ultimately, to regaining trust in the world. The contributors to this book agree that no one is exempt from the task at hand, that each of us must initiate action, that we cannot wait for others to begin the work of healing our world.

Jean Améry insisted that "reality is reasonable only so long as it is moral."[9] In solidarity with his fellow philosopher and recalling a passage from Dostoevsky's *The Brothers Karamazov*, Emmanuel Levinas proclaims that although we humans are responsible for one another, each individual "I" has more responsibility than all the others.[10] As it furthers the mission to keep working toward the elimination of torture, *Losing Trust in the World* embraces that responsibility.

NOTES

1   Jean Amery, *At the Mind's Limits: Contemplations by a Survivor on Auschwitz and Its Realities*, trans. Sidney Rosenfeld and Stella P. Rosenfeld (Bloomington: Indiana University Press, 1980), 28.

2   Ibid., 24.

3   George Hunsinger, "Torture Is the Ticking Time Bomb: Why the Necessity Defense Fails," in *Torture Is a Moral Issue: Christians, Jews, Muslims, and People of Conscience Speak Out*, ed. George Hunsinger (Grand Rapids, MI: William B. Eerdmans, 2008), 51.

4 Juan E. Méndez, "Foreword," in *The Phenomenon of Torture: Readings and Commentary,* ed. William F. Schulz (Philadelphia: University of Pennsylvania Press, 2007), xvii.

5 Rejali is quoted in Hunsinger, "How To End Torture," in *Torture Is a Moral Issue,* 250–51.

6 Rejali quoted in Hunsinger, "How to End Torture," 251. Hunsinger indicates that his quotations from Rejali are from Lawrence J. Maushard, "Interview with Darius Rejali," *Willamette Week* (Portland, OR), November 28, 2007.

7 Méndez, "Foreword," in Schulz, ed., *The Phenomenon of Torture,* xvii.

8 The text of "Amnesty International's 12-Point Program for the Prevention of Torture and Other Cruel, Inhuman or Degrading Treatment or Punishment by Agents of the State" is accessible at https://www.amnesty.org/en/documents/act40/001/2005/en/.

9 Jean Améry, *Radical Humanism: Selected Essays,* trans. Sidney Rosenfeld and Stella P. Rosenfeld (Bloomington: Indiana University Press, 1984), 65.

10 Emmanuel Levinas, *Ethics and Infinity: Conversations with Philippe Nemo,* trans. Richard A. Cohen (Pittsburgh, PA: Duquesne University Press, 1985), 99.

Selected Bibliography

Focused on work done in the twenty-first century, this bibliography supplements the sources cited by the contributors. The books noted here are primarily of two kinds. Some concentrate explicitly on torture and its implications for ethics, politics, international relations, and religion. Others explore the Holocaust and genocide in torture-related ways. Some of these books center on Jean Améry, whose experience of torture grounds this volume.

Aguilar, Mario I. *Religion, Torture and the Liberation of God*. New York: Routledge, 2015.

Allhoff, Fritz. *Terrorism, Ticking Time-Bombs, and Torture: A Philosophical Analysis*. Chicago: University of Chicago Press, 2012.

Bagaric, Mirko, and Julie Clarke. *Torture: When the Unthinkable Is Morally Permissible*. Albany: State University of New York Press, 2007.

Bernstein, J. M. *Torture and Dignity: An Essay on Moral Injury*. Chicago: University of Chicago Press, 2015.

Biswas, Shampa, and Zahi Zalloua, eds. *Torture: Power, Democracy, and the Human Body*. Seattle: University of Washington Press, 2011.

Brecher, Bob. *Torture and the Ticking Bomb*. Oxford: Blackwell Publishing, 2007.

Brudholm, Thomas. *Resentment's Virtue: Jean Améry and the Refusal to Forgive*. Philadelphia: Temple University Press, 2008.

Card, Claudia. *Confronting Evils: Terrorism, Torture, Genocide*. Cambridge, UK: Cambridge University Press, 2010.

Carlson, Julie A., and Elisabeth Weber, eds. *Speaking about Torture*. New York: Fordham University Press, 2012.

Cheyette, Bryan. *Diasporas of the Mind: Jewish and Postcolonial Writing and the Nightmare of History*. New Haven, CT: Yale University Press, 2013.

Clarke, Alan W. *Rendition to Torture.* New Brunswick, NJ: Rutgers University Press, 2012.

Clucas, Bev, Gerry Johnstone, and Tony Ward, eds. *Torture: Moral Absolutes and Ambiguities.* Baden-Baden: Nomos, 2009.

Cole, David, ed. *The Torture Memos: Rationalizing the Unthinkable.* New York: New Press, 2009.

Connerton, Paul. *The Spirit of Mourning: History, Memory, and the Body.* Cambridge, UK: Cambridge University Press, 2011.

Conroy, John. *Unspeakable Acts, Ordinary People.* Berkeley: University of California Press, 2001.

Danner, Mark. *Torture and Truth: America, Abu Ghraib, and the War on Terror.* New York: New York Review Books, 2004.

De Vito, Daniela. *Rape, Torture, and Genocide: Some Theoretical Implications.* Hauppauge, NY: Nova Science Publishers, 2011.

Del Rosso, Jared. *Talking about Torture: How Political Discourse Shapes the Debate.* New York: Columbia University Press, 2015.

Edmonds, Bill Russell. *God Is Not Here: A Soldier's Struggle with Torture, Trauma, and the Moral Injuries of War.* New York: Pegasus Books, 2015.

Farrell, Michelle. *The Prohibition of Torture in Exceptional Circumstances.* Cambridge, UK: Cambridge University Press, 2013.

Flynn, Michael, and Fabiola F. Salek, eds. *Screening Torture: Media Representations of State Terror and Political Domination.* New York: Columbia University Press, 2012.

Fried, Charles, and Gregory Fried. *Because It Is Wrong: Torture, Privacy and Presidential Power in the Age of Terror.* New York: W. W. Norton, 2010.

Gardell, Mattias. *Return of Torture.* New York: Routledge, 2015.

Geddes, Jennifer L., John K. Roth, and Jules Simon, eds. *The Double Binds of Ethics after the Holocaust: Salvaging the Fragments.* New York: Palgrave Macmillan, 2009.

Gerrity, Ellen, Terrance M. Keane, and Farris Tuma, eds., *The Mental Health Consequences of Torture.* Dordrecht: Kluwer, 2001.

Ginbar, Yuval. *Why Not Torture Terrorists? Moral, Practical, and Legal Aspects of the "Ticking Bomb" Justification for Torture.* Oxford: Oxford University Press, 2008.

Gordon, Rebecca. *Mainstreaming Torture: Ethical Approaches in the Post-9/11 United States.* Oxford: Oxford University Press, 2014.

Graessner, Sepp, Norbert Gurris, and Christian Pross, eds. *At the Side of Torture Survivors: Treating a Terrible Assault on Human Dignity.* Baltimore, MD: Johns Hopkins University Press, 2001.

Greenberg, Karen J., ed. *The Torture Debate in America.* Cambridge, UK: Cambridge University Press, 2006.

Gross, Michael L. *Moral Dilemmas of Modern War: Torture, Assassination, and Blackmail in an Age of Asymmetic Conflict.* Cambridge, UK: Cambridge University Press, 2010.

Gushee, David, Jillian Hickman Zimmer, and J. Drew Zimmer, eds. *Religious Faith, Torture, and Our National Soul.* Macon, GA: Mercer University Press, 2010.

Hajjar, Lisa. *Torture: A Sociology of Violence and Human Rights*. New York: Routledge, 2013.

Hayes, Peter, and John K. Roth, eds. *The Oxford Handbook of Holocaust Studies*. Oxford: Oxford University Press, 2010.

Heidelberger-Leonard, Irène. *The Philosopher of Auschwitz: Jean Améry and Living with the Holocaust*. Translated by Anthea Bell. London: I. B. Taurus, 2010.

Hilde, Thomas G., ed. *On Torture*. Baltimore, MD: Johns Hopkins University Press, 2008.

Hunsinger, George, ed. *Torture Is a Moral Issue: Christians, Jews, Muslims, and People of Conscience Speak Out*. Grand Rapids, MI: Wm. B. Eerdmans, 2008.

Ignatieff, Michael. *The Lesser Evil: Political Ethics in an Age of Terror*. Princeton, NJ: Princeton University Press, 2004.

Jeffreys, Derek S. *Spirituality and the Ethics of Torture*. New York: Palgrave Macmillan, 2009.

Kamm, F. M. *Ethics for Enemies: Terror, Torture, and War*. Oxford: Oxford University Press, 2011.

Kelly, Tobias. *This Side of Silence: Human Rights, Torture, and Recognition of Cruelty*. Philadelphia: University of Pennsylvania Press, 2012.

Kershnar, Stephen. *For Torture: A Rights-Based Defense*. Lanham, MD: Lexington Books, 2011.

Kramer, Matthew H. *Torture and Moral Integrity: A Philosophical Enquiry*. Oxford: Oxford University Press, 2014.

Lazreg, Marnia. *Torture and the Twilight of Empire: From Algiers to Baghdad*. Princeton, NJ: Princeton University Press, 2008.

Levi, Primo. *The Drowned and the Saved*. Translated by Raymond Rosenthal. New York: Summit Books, 1988.

Luban, David. *Torture, Power, and Law*. Cambridge, UK: Cambridge University Press, 2014.

McCoy, Alfred. *A Question of Torture: CIA Interrogation, from the Cold War to the War on Terror*. New York: Metropolitan Books, 2006.

———. *Torture and Impunity: The U.S. Doctrine of Coercive Interrogation*. Madison: University of Wisconsin Press, 2012.

Méndez, Juan E. *Taking a Stand: The Evolution of Human Rights*. New York: Palgrave Macmillan, 2011.

Miles, Stephen H. *Oath Betrayed: America's Torture Doctors*, 2nd ed. Berkeley: University of California Press, 2009.

Moyn, Samuel. *Human Rights and the Uses of History*. London: Verso, 2014.

Mukherjee, Amrita. *Torture and the United Nations: Charter and Treaty-Based Monitoring*. London: Cameron May, 2008.

Ohlen, Jens David. *The Assault on International Law*. Oxford: Oxford University Press, 2015.

O'Mara, Shane. *Why Torture Doesn't Work: The Neuroscience of Interrogation*. Cambridge, MA: Harvard University Press, 2015.

Osiel, Mark. *The End of Reciprocity: Terror, Torture, and Law of War.* Cambridge, UK: Cambridge University Press, 2009.

Parry, John. *Understanding Torture: Law, Violence, and Political Identity.* Ann Arbor: University of Michigan Press, 2010.

Patterson, David, and John K. Roth, eds. *Fire in the Ashes: God, Evil, and the Holocaust.* Seattle: University of Washington Press, 2005.

Perry, John. *Torture: Religious Ethics and National Security.* Maryknoll, NY: Orbis, 2005.

Rejali, Darius. *Torture and Democracy.* Princeton, NJ: Princeton University Press, 2009.

Rittner, Carol, and John K. Roth, eds. *Rape: Weapon of War and Genocide.* St. Paul, MN: Paragon House, 2012.

———, eds. *Teaching about Rape in War and Genocide.* New York: Palgrave Macmillan, 2015.

Rosenfeld, Alvin H. *The End of the Holocaust.* Bloomington: Indiana University Press, 2011.

Roth, John K. *Ethics During and After the Holocaust: In the Shadow of Birkenau.* New York: Palgrave Macmillan, 2005.

———. *The Failures of Ethics: Confronting the Holocaust, Genocide, and Other Mass Atrocities.* Oxford: Oxford University Press, 2015.

Roth, Kenneth, Minky Worden, and Amy D. Bernstein, eds. *Torture: Does It Make Us Safer? Is It Ever OK?* New York: New Press, 2005.

Sands, Philippe. *Torture Team: Rumsfeld's Memo and the Betrayal of American Values.* New York: Palgrave Macmillan, 2008.

Schiemann, John W. *Does Torture Work?* Oxford: Oxford University Press, 2015.

Schuchalter, Jerry. *Poetry and Truth: Variations on Holocaust Testimony.* New York: Peter Lang, 2009.

Sebald, W. G. *On the Natural History of Destruction.* Translated by Anthea Bell. New York: Random House, 2003.

Shue, Henry. *Fighting Hurt: Rule and Exception in Torture and War.* Oxford: Oxford University Press, 2016.

Simon, Thomas W. *Genocide, Torture, and Terrorism: Ranking International Crimes and Justifying Humanitarian Intervention.* New York: Palgrave Macmillan, 2015.

Steinhoff, Uwe. *On the Ethics of Torture.* Albany: State University of New York Press, 2013.

Stritzke, Werner G. K., Stephan Lewandowsky, David Denemark, Joseph Clare, and Frank Morgan, eds. *Terrorism and Torture: An Interdisciplinary Perspective.* Cambridge, UK: Cambridge University Press, 2009.

Thomas, George C., III, and Richard A. Leo. *Confessions of Guilt: From Torture to Miranda and Beyond.* Oxford: Oxford University Press, 2012.

Todorov, Tzvetan. *Torture and the War on Terror.* Translated by Gila Walker. Kolkata: Seagull Books, 2009.

Wachsmann, Nikolaus. *Hitler's Prisons: Legal Terror in Nazi Germany.* New Haven, CT: Yale University Press, 2004.

———. *KL: A History of the Nazi Concentration Camps*. New York: Farrar, Straus and Giroux, 2015.

Wilson, John P., and Boris Droždek. *Broken Spirits: The Treatment of Traumatized Asylum Seekers, Refugees, and War and Torture Victims*. New York: Brunner-Routledge, 2004.

Wisnewski, J. Jeremy. *Understanding Torture*. Edinburgh: University of Edinburgh Press, 2010.

Wisnewski, J. Jeremy, and R. D. Emerick. *The Ethics of Torture*. London: Continuum, 2009.

Wolfendale, Jessica. *Torture and the Military Profession*. New York: Palgrave Macmillan, 2007.

Zolkos, Magdalena, ed. *On Jean Améry: Philosophy of Catastrophe*. Lanham, MD: Lexington Books, 2011.

———. *Reconciling Community and Subjective Life: Trauma Testimony as Political Theorizing in the Work of Jean Améry and Imre Kertész*. New York: Continuum, 2010.

Editors and Contributors

EDITORS

LEONARD GROB is Professor Emeritus of Philosophy at Fairleigh Dickinson University. Along with Henry Knight, he is also is the founding codirector of the Stephen S. Weinstein Holocaust Symposium, which has met biennially at Wroxton College in the United Kingdom since 1996. Grob has published extensively in the areas of peace studies and the philosophy of dialogue, concentrating on Martin Buber and Emmanuel Levinas. These interests led to *Encountering the Stranger: A Jewish-Christian-Muslim Trialogue* (2012), a volume edited with John K. Roth. The memoir "Goodbye Father," which describes Grob's "roots journey" to Ukraine, appeared in the journal *Judaism*. His experience in uncovering the history of the destruction of his father's family during the Holocaust led him to study that genocide, which has been a focal point during the second half of his career. Grob has authored articles and chapters on topics such as post-Holocaust education, ethics after the Holocaust, the ethics of rescue, and relationships between memory of the Holocaust and Israeli politics. Grob focused on the latter topic in *Anguished Hope: Holocaust Scholars Confront the Palestinian-Israeli Conflict* (2008), also edited with Roth.

JOHN K. ROTH is the Edward J. Sexton Professor Emeritus of Philosophy and the founding director of the Center for the Study of the Holocaust, Genocide, and Human Rights (now the Mgrublian Center for Human Rights) at Claremont McKenna College. Roth has published hundreds of articles and reviews and authored, coauthored, or edited more than fifty books, including *The Oxford Handbook of Holocaust Studies* (2010), *Encountering the Stranger: A Jewish-Christian-Muslim Trialogue* (2012), *Rape: Weapon of War and Genocide* (2012), *Teaching about Rape in War and Genocide* (2015), and *The Failures of Ethics: Confronting the Holocaust, Genocide, and Other Mass Atrocities* (2015). With David Patterson, he edits the Stephen S. Weinstein Series in Post-Holocaust Studies, which is published by the University of Washington Press. Named the 1988 US National Professor of the Year by the Council for Advancement and Support of Education and the Carnegie Foundation for the Advancement of Teaching, Roth has also received the Holocaust Educational Foundation's Distinguished Achievement Award for Holocaust Studies and Research.

CONTRIBUTORS

MARGARET BREARLEY is an independent scholar and activist. Having studied at Oxford, Cambridge, and Münster, she has held academic posts at Birmingham University; the Centre for Judaism and Jewish-Christian Relations, Selly Oak Colleges; and the Institute of Jewish Affairs, London. She founded and led the Kinmos Day-care Centre for the Mentally Ill in Birmingham and the West Midlands Israel Information Centre. She has lectured in Israel, Germany, Finland, the United States, and throughout Britain, and has published many articles and book chapters, especially on anti-Judaism, genocide, ideological sources of the Holocaust, and the Roma people. Brearley has been a consultant to several films and documentaries, judge for the Times Preacher of the Year competition in the United Kingdom, and honorary Advisor on the Holocaust to the Archbishops' Council. Consequent upon the death of her elder son, she is currently Chair and acting honorary CEO of the Compassionate Friends, a national charity providing peer support for bereaved parents.

SUZANNE BROWN-FLEMING directs the visiting scholar programs at the United States Holocaust Memorial Museum's Jack, Joseph and Morton Mandel Center for Advanced Holocaust Studies. A Mandel Center Fellow (2000), she is the author of *The Holocaust and Catholic Conscience: Cardinal Aloisius Muench and the Guilt Question in Germany* (2006). More recently, her book *Nazi Persecution and Postwar Repercussions: The Inter-*

national Tracing Service Archive and Holocaust Research (2016) is part of the USHMM series *Documenting Life and Destruction: Holocaust Sources in Context.* Along with Rebecca Boehling, Suzanne Urban, and Elizabeth Anthony, Brown-Fleming has also edited *Freilegungen: Spiegelungen der NS-Verfolgung und ihrer Konsequenzen, 2015 Jahrbuch des International Tracing Service* (Excavations: Reflections of Nazi persecution and its consequences, 2015 yearbook of the International Tracing Service). In addition to service on the executive council of the American Catholic Historical Association, she is a member of the editorial board for the journal *Contemporary Church History Quarterly.*

DOROTA GLOWACKA is Professor of Humanities in the Contemporary Studies Programme at the University of King's College in Halifax, Canada. Her research interests include Holocaust and genocide studies, Polish-Jewish relations after the Shoah, continental philosophy, gender studies, and philosophies of race. She is the author of *Disappearing Traces: Holocaust Testimonials, Ethics, and Aesthetics* (2012); coeditor of *Between Ethics and Aesthetics: Crossing the Boundaries* (2002) and *Imaginary Neighbors: Mediating Polish-Jewish Relations after the Holocaust* (2007); and guest editor of the issue of *Culture Machine* entitled "Community" (2006). In addition, Glowacka has published—in Polish and French as well as in English—more than fifty journal articles, book chapters, reviews, and encyclopedia entries, many of them dealing with the Holocaust and Polish-Jewish relations. Her current research focuses on issues of gender and race in relation to histories of atrocity.

PETER J. HAAS, the Abba Hillel Silver Professor Emeritus of Jewish Studies at Case Western Reserve University, was ordained as a Reform rabbi in 1974, served as an active US Army chaplain for three years, and remained in the Army National Guard for another nineteen years. He joined the faculty at Vanderbilt University in 1980, where he taught courses in Judaism, Jewish ethics, the Holocaust, Western religion, and the Middle East conflict before moving to Case Western Reserve University in 2000, where he chaired the Department or Religious Studies from 2003 to 2015. In addition to lecturing in Germany, Italy, Belgium, and Israel, as well as widely throughout the United States, Haas has published extensively on ethics and on Jewish and Christian thought after the Holocaust. His books include *Morality after Auschwitz: The Radical Challenge of the Nazi Ethic*

(2014 [1988]), *The Jewish Tradition*, volume 1 in the series *Human Rights and the World's Major Religions* (2005), and *Biblical Interpretation in Judaism and Christianity* (2006).

BJÖRN KRONDORFER directs the Martin-Springer Institute at Northern Arizona University, where he is the Endowed Professor of Religious Studies in the Department of Comparative Cultural Studies. His fields of expertise encompass gender, culture, Holocaust studies, Western religious thought, and reconciliation studies. His books include *Remembrance and Reconciliation: Encounters between Young Jews and Germans* (1995), *Men and Masculinities in Christianity and Judaism* (2009), and *Male Confessions: Intimate Revelations and the Religious Imagination* (2010). These works have helped to define the field of Critical Men's Studies in Religions. In addition, Krondorfer has published three volumes in German on the cultural and theological legacy of the Holocaust. In his numerous international academic appointments and lectureships, Krondorfer facilitates intercultural encounters and works on reconciliation and social repair. Currently, he is exploring the connections among traumatic memory, reconciliation, and restorative justice.

DAVID PATTERSON holds the Hillel Feinberg Chair in Holocaust Studies in the Ackerman Center for Holocaust Studies at the University of Texas at Dallas. A winner of the National Jewish Book Award and the Koret Jewish Book Award, he has published thirty-five books and more than two hundred articles and book chapters. His books include *Sun Turned to Darkness* (1998), *Along the Edge of Annihilation* (1999), *Open Wounds: The Crisis of Jewish Thought in the Aftermath of Auschwitz* (2006), *Wrestling with the Angel* (2006), *Emil L. Fackenheim: A Jewish Philosopher's Response to the Holocaust* (2008), *A Genealogy of Evil: Ant-Semitism from Nazism to Islamic Jihad* (2011), *Genocide in Jewish Thought* (2012), and *Anti-Semitism and Its Metaphysical Origins* (2015). In addition, he is the editor and translator of *The Complete Black Book of Russian Jewry* (2002) and coeditor (with Alan L. Berger) of the *Encyclopedia of Holocaust Literature* (2002).

SARAH K. PINNOCK, Professor of Religion at Trinity University (Texas), co-chairs the American Academy of Religion's group on Religion, Holocaust, and Genocide. In addition to her appointment as a Fulbright fellow in Latvia (2006–7), she has received scholarly support from the Social

Sciences and Humanities Research Council and the German Academic Exchange. Her teaching and research concentrate on the problem of evil, feminist theology, death and dying, and the Holocaust. Pinnock's published work includes "Atrocity and Ambiguity: Recent Developments in Christian Holocaust Responses" in the *Journal of the American Academy of Religion* (2007), "Vulnerable Bodies: Feminist Reflections on the Holocaust and Nature" in *Holocaust and Nature* (2013), *Beyond Theodicy: Jewish and Christian Continental Thinkers Respond to the Holocaust* (2002), *The Theology of Dorothee Soelle* (2003), and the forthcoming volume *Facing Death: Confronting Mortality in the Holocaust and Ourselves*.

DIDIER POLLEFEYT is the Vice Rector for Education at the Katholieke Universiteit Leuven, Belgium, where he also is a full professor in the Faculty of Theology and Religious Studies. His teaching and research focus on religious education, ethics, Jewish-Christian relations, and post-Holocaust theology. In addition to serving on Belgium's National Catholic Commission for the Relations with Judaism, Pollefeyt is a widely published author. His numerous books include *Jews and Christians: Rivals or Partners for the Kingdom of God?* (1997), *Anti-Judaism and the Fourth Gospel* (2001), *Incredible Forgiveness* (2004), *Hermeneutics and Religious Education* (2004), *Interreligious Learning* (2007); *Children's Voices: Children's Perspectives in Ethics, Theology and Religious Education* (2010); *Never Revoked: Nostra Aetate as Ongoing Challenge for Jewish-Christian Dialogue* (2011), *Holocaust and Nature* (2013), and *Identity in Dialogue* (2014).

Index

Abeles, Margi, 147, 148

Abu Ghraib prison, 16, 31, 50, 53, 58n42, 126

ACLU (American Civil Liberties Union), xviin3

actions against torture and loss of trust: active awareness as, 12–13; artifacts for making, re-creating, and repairing in, 146–47; attention to the howl needed in, 47–48, 56; call to action in, 148–49, 190–92; in everyday ethical practice, 13–14; honoring personhood of Other/ others, 181, 183–84; listening to sur- vivors' voices, 4, 49, 143–44, 147–49, 179; making choices in, 15, 16; multiple others in questions of justice and, 14–15; overview of, 131–34; questions about, 145–46; resistance to ideologi- cal sincerity and "truth," 33–34, 38; responsibility for others, 13–15, 18, 48– 49, 50, 117–18, 123–25, 126–27, 192. *See also* communities; "crying out"; ethics; "responsibility to protect"; responsible witnessing; therapeutic care for vic- tims; *tikkun olam*

Adorno, Theodor, 54

Afghanistan, rape/torture in, 181–82. *See also* war on terror

After Auschwitz (Rubenstein), 116

Agamben, Giorgio: on bare life, 48, 56n2; on humans and language, 43–44, 50– 51; on modernity and Holocaust, 39n12; reading of, 54

Ahmadinejad, Mahmoud, 159

AI (Amnesty International), xii, xiii, 136, 148, 191–92

Akayesu, Jean-Paul, 172

Algerian War (1954–62), 121, 149

Alleg, Henri, 121

al-Qaeda, 58n41, 126, 159

Alter, Jonathan, 24

ambiguity, disallowed, 30–31

Amboss und Hammer (Anvil and hammer, Neuhäusler), 69

Amcha (Israeli Center of Holocaust Survivors and Their Children), 144

American Civil Liberties Union (ACLU), xviin3

American Psychological Association (APA), xvii–xviiin6

Améry, Jean: call to stop torture, 15, 16–17, 52; on "crying out under tor- ture," 52, 171; despair and suicide of, 128, 134n1; justifications for torture and, 115, 123, 128; on loss of trust in the world, xi, xvi, 4, 8–9, 14–15, 134, 173, 189–90; name of, xixn13; Nazis' torture of, xiv–xv, 8–9, 14, 30, 31–32, 173; on rape and torture, 134, 173, 182, 188n27; on reality as reasonable only if moral, xi, 5, 192; on resentments, xv, 15, 17, 18; on skin as shield, 161; on teaching, learning, and remembering, 11; on torture, pain, and language, 4, 44, 45, 46; on torture as essence of Nazism, 133, 141, 154–57, 163–64, 182,

Améry, Jean (*continued*)
190; on torture as existential destruction, 102, 103, 104, 135, 137, 138, 154, 156;
works: "Torture," xv–xvi, 4, 31–32, 183,
184. See also *At the Mind's Limits*
Amnesty International (AI), xii, xiii, 136,
148, 191–92
amputation, 95, 109, 161
animals: problematic distinctions of
humans and, 43–44, 47–48, 50–56;
Torah's prohibition against causing
pain to, 88, 93, 95, 96
antisemitism: Grüber's testimony and,
116; in Islamic jihadism, 133, 154–57,
164; in Nazi Germany's ideology and
laws, 25, 165–66. See also genocide;
Islamic jihadism; Nazism; race and
ethnicity
APA (American Psychological Associa-
tion), xvii–xviii*n*6
Aqsa Martyrs, al-, 159
Arab leadership, Nazi links to, 157–58
Arar, Maher, 44–45
Arendt, Hannah, 29, 33, 54
Argentina, torture in, 31, 45
Aristotle, 43, 54
Asad, Talal, 26, 28
Assad, Bashir al-, 171
Association for the Prevention of
Torture, xvii*n*3, 132
At the Mind's Limits (Améry): despair
in, 134n1; reading of, 7–8; "Torture"
essay in, xv–xvi, 31–32, 183
Auden, W. H., 147
Augustine (saint), 110
Auschwitz: absence of language in, 51;
"Boger swing" in, 119–20; Hebrew
prayer in shadows of, 10–11; meaning
of, 13; medical experiments at, 119;
prisoners in, xiv, 32, 72, 155, 173; tor-
ture in, 154, 155
authoritarian regimes: abuse of power
in, 117–18; camps as verifying ideology of, 33–34; political repression in,

23–24; torture as ready tool of, 31,
39n14, 123, 149. See also ideological
sincerity; totalitarianism; *and specific
regimes*
autocannibalism, 174, 178, 180
Avrahami, Yossi, 160
awareness. See direct awareness

Babi Yar, 154
Bamber, Helen, 136, 138, 139
Ban Ki-moon, 181–82, 183
Banna, Hasan al-, 157, 159–60, 161
Baobab Centre (London), 139
Baraitser, Marion, 139
bare life: "inclusive exclusion" of, 56n2;
politicization of, 43–44; prelinguistic
voice of, 47–48; unnameability in, 51
Barnett, Jamie, 5
Bataille, Georges, 39n15
Bauman, Zygmunt, 39n12
Behnia, Behnam, 138
Benedict XVI (pope), 100
Bentham, Jeremy, 55
Bergen-Belsen, xiv
Berkovits, Eliezer, 116
Berlin-Alexanderplatz prison, 67
bin Laden, Osama, 161
Birkenau, 154. See also Auschwitz
Blobel, Paul, 76
blood: jihadist lust for, 160–62; soul
as in, 154–55, 158
Bloodlands (Snyder), 46
Boder, David, 180, 187–88n24
body, mind, and spirit: evils designed
to assault, 23–24; meaning of torture
in context of incarnation, 104–5;
rejecting dichotomy in, 13; torture
and appropriation of soul, 153–57, 159–
63, 164–67; torture as radical destruction of victim's, 102, 103, 104–5, 135,
137, 138, 154, 156; "truth" impressed
on, 28–31. See also pain; suffering;
torture; trust in the world
Boger, Wilhelm, 119–20

Bosnia: genocide in, 126; Muslims in SS from, 157

Bosnia-Herzegovina, rape/torture in, 181–82

Boyle, Danny, 42

Brazil, torture in, 49

Brearley, Margaret: essay by, 135–45; questions for, 145–46; referenced, 132–33; response by, 146–49

Breendonk (detention camp), xiv

Brown-Fleming, Suzanne: essay by, 67–76; questions for, 76–77; referenced, 62–63; response by, 77–79

Browning, Christopher, 26

Broyde, Michael J., 91, 92, 94, 96

Buber, Martin, 21n36, 124

Buchenwald, 142

Bush, George W., xiii–xiv, xvii–xviiin6, 56n2, 121. *See also* euphemistic language about torture; war on terror

Busta (SS-Hauptscharfüher), 70

Butler, Judith, 50, 59n48

bystanders: danger of, 190–91; dynamics of indifference, 103–4, 105; questions about witnessing and indifference, 15, 18

Calvin, John, 117

Cambodia, killing fields of, 23

camps: for displaced persons (DP), 142. *See also* concentration and extermination camps; detention camps

Catholic Church: absolutist view of torture in, 99–100, 105–6; on capital punishment, 106–7; clemency campaign of, 76; Concordat of Third Reich with, 68; grandfather's break with, 77; moral theology tradition in, 109–10; Nazi campaign against, 72; post-Holocaust understanding of torture in, 102–5; postwar chapel on site of Dachau, 68, 80n12; priests imprisoned by Nazis, 72, 81nn40,41. *See also* Neuhäusler, Johann Baptist

Cavanaugh, William, 31

Center for Victims of Torture, xviin3, 21n37, 132

Central Intelligence Agency (CIA), xiii–xiv, xviiin7, 41n34, 48

Charny, Israel, 141

Charter of Allah (Hamas), 160, 162

Cheney, Dick, xiii

children as survivors and children of survivors, 144

Chile, torture in, 31

Christianity: belief in God's will, 116–17; on God, responsibility, and suffering, 122–23; responsibility for Other in, 124. *See also* Catholic Church; religious beliefs

Ci, którzy przez Dachau (Those who went through Dachau, Domogała), 68, 72–73, 81n40

CIA (Central Intelligence Agency), xiii–xiv, xviiin7, 41n34, 48

Code of Jewish Law (*Mishneh Torah*), 86–87

Colombia, rape/torture in, 181–82

Committee against Torture, xviin3

communities: connections to others in, 55–56; genocide as assault on, 23–24; Holocaust survivors' bonding and self-healing in, 141, 142–43, 147; individual as always being-with-others in, 16; obligation to do good in, 13–15; public violence in, 25–26; responsibilities of international, 175; role in abolishing torture, 190–91. *See also* actions against torture and loss of trust; survivors of Holocaust; *and specific organizations*

The Complete Black Book of Russian Jewry (trans. Patterson), 166

concentration and extermination camps: absence of language in, 50–51; common experiences in, 141–43; medical experiments at, 119; mundane examples of "useless violence" in, 120;

concentration and extermination camps
(*continued*)
Muselmann of, 43, 166; torture and
torturous conditions in, 166–67. *See
also* detention camps; *and specific
camps*
concentration camp survivor syndrome,
143
Concordat of Vatican and Third Reich
(1933), 68
"concussive events," 146
confession: accuracy/inaccuracy of,
xviin5, 6n2, 37, 44–47, 88; as "confirmation" of torturer's "truth," 5, 28,
29–31, 36, 44–45, 161–62; conveyor
method to obtain, 46–47; drugs to
facilitate, 119; film's depiction of, 42;
as purpose of torture, xii, 86–88, 104–
5, 120. *See also* ideological sincerity
"conveyor method," 46–47
Counterintelligence Interrogation (CIA),
41n34, 48
Crane, Jonathan K., 39n6
"crying out": for action, 178–79; for educational reform, 181; under torture,
52, 171
culture: of impunity, xiii, xv–xvi, 27; of
torture, 100–101; of violence, 119–21

Dachau: coupon system in, 73; first history of, 82n54; medical experiments
in, 119; Monument of Atonement in
the Concentration Camp at, 80n14;
Neuhäusler as special prisoner (*Sonderhäftling*) in, 63, 67, 69–70, 73; postwar
Catholic chapel on site of, 68, 80n12;
prisoners deported to Auschwitz
from, 72; torture heard and seen in,
62, 63, 70–73, 74, 75
"Dachau" trials (US Army), 68, 69, 74
Danish Institute against Torture, xviin3
Danner, Mark, 41n34
Darfur (Sudan), rape/torture in, 181–82,
184

David (king), 85
Davidson, Shamai, 141, 144–45
Davis, Javal, 53
dehumanization: of detainees in camps,
50, 54–55; ideologies of superiority
reinforced in, 119; Nazism's calculated
use of, 155–57; of victims of torture, 7,
9–10, 89–90, 126
delegitimization of torture. *See* actions
against torture and loss of trust
Democratic Republic of Congo (DRC):
rape/torture in conflict in, 23, 181–82;
terminology in war of, 174–75, 178
denazification, 119–21
Denmark: Institute against Torture in,
xviin3; therapeutic care for victims
of torture in, 136
deontological (absolutist) view: approach
to, 61–62, 64–65; critique of, 101, 110–
12; examples of, 99–100; proportionalist view compared with, 104, 105–6;
static vs. living (or enacted) position
in, 107, 109–10; torture never legitimate in, 99. *See also* proportionalist
(consequentialist) view
Dershowitz, Alan, 24, 56n1
Desbois, Patrick, 188n28
Des Pres, Terrence, xixn12, 142
detention camps: abusive conditions
in, xii, xiii, 16; bare life in, 43, 51;
Breendonk, xiv; dehumanization
and bestialization of those in, 50,
54–55; ensuring against secrecy of,
191–92; Guantánamo Bay, 16, 54,
59n50, 110, 121, 126; voices of survivors from, 53, 54, 58n41, 59n50.
See also Abu Ghraib prison; concentration and extermination camps
direct awareness: ambiguities and
dilemmas in, 73–77; limits of, 62–63;
torture heard and seen, 62, 63, 70–73.
See also Neuhäusler, Johann Baptist
Dirty War (Argentina), 45
displaced persons (DP) camps, 142

The Dominion of the Dead (Harrison), 180

Domogała, Jan, 68, 72–73, 81n40

"done to death," 171, 178–80, 186n4

Dorfman, Ariel, 9, 135

Dostoevsky, Fyodor, 19, 189, 192

DRC. *See* Democratic Republic of Congo

Eichmann, Adolf, 116

Eicke, Theodor, 68, 119

Eitinger, Leo, 143, 145

Elsasser und Lothringer in Dachau (Alsatian and Lorrainan prisoners in Dachau, Goldschmitt), 72

empathy, 12, 33–34. *See also* responsible witnessing

England, Lynndie, 50

"enhanced interrogation": brutal tactics of, xiii–xiv, 121, 123; dehumanization in, 50, 54–55, 89–90, 126; Geneva Convention violated in, 121; German term for, xiv; Islamic jihadism torture compared with, 164–65; justification of, 127; psychologists' complicity in, xvii–xviiin6. *See also* euphemistic language about torture; torture

ethical subject, 48–49

ethics: debates on absolute nature of evil in, 61–65; everyday actions as practice of, 13–14; in honoring personhood of Other/others, 181, 183–84; as "optics," or way of seeing, 21n32; politics in relation to, 15, 19, 35–36; of resistance to ideological sincerity and "truth," 33–34, 38; of responsibility for others, 13–15, 18, 48–49, 50, 117–18, 123–25, 126–27, 192; stance on suffering as useless in, 11, 48–49, 117–18; witnessing torture as intensifying responsibility, 49–52. *See also* deontological (absolutist) view; morality; proportionalist (consequentialist) view

Ethics of the Patriarchs (late Mishnaic tractate), 87

ethnicity. *See* race and ethnicity

euphemistic language about torture: commitment to expose, xvi; questions about, xixn12; "third degree" and "harsh" interrogations, 31, 41n35; torture justified by using, 110. *See also* "enhanced interrogation"; "extraordinary rendition"

Evans, Gareth, 177

evil: Catholic understanding of, 99–102; debates on absolute nature of, 61–65; embedded in perpetrators of torture, 105; lesser and greater, 19, 24, 29, 42–43, 64–65, 100, 101; moral complexities in identifying, 108–9; new interpretation of, 102–3; in proportionalist view, 106–7; torture as always, xvi, 14, 23, 53, 61, 101, 102–3. *See also* Holocaust; theodicy; "ticking time bomb"

"excremental assault," xixn12, 142

"extraordinary rendition," arrests under provisions of, 45. *See also* torture

Fackenheim, Emil L., 116, 154, 156, 163, 166

"The Fall of Icarus" (Auden), 147

Fatah, 159

Faulhaber, Michael, 68

Feinstein, Dianne, xiii

Filártiga, Joel, 49

Filártiga, Joelito, 49

film, 42, 53, 58n42

"Final Solution," 164

45 Aid Society, 142

Foucault, Michel, 24, 39n13

France, use of torture in Algeria, 121, 149

Franco, Francisco, 49

Frankl, Viktor, 140

Frederick Leopold (prince of Prussia), 69

Freedom from Torture (earlier called Medical Foundation for the Care of Victims of Torture), 136, 137, 138, 140–41, 145

García, Antonia, 49

gardening, 140–41

Gaza: Purity of Arms doctrine questioned in, 90; torture in, 165; university in, 158

Gdańsk (Poland), 53

generosity, 147

Geneva Convention Relative to the Treatment of Prisoners of War (1949), 99, 121, 126

genocide: ethnic cleansing in, 177–78; heeding early signs of, 17; individual murder compared with, 9; justification of torture and, 118; lessons for Israel, 92–93; multiple forms of violence in, 23–24; rape/torture-as-policy linked to, 172–74, 181–83; torture in relation to, 33, 35, 126, 190. *See also* Holocaust; rape/torture-as-policy; *and specific countries*

Genocide Watch, 17

German Labor Front, 77, 78

Germano, William, 6n1

Germany, postwar outlook, 76–77. *See also* Nazism

Gestapo: "enhanced interrogation" procedures of, xiv; Neuhäusler's testimony for some members, 68, 69, 73–76. *See also* Nazism

Gilmore, Leigh, 31

Glowacka, Dorota: essay by, 42–52; questions for, 52–53; referenced, 4, 5; response by, 53–56

God: authoritarian images of, 117; humans created in image of, 124; torturers' appropriation of, 153–57, 159–63, 164–67. *See also* religious beliefs; theodicy

Goldermann, Eduard, 77–78

Goldhagen, Daniel Jonah, 25, 26

Goldschmitt, François, 72

Gordon, Elizabeth, 136

governments: belief in benefits from torture, xiii; distrust of power inherent in, 111; good of the many argument of, 15, 19, 37, 62, 64; instability of torturing regimes, 37, 40n25; responsibilities of, 175–76; role in abolishing torture, 191–92; speaking subjects decided by, 58n41; state of exception declared (e.g., emergency), 56n2; torture authorized by, 24–25, 27–29, 31, 40n17, 42–43, 84–85, 91, 92, 118, 123, 126–27; UN power in relation to, 176. *See also* authoritarian regimes; liberal democracies; rape/torture-as-policy; "ticking time bomb"; totalitarianism; *and specific countries*

Great Britain, torture used by, 149

Grob, Leonard: epilogue by, 189–92; essay by, 7–15; prologue by, xi–xix; questions for, 15; referenced, 4–5; response by, 16–19

Gross, Jan, 25, 26

Grüber, Heinrich, 116, 123

Grut, Jenny, 140

Guantánamo Bay detainees, 16, 54, 59n50, 110, 121, 126

Haas, Peter J.: essay by, 83–92; questions for, 92–93; referenced, 40n22, 63–64, 102–3; response by, 93–96

Haj, Sami Al, 59n50

Halabiya, Ahmad Abu, 158

halachic debates: context of, 83–85; current practice compared with earlier, 63–64; Israeli sources on human dignity and, 88–89; Jewish classical sources on punishments and, 85–88; role of diaspora voices in, 90–91, 94; self-sufficiency of Torah vs. including other sources in, 94–95; on use of torture, 39n6, 64, 89–92, 93–96. *See also* Jewish legal tradition

Hamas, 158, 159, 160, 162

Harrison, Robert Pogue, 180

"harsh interrogation methods." *See* torture

Hassan, Judith, 144–45

Hatley, James, 10, 11, 12

hatred: inscribed on bodies of victims, 138; for Jewish people, 133, 155–56, 162–63; for race, group, or humanity, 16, 24, 26, 32–33, 100, 156. *See also* anti-semitism

Hayman, Sheila, 140

"heartroom," 141

Helfgott, Ben, 142

Hezbollah, 89, 90, 159, 160

Himmler, Heinrich, 31, 117, 118

Hitler, Adolf: accession to chancellorship, 68; Arab leaders linked to, 157; as God's henchman, 116, 123; legacy of, 132, 134n1; Maududi on, 159; as murderer, 166; state of emergency declared by, 56n2. *See also* Nazism

Hitler's Willing Executioners (Goldhagen), 25, 26

Hodapp (SS-doctor), 75

Hoffman, David H., xvii–xviiin6

holiness of human being, 153–57, 167

Holocaust: Catholic understanding of torture in light of, 65, 102–5; human reciprocity between survivors, 142–43; as human suffering writ large, 8–10; lessons of, 90–93, 96; life of responsibility to others in aftermath of, 13–15, 18, 48–49; post-Holocaust rape/torture in relation to, 180–83; power imbalances underlying, 121, 126; rape in, 188n28; as regression to premodern vs. form of modernity, 26, 39n12; theodicy in relation to, 65, 115–28; "torture" used in relation to, xixn12; type of violence in, xiv, 25–26, 31–34. *See also* bystanders; concentration and extermination camps; the howl; Nazism; pain; responsible witnessing; suffering; survivors of Holocaust; torture

Holocaust studies, xv–xvi, 103, 132, 182

Holocaust Survivors' Centre (London), 144

Homeland Security Act (US, 2002), 45

Homo Sacer (Agamben), 43–44

Horthy, Miklós, 69

the howl: bearing witness to, 53–56; of both French and Algerian victims, 121; human rights and, 47–48; implications of excluding from definition of human, 50–52; as prelinguistic response, 5, 45, 56; questions about, 52–53; scream remaining within soul, 155; special prisoners' hearing and seeing of, 62, 63, 70–73; torturers' demand for, 161–62; of useless suffering, 48–49

HRFT (Human Rights Foundation of Turkey), xvi–xviin2, 186–87n10

Hugo, Victor, 78

humanity and human dignity: capacity for language (*logos*) as defining characteristic of, 43–44, 50–51, 54–55; holiness of human being and, 153–57, 167; integrity of human and, 99–100; inviolability of human rights based in, 28; Israeli sources encoding, 63, 88–89, 92–93; Jewish legal tradition's prohibitions against causing pain to, 85–88; problematic distinctions of animals and, 43–44, 47–48, 50–56; proportionalists' radical respect for, 101; responsibility for each other, 13–15, 18, 48–49, 50, 117–18, 123–25, 126–27, 192; torture as violation of, 25, 39n6, 124. *See also* actions against torture and loss of trust; communities; dehumanization; holiness of human being

human rights: basis for Israeli legal sources, 63, 89; documented violations of, 185n1; Guantánamo detainees excluded from, 50, 54; human dignity basis for, 28; international agreements on, 94–95, 99; national sovereignty privileged over, 176; speech in discourse of, 47–48

Human Rights Foundation of Turkey
  (HRFT), xvi–xvii*n*2, 186–87n10
Human Rights Watch, xvii*n*3
Hunsinger, George, 190
Husseini, Haj Amin al-, 157
Hygiene Institute (Auschwitz), 119

ICISS (International Commission on
  Intervention and State Sovereignty),
  177–78
ICTR (International Criminal Tribunal
  for Rwanda), 172–73, 174
ICTY (International Criminal Tribunal
  for the former Yugoslavia), 172
ideological sincerity: as necessity for
  torturer, 28; in seeking information
  and "truth," 28–31, 36–38; specific acts
  of political power operating in, 31–34;
  torture as mode of, 25–26. *See also*
  "truth"
ideology: definition of, 28–29; ethics
  manipulated in, 102–3; torture as
  defense of, 5, 28–31; torture as means
  of communicating, 27–28
Ignatieff, Michael, 38n2
Al Ikhwan Al Muslimin (newspaper),
  157
"impossible possibility," 65, 106–7, 108,
  110
impunity, culture of, xiii, xv–xvi, 27
indifferent bystanders. *See* bystanders
interhuman domain: call to enter, 12–
  13; other's pain in, 48–49. *See also*
  humanity and human dignity
International Association of Genocide
  Scholars, 17
International Coalition for the Responsibility to Protect, 187n21
International Commission on Intervention and State Sovereignty (ICISS),
  177–78
International Council of Nurses, 136
International Criminal Tribunal for
  Rwanda (ICTR), 172–73, 174

International Criminal Tribunal for
  the former Yugoslavia (ICTY), 172
International Crisis Group, xvii*n*3, 177
international law: applicability to non-
  state actors, 186–87n10; "enhanced
  interrogation" as violating, xiii–xiv;
  R2P in relation to, 134, 177–78; rape
  defined as crime in, 172–74. *See also*
  specific conventions
International Rehabilitation and
  Research Centre for Torture Victims
  (RCT, Denmark), 136
International Rehabilitation Council
  for Torture Victims (IRCT), xvi–
  xvii*nn*2,3, 136, 186–87n10
International Rescue Committee, xvii*n*3
International Tracing Service (ITS), 73
Iran. *See* Islamic Republic of Iran
Iraq War (2003–): Abu Ghraib prison
  in, 16, 31, 50, 53, 58n42, 126; torture
  used in, xiii–xiv, xvii–xviii*n*6, xviii*n*8,
  16, 121, 123, 149. *See also* war on terror
IRTC (International Rehabilitation
  Council for Torture Victims),
  xvi–xvii*nn*2,3, 136, 186–87n10
ISIS (Islamic State of Iraq and Syria),
  24, 159, 171, 185n1
Islam: justification of torture based on
  belief in, 126; Muslims opposed to
  jihadist usurpation of, 155. *See also*
  Islamic jihadism
Islamic Jihad (group), 159
Islamic jihadism: appropriation of God
  in, 159–63; "enhanced interrogation"
  compared with torture in, 164–65;
  essence of torture in Nazism and,
  133, 154–57; Nazi connections to, 157–
  63, 164–67. *See also* post-Holocaust
  torture
Islamic Republic of Iran: Khomeini's
  models for, 158, 161; torture in, 159
Islamic State of Iraq and Syria (ISIS),
  24, 159, 171, 185n1
Israel: debates on torture in, 39n6, 64,

89–92, 93–96; Holocaust survivors in, 143, 144; human dignity in documents of, 63, 88–89; jihadists' call to destroy, 158, 162–63; political and legal structure of, 83–84; relationship between Jewish legal tradition and laws of, 83–85, 93–94. *See also* "enhanced interrogation"; Gaza; halachic debates; Jewish legal tradition; Jewish people; Judaism; West Bank

Israel Defense Forces (IDF): call to focus on mission, 91; as "morally superior" to enemy, 89; Purity of Arms (*Tohar HaNeshek*) doctrine, 63, 88, 89, 90, 92–93

Israeli Basic Law: Human Dignity and Liberty, 63, 89

Israeli Center of Holocaust Survivors and Their Children (Amcha), 144

Israeli Declaration of Independence, 89

Israeli High Court of Justice, 84, 85, 89

Israeli Penal Code, 88–89

Israeli Supreme Court, 84

ITS (International Tracing Service), 73

Izzadeen, Abu, 160

Jackson, Andrew, 95–96

Jawahir (Salamat girl), 184

Jedwabne (Poland), 26

Jewish legal tradition: Israeli law in relation to, 83–85, 93–94; prohibition against causing pain to animals, 88, 93, 95, 96; self-sufficiency of Torah vs. including other sources in, 94–95; torture addressed in sources of, 85–88. *See also* halachic debates

Jewish people: Aryanization of, 155–56; commitment to protecting innocents, 94; emergence of political control by, 83–84; hatred for, 133, 155–56, 158, 162–63; multiple forms of extreme violence used against, 25–26; as object of Nazi mastery, 8–10; role of diaspora voices in halachic debates, 90–91, 94; three

qualities of, 149; torturous conditions imposed on, 78, 166–67; "we" rebuilt by, 142–43; women and girls raped in WWII and Holocaust, 182–83, 188n28. *See also* Holocaust; Israel; Judaism

The Jewish Week (periodical), 91

jihadism. *See* Islamic jihadism

John Paul II (pope), 100

Joos, Josef, 72, 73

Judaism: call of suffering other in, 13; on God, responsibility, and suffering, 123; jihadists' aim to destroy, 158–63; respect for other in, 9–10; responsibility for Other in, 124; Shema ritual in, 10–11; topic of torture in and discussions of, 85–88. *See also* halachic debates; Israel; Jewish legal tradition; Jewish people

justice: Levinas's ethics and, 19, 112; multiple others in questions of, 14–15; retributive type of, 127. *See also* humanity and human dignity; responsible witnessing

justification of torture: absolute vs. relative in debates on, 61–62, 64–65; ambiguities and dilemmas in, 73–77; criteria for, 64–65, 101, 107; efficiency as (utilitarian justification), 29, 30, 32, 36–38, 42–43; good of the many argument in, 15, 19, 37, 62, 64; governmental authorization as, 24–25, 27–29, 31, 40n17, 42–43, 84–85, 91, 92, 118, 123, 126–27; intellectual rigor and open discussion about, 100–101, 109–12; national security as, 4, 121, 123; neuroscientific evidence against "torture works," xviin5, 6n2; pain as lesser evil than death (utilitarian argument), 42–43; political and race-based types of, 118, 120, 126; by regimes that use torture, 135; suspicion, resistance, and rejection of, xvi; victims' invention of information as denial of, xiv, xixn14. *See also* halachic debates; Nazism;

justification of torture (*continued*)
proportionalist (consequentialist)
view; theodicy; "ticking time bomb"
just war theory (Catholicism), 110

Katznelson, Yitzhak, 166
Kenya, British use of torture in, 149
Khalkhali, Sadeq, 158
Khomeini, Ruhullah, 158, 161
Kohlhofer (witness), 73
Kolmar, Gertrud, 56
Kosiński, Jerzy, 25–26, 39n9
Kreuz und Hakenkreuz (Cross and
swastika, Neuhäusler), 72
Kristof, Nicholas D., 174–75, 178, 184
Krondorfer, Björn: essay by, 23–34; ques-
tions for, 34; referenced, 4–5; response
by, 35–38
Kurnaz, Murat, 54

Landau, Moshe, 84
Landau Commission (Israel), 84
Langbein, Hermann, 75
language: as "agent of physical pain,"
139–40; human beings defined as
having, 43–44, 50–52, 54–55; in
human rights discourse of, 47–48;
legal, objectified, and sincere type
of, 29–30; new terms for torture and
rape in, 174–76; pain as destroying,
5, 43, 45–47, 161–62; of torture, 25.
See also euphemistic language about
torture; speech under torture
Lansen, Johan, 136–37
Laub, Dori, 137, 140, 142, 143–44
law: antisemitism in Nazi Germany's,
165–66; Sharia, 161, 162–63, 165. *See
also* Geneva Convention; international law; liberal democracies
Lebanon War (2006), 63, 89, 90
Leben auf Widerruf (Life is revoked,
Joos), 72, 73
legitimation. *See* justification of torture
Levi, Primo: on absence of language, 51;

on justifications for torture, 115; *Muselmann* described by, 166; on purposes
of camps, 120; on teaching, learning,
and remembering, 10–11; on violence
of torture, 46
Levinas, Emmanuel: active awareness
of other's suffering, 12–13; call for
responsibility for other, 13–15, 48–49,
50, 117–18, 124–25, 126–27, 192; on
humanity and language, 53, 54, 55;
on meaning of Auschwitz, 13; on
meaning of torture, 104–5, 153–54;
"metaethics" of, 21n32; on murder,
9, 154; Other as viewed by, 112, 113n14;
on suffering, 11–13; on theodicy, 116,
117–18, 127; on the Third, 15, 18–19
Lewis, Bernard, 157
liberal democracies: bystanders and protest in, 104; decision to use torture
made publicly in, 101; ideological sincerity in, 34; Islamic jihadists' and
Nazis' contempt for, 159; mode of sincerity in, 29; permissibility of torture
in, 33; torture as corrosion of, 127; torture prohibited in, 165
Libya, torture in, 159
Linden, Sonja, 140
List, Wilhelm, 76
listening: as basis for R2P, 183–84; to
survivors' voices, 4, 49, 143–44, 147–
49, 179; to those "done to death," 171,
178–80, 186n4. *See also* actions against
torture and loss of trust; responsible
witnessing
logotherapy, 140
lost trust. *See* actions against torture
and loss of trust; trust in the world
Luxembourg, liquidation of businesses
and organizations in, 77–78

Maimonides, 86–87
Malaysia, British use of torture in, 149
Marcel, Gabriel, 124
Marcuse, Harold, 69, 80n14

Maududi, Abdul Al'a, 159

Mayerfield, Jamie, 62

Medical Foundation for the Care of
Victims of Torture (later called Freedom from Torture), 136, 137, 138, 140–
41, 145

Méndez, Juan E., 52, 191

Mendl of Vorki, 149

Metz, Johann Baptist, 116

Mishneh Torah (Code of Jewish Law),
86–87

Misseriya (tribe), 188n32

Monument of Atonement in the Concentration Camp at Dachau, 80n14

morality: absolute vs. relative in, 61–62,
64–65; dilemmas in, 11, 73–76, 104,
106, 107–12; in fighting a war (*jus in
bello*), 88, 91, 93–94; new modes of
evaluating, 102–3; permissability of
torture based in, 24; of perpetrators,
29, 40n22; reality as reasonable only
if based in, xi, 5, 192; torture as labor
of necessity in, 28; torture as under-
mining, 99–100. *See also* ethics; ideological sincerity

Morality after Auschwitz (Haas), 102–3

Moratorium Commissioner for Organizational Matters (Luxembourg),
77–78

Muir, Edwin, 147–48

Müller, Heinrich, xiv

Müller, Josef, 70

Murawiec, Laurent, 157, 160

murder: Code of Jewish Law on, 86;
definition of, 166–67; methods of,
26–27, 75; prohibition of, 9, 99, 112,
154; responsibility in face of, 13–14;
torture in relation to, xixn12, 106–7,
109; as ultimate dehumanizing act,
9–10. *See also* concentration and
extermination camps; murder camp;
theodicy; "ticking time bomb"

murder camp, 154. *See also* murder

Muselmann, 43, 166

Muslim Brotherhood, 157, 158, 159

Muslims. *See also* Islam

National Emergencies Act (US, 1976),
56n2

National Office for the Investigation of
War Crimes in Luxembourg, 77–78

National Religious Campaign against
Torture (NRCAT), 16–17, 132, 190

Nationalsozialistische Deutsche Arbeiterpartei (NSDAP), 157

Natural Growth Project, 140–41

Navab-Safavi, Muhammed, 158

Nazism (National Socialism): absolute
sovereignty as goal, 12–13; anti-
Christian measures of, 63; Bosnian
Muslim unit of (13th Handschar Div.
of SS), 157; clergy imprisoned, 72,
81nn40,41; Concordat of Vatican with
Third Reich (1933), 68; contributor's
grandfather in, 77–79; ethical absolutism and moral relativism in, 110;
extra-judicial system of, 118; first step
toward torture, 165–66; imagination
as only limit of, 166–67; Islamic jihadism connections of, 157–63, 164–67;
liquidation of businesses and organizations for, 77–78; multiple forms
of extreme violence used by, 25–26;
new modes of moral evaluation in,
102–3; object of power is power in,
46–47; psychological warfare of, 141–
42; racial and antisemitic ideology of,
25–26; rape used by, 188n28; state of
emergency declared, 56n2; theodicy's
parallels with, 117; torture as essence
of, 8–10, 11, 31, 102, 118–21, 122, 123,
125, 126, 133, 141, 154–57, 163–64, 182,
190; *verschärfte Vernehmung* in, xiv.
See also bystanders; concentration
and extermination camps; Hitler,
Adolf; Holocaust; ideological sincerity; Islamic jihadism

Nehemiah (biblical), 85

Neighbors (Gross), 25, 26

Neuhäusler, Johann Baptist: background, 62–63, 67–68; personal history and perspective on, 77–79; questions about, 76–77; as special prisoner (*Sonderhäftling*) in Dachau, 63, 67, 69–70, 73; testimony for German war criminals, 68, 69, 73–76, 82n58; torture heard and seen by, 62, 63, 70–73

neuroscience, evidence against "torture works," xviin5, 6n2

"Never Again," 17, 64, 93, 178

Newsweek, 24

New York Times, xvii–xviiin6, 174–75, 184

Niederlahnstein, Nazi Party victory in, 78

Niemöller, Martin, 69, 75

Nietzsche, Friedrich, 159

Night (Wiesel), 115–16

1984 (Orwell), 45

NKVD (Soviet), 46–47

non-state actors, international law's application to, xvi–xviin2. *See also specific groups*

Norjitz, Vadim, 160

Nowak, Manfred, 173

NRCAT (National Religious Campaign against Torture), 16–17, 132, 190

NSDAP (Nationalsozialistische Deutsche Arbeiterpartei), 157

Obama, Barack, xviiin8

Ohlendorf, Otto, 76

O'Mara, Shane, xviin5, 6n2

Ordinary Men (Browning), 26

Orwell, George, 45, 46

Other/others: call to honor personhood of, 181, 183–84; call to responsibility for, 13–15, 18, 48–49, 50, 117–18, 123–25, 126–27, 192; holiness of, 153–55, 167; justification for suffering of, 122; Levinas's view of, 112, 113n14; sadism

as "radical negation" of, 39n15; torture as absolute appropriation of, 153–57, 159–63, 164–67; use of term, 113n14, 128n12. *See also* ethics; humanity and human dignity; suffering

Outcome Document (UN World Summit, 2005), 175–76, 177

pain: human and animal undistinguished in, 47–48; ideological sincerity in inflicting, 32–34; language destroyed in, 5, 43, 45–47, 161–62; as manifestation of negating human being, 161–63; prohibitions against undeserved and unnecessary, 88, 92, 93, 95–96; radical incommunicability of, 44–47; of survivors, 137–38; in theodicy, 114–15; Torah's prohibition against causing pain to animals, 88, 93, 95, 96; as transcending every kind of proportionality, 102; verbal and physical acts combined in, 35–36. *See also* suffering; therapeutic care for victims

The Painted Bird (Kosiński), 25–26, 39n9

Palestine: call to massacre Jews, 158; Israeli call to abandon Purity of Arms doctrine in fight against, 90

Palestinian Authority, Fatwa Council, 158

Palestinian Intifada (1987), 84

Palestinian Intifada (2000), 63, 89

Patterson, David: essay by, 153–63; questions for, 163–64; referenced, 132, 133; response by, 164–67

perpetrators of torture: always accountable for actions, 111–12; authorized behavior of, 24–25, 27–29, 31, 40n17, 42–43, 84–85, 91, 92, 118, 123, 126–27; belief in efficiency of torture, 32–33; calculated destruction of soul by, 155–57; call to publicly monitor, 191; at Dachau, 70–73; hatred inscribed on victims' bodies, 138, 162–63; liability

of, 85, 88–89; moral codes of, 28, 29–
30, 40n22, 119, 122; negative repercussions of torture for, 18, 105, 124; power
and sovereignty over prisoner, 45–47,
122, 135; reconciliation with, rejected,
17; as seeking information and "truth,"
27–31; suffering justified by, 114–15;
training for, 27–28, 39n14, 41n34, 68;
"truth" imposed by, 35–38; truth-
telling witnesses shut out by, 49; on
uselessness of threat of death, 48. *See
also* ideological sincerity; *and specific
countries and regimes*
Perry, John, 24, 39n14
Peters, Edward, 136
physicians and doctors, complicity of,
75, 118–19. *See also* therapists
Physicians for Human Rights USA
(PHR USA), xvi–xviin2, 186–87n10
Pinnock, Sarah K.: essay by, 114–24;
questions for, 124–25; referenced, 65;
response by, 125–28
Pinto da Silva, Murilo, 49
Piorkowski, Alex, 68
Pius XII (pope), 68
Pohl, Oswald, 76
political realm: ethics in relation to, 15,
19, 35–36; human capacity for, 43–44,
50–52; responsibility for one another
in, 50; torture as tool of, 24–25, 29,
31–34, 35, 37–38, 65. *See also* ideological sincerity
Pollefeyt, Didier: essay by, 99–107; questions for, 107–8; referenced, 64–65;
response by, 108–12
polls. *See* public opinion
Popitz, Heinrich, 35
post-Holocaust torture: characteristics
of, 154–55; "enhanced interrogation"
vs. Islamic jihadism torture in, 164–
65; Holocaust in relation to, 180–83;
jihadist appropriation of God in, 159–
63; questions about, 189–92; recognition and knowledge of, 133, 148–49.

See also Islamic jihadism; rape/torture-
as-policy; war on terror
posttraumatic stress disorder (PTSD),
137, 144
Praust (SS personnel), xiv
Precarious Life (Butler), 50, 59n48
Prevention through Documentation
Project, Redress Trust part of, xvi–
xviin2, 186–87n10
Primo Levi Centre (France), 139
*Prisoner without a Name, Cell without
a Number* (Timerman), 45, 51
proportionalist (consequentialist) view:
approach to, 61–62, 64–65; avoiding
slippery slope in, 100–101; considered
in light of Holocaust, 102–5; intellectual rigor and open discussion in, 109–
12; moral complexities involved in,
108–9; reconsideration of, 105–7. *See
also* deontological (absolutist) view
Protestantism, belief in God's will, 116–
17
psychologists and psychiatrists: complicity in torture, xiii, xvii–xviiin6;
parallels between torture and Holocaust survivors recognized by, 141–45.
See also therapeutic care for victims;
therapists
public dialogue: on abolishing torture,
191–92; on decision to use torture,
101, 111–12; torture not exempt from
ethical and Socratic approach, 62–63.
See also euphemistic language about
torture
public opinion: anti-torture (1970s), 136;
French use of torture in Algeria, 121;
moral permissability of torture, 24;
US use of "enhanced interrogation,"
xiii–xiv
public space: performances of spectacular violence in, 27–28, 39n13; rituals of
violence and torture in, 25–26
Purity of Arms (*Tohar HaNeshek*) doctrine (Israel), 63, 88, 89, 90, 92–93

Qaeda, al-, 58n41, 126, 159
The Question (Alleg), 121
Quran, 159, 161. *See also* Islam
Qutb, Sayyid, 157, 158, 159, 161, 162–63

Rabbinical Council of America, 90
race and ethnicity: justification of tor-
    ture based on, 89–90, 118, 120, 126;
    as metaphysical category, 133, 157–58,
    162–63; torture and rape in ethnic
    cleansing, 177–78. *See also* antisemi-
    tism; genocide
rape: definitions of, 172–73, 174; torture
    as, xii, 134, 154, 155, 173, 182, 188n27;
    use of term, 187n13
rape/torture-as-policy: "crying out" for
    action against, 178–79; defined in
    international criminal tribunals, 172–
    74; documentation of, 185nn1,2; "done
    to death" by, 171, 179–80, 186n4; Holo-
    caust in relation to post-Holocaust,
    180–83; ICISS report detailing, 177–78;
    intertwined nature of, 134; listening to
    victims of, 183–84; new words in, 174–
    76; use of term, 187n13; widespread use
    of, 23. *See also* genocide; "responsibil-
    ity to protect"; *and specific regimes*
Raphaely, Mary, 138, 140
RCT (International Rehabilitation and
    Research Centre for Torture Victims,
    Denmark), 136
Redress Trust, of Prevention through
    Documentation Project, xvi–xviin2,
    186–87n10
rehabilitation. *See* therapeutic care for
    victims
Rejali, Darius, 191
religious beliefs: ambiguities in actions
    and, 76–77; anti-torture organization
    based in, 16; "be angry and sin not,"
    148; God, responsibility, and suffer-
    ing, 122–24; justification of torture
    based on, 126; of perpetrators, 29;
    on punishments, 85, 161, 162–63, 165;

"Thou shalt not murder," 9, 112; tor-
    ture as violation of, 25, 39n6. *See also*
    Catholic Church; Christianity; Islam;
    Protestantism; theodicy
re-rape, 174, 178, 180
resentments, xv, 15, 17–18
resilience, 140–41, 144, 148–49
Resolution 2016 (UN, 2013), 183–84
"responsibility to protect" (R2P): broad-
    ened scope of, 181; coalition website
    on, 187n21; concept of, 177–78, 180;
    emerging norm of, 134, 183–84; expec-
    tation for governments, 175–76
responsible witnessing: approach to,
    4; in concrete acts of justice, 14–15,
    16; continuing to be troubled in, 11–
    12; "egoistic ambition" jettisoned in,
    12–14; Levi's call for, 10–11; reflections
    on possibility of, 7–8, 21n36; "seeing
    through" in, 180; silence followed by
    action in, 179; suffering of others as
    call for, 117–18, 124–25, 126–27; wit-
    nessing torture as intensifying, 49–
    52. *See also* speech under torture
Risen, James, xvii–xviiin6
rogue states, torture in, 33
Rosen, David, 63, 89–90
Rosenberg, Alfred, 157–58, 159, 162
Rosenthal, Andrew, xvii–xviiin6
Roth, John K.: epilogue by, 189–92; essay
    by, 171–80; prologue by, xi–xix; ques-
    tions for, 180–81; referenced, 116, 132,
    134; response by, 181–84
R2P. *See* "responsibility to protect"
Rubenstein, Richard, 116, 117
Ruff, Mark, 68
Rwanda: genocide in, 126; rape/torture
    in, 172–73, 174, 178, 182; violence in, 23

Sachsenhausen-Oranienburg, 67, 70
sadism: misconceptions about torture
    and, 24, 27, 28, 31; testimony on, 71,
    102, 119, 138; theodicy and, 117; use of
    term, 39n15

Salamat (tribe), 184, 188n32

Sanhedrin (Babylonian Talmudic tractate), 86

Santilli, Paul C., 186n4

Sartre, Jean-Paul, 115, 121

Saudi Arabia, torture in, 159

Scarry, Elaine: on artifacts for making,
re-creating, and repairing, 146–47;
on pain, 45, 46, 48, 139, 161–62; on
screams, 49, 53; on torture process
and regime's language, 29, 30; on victims' voices, 145

Schlapobersky, John, 147, 148, 149

Schmidt, Franz, 77–78

Schuschnigg, Kurt von, 69

screams. *See* the howl

secrecy: as key to torture, 5, 26, 27–28,
39n14, 49; public rejection of, 191–92

Seligman, Adam, 29

Sendler, Irena, 44

September 11, 2001, terrorist attacks
(9/11): morality of torture debated
after, 24; state of emergency declared
after, 56n2; torture increased after, 16,
42–43, 121; US destabilized by, 40n25.
See also "enhanced interrogation";
Guantánamo Bay detainees; war
on terror

sexual violence: steps to curb and eliminate, 183–84; UN report on, 181–82, 183.
See also rape; rape/torture-as-policy

Shalvata (London), 144

Shalvata Mental Health Center (Israel),
144, 145

Sharia law, 161, 162–63, 165

Shoah. *See* Holocaust

Shue, Henry, 61

Sierra Leone, rape/torture in, 181–82

sincerity, 29. *See also* ideological
sincerity

Slumdog Millionaire (film), 42

Snyder, Timothy, 46

social engineering, 120–21

social justice. *See* justice

social world: social contract voided by
act of torture, xi, xvi, 4, 8–9, 14–15;
torture as total inversion of, 135

Soelle, Dorothee, 116–17, 118

soul. *See* body, mind, and spirit; holiness
of human being

Soviet Union, torture in, 46–47

space. *See* public space; torture chambers

Spain, torture in, 49

spectacle, performances of violence as,
27–28, 39n13

speech under torture: in definition of
torture, 5, 43; perpetrators' power to
silence, 44–47; suffering voiced in,
139–40. *See also* the howl; language

Stadlen, Naomi, 141

Stalin, Joseph, 46

Standard Operating Procedure (film),
58n42

Steiner, George, 186n4

Stephen S. Weinstein Holocaust Symposium, xv

Stöhr, Heinrich, 75

Sudan (Darfur), rape/torture in, 181–82,
184

Sudanese National Islamic Front, 159

suffering: active attentiveness to, 10–13;
approach to and questions about, 7–
8; concrete and specific responses to,
13–15; emphasis on, 43; as end in itself
in camps, 120; instrumentalized as
means to end, 114–15, 125, 127–28; justified in theodicy, 114–18, 121–24, 125,
127–28; possibility of torture because
of care for others', 112; prohibitions
against undeserved and unnecessary,
88, 92, 93, 95–96; in torture during the
Holocaust, 8–10. *See also* the howl;
pain; therapeutic care for victims;
uselessness of suffering

suicide: Améry's, 128, 134n1; persons
driven to commit, 68, 70, 142

suicide bombings, 89, 94

Sullivan, Andrew, xiv

Surin, Kenneth, 116

Survival in Auschwitz (Levi), 10–11

survivors of Holocaust: bonding and self-healing among, 141, 142–43, 147; listening to voices of, 4, 49, 143–44, 147–49, 179; organizations of, 133, 144, 148; pain of, 137–38; parallels between torture victims and, 141–45. *See also* therapeutic care for victims; victims of torture

Syrian Arab Republic: rape/torture in conflict in, 181–82; torture and human rights violations in, 159, 171, 185nn1,2

Szymborska, Wisława, 108

Tal, Wasfi al-, 160

Talmud, 39n6, 86–88, 158

Taussig, Michael, 135

Teller, Moshe, 145

terrorists: dehumanization of, 50, 54–55, 89–90, 126; deployment of term, 58n41; human dignity vs. state preservation in treatment of, 64; torture justified as deterrent to, 100, 127. *See also* "ticking time bomb"; war on terror; *and specific groups*

theodicy: approach to critique of, 65, 114–15; ethical objections to, 117–18, 124, 127; justification of suffering and torture in, 121–24, 125, 127–28; theological challenges to, 115–17

therapeutic care for victims: active support for, 18; approaches in, 139–41; artifacts for making, re-creating, and repairing in, 146–47; Catholic efforts and, 76; centers established for, 136–37; complexities and challenges in, 138–39, 141–45; multiple modalities in, 137–38; overview of, 132–33. *See also* victims of torture

therapists: attributes of, 138–39; creativity and challenges for, 132–33; goals of, 136–37; parallels between torture

and Holocaust survivors recognized by, 141–45; therapeutic presence of, 147–49. *See also* therapeutic care for victims

"third degree" interrogations. *See* torture

Thomas Aquinas (saint), 110

"ticking time bomb": Améry's case compared with, 103; dilemmas in, 104, 107–8; good of the many argument in, 15, 19, 37, 62, 64; justification for torture in, 64–65, 101, 107, 127; in proportionalist (consequentialist) view of torture, 100–101, 105–7, 109–11; public accountability in decisions on, 111–12; torture as, 190–91

tikkun olam ("repair or healing of the world"), xv, 14–15, 18. *See also* actions against torture and loss of trust; responsible witnessing

Timerman, Jacobo, 31, 32, 45, 51

Torah, 86–88, 93, 94

torture: as always evil, xvi, 14, 23, 53, 61, 101, 102–3; as always unacceptable, 4, 5, 25, 99, 128; approach to questions about, xi–xvi; artifacts for countering destruction of, 146–47; call to work for world free from, 14–15, 16, 33–34, 38, 131–34; characteristics delineated, 27–28, 35, 137–38; "crying out under," 52, 171; definitions of, xii, xiii, 3–5, 125–26, 153, 165–67, 171–72; dynamics of, 28–31; eradication unlikely, 149; as essence of Nazism, 8–10, 11, 31, 102, 118–21, 122, 123, 125, 126, 133, 141, 154–57, 163–64, 182, 190; explication impossible, 7–8; genocide linked to, 33; as gratuitous and inefficient, 11, 12, 24–25, 28, 32–33, 40n20, 46, 115; as impossible possibility, 65, 106–7, 108, 110; individual nature of, 23–24, 34; misconceptions about, 24–28, 36–38, 40n20; as moral possibility, 100–101,

106–7; normalization of, 42; as political act of coercive violence, 24–25, 29, 31–34, 65; questions about, 189–92; social normativity and institutionalization of, xviii*n*8, 33, 42–43, 118–21, 122, 123, 125; as totalitarian appropriation of human being, 153–57, 159–63, 164–67. *See also* actions against torture and loss of trust; body, mind, and spirit; bystanders; Holocaust; the howl; ideological sincerity; Islamic jihadism; justification of torture; language; Nazism; perpetrators of torture; rape/torture-as-policy; responsible witnessing; victims of torture; war on terror

"Torture" (Améry), xv–xvi, 4, 31–32, 183, 184. See also *At the Mind's Limits*

torture chambers: confined or open, 154; key role of, 32–33; secrecy of, 5, 26, 27–28, 39n14, 49; special prisoners' proximity to, 70–72

Torture in the Eighties (AI), 136

torturers. *See* perpetrators of torture

"Tortures" (Szymborska), 108

totalitarianism: bystanders and protest in, 103–4; mode of sincerity in, 29, 33–34; object of power is power in, 46–47; torture as tool of, 159–63, 164. *See also* authoritarian regimes; Islamic jihadism; Nazism

training manuals for torturers, 27–28, 41n34, 68

trust in the world: approaches and obstacles to rebuilding, 138–39; "cautious" type of, manifested, 18; goal of restoring, xi, 131–32; loss of, xi, xvi, 4, 8–9, 14–15, 134, 138, 173, 189–90. *See also* actions against torture and loss of trust

"truth": questions about concept, 34; torture as means of establishing, 5, 24–25, 27–31, 36–38; unequal power and imposition of, 35–37; use of quotation marks, 40n26; victims as ready to tell/confess, 44–45. *See also* ideological sincerity

"12-Point Program for the Prevention of Torture" (AI), 191–92

United Nations: establishment of, 175–76; rape as torture recognized by, 173; "Sexual Violence in Conflict" report, 181–82, 183

United Nations Commission on Human Rights, 173

United Nations Convention against Torture and Other Cruel, Inhuman or Degrading Treatment or Punishment: adoption of, xii, 171–72; on authorized perpetrators, 40n17; governmental laws to support, 192; human being defined in, 47; human dignity as basis of, 39n6; Krondorfer's definition compared with, 4–5; supplement to, xvi–xvii*n*2; torture defined in, xii, xiii, 125–26, 171–72; US violation of, 42–43

United Nations Declaration on Human Rights, 94–95

United Nations Human Rights Council, 185n1

United Nations Security Council, 176, 183–84

United Nations Voluntary Fund for Victims of Torture (UNVFVT), xvi–xvii*n*2, xvii*n*3, 136, 186–87n10

United Nations World Summit (2005), Outcome Document of, 175–76, 177

United States: asylum applicants in, 136; attitudes on torture among Jews in, 90–91, 94; beneficiaries of torture in, 121; destabilized (2001), 40n25; exceptionalism argument in, 191; state of emergency declared, 56n2; torture used by, xiii–xiv, xvii–xviii*n*6, xviii*n*8, 16, 121, 123, 149; treatment of Abu Ghraib prisoners by, 16, 31, 50, 53,

United States (*continued*)
58n42, 126; use of torture normalized
in, 42–43. *See also* detention camps;
"enhanced interrogation"; September
11, 2001, terrorist attacks (9/11); war
on terror
United States Army, "Dachau" trials, 68,
69, 74
United States Holocaust Memorial
Museum, 185n1
United States Immigration and Naturalization Service, 45
United States Senate Select Intelligence
Committee, xiii–xiv, xviii*n*7
United to End Genocide, 17
Universal Declaration of Human Rights
(1948), 99
UNVFVT (United Nations Voluntary
Fund for Victims of Torture), xvi–
xvii*n*2, xviii*n*3, 136, 186–87n10
uselessness of suffering: in Holocaust,
115, 122; Levinas on, 11, 48–49, 117–18;
theodicy and, 65, 116, 121–24
"Useless Suffering" (Levinas), 11, 48–49

Veritatis Splendor (encyclical), 100
verschärfte Vernehmung (enhanced
interrogation), xiv. *See also* "enhanced
interrogation"
victims of torture: assuming responsibility for, 14–15, 18, 48–49; commitment to assist, xvi, 192; dehumanized
existence of, 7, 9–10, 89–90, 126; differences among, 133; as individuals,
179; listening to voices of, 4, 49, 143–
44, 147–49, 179; parallels between
Holocaust survivors and, 141–45; politicized but with zero political power,
43–44; in proportionalist moral position, 108–9; psychological, physical,
and long-term damage to, 137–38; self-
silencing of, 139–40, 143; shattered sense
of self, 45–47; theodicy as denying
voices of, 114, 117–18, 128; as therapists,

139; torturers' view of guilt, 30–31;
"truth" imposed on, 35–38. *See also*
actions against torture and loss of
trust; the howl; pain; responsible
witnessing; speech under torture;
survivors of Holocaust; therapeutic
care for victims
violence: accounts of extreme, 25–26,
33–34; deliberate physical injury as
most direct, 35; multiple extreme
forms of, 23–28. *See also* murder;
rape/torture-as-policy; sexual violence; torture
Vittel Diary (Katznelson), 166
Volksgerichtshof tribunals, 118

Wagner (Dachau prisoner), 75
Wajs (SS personnel), xiv
Walzer, Michael, 62, 101
Wardi, Dina, 141
Warhaftig, Itamar, 89
War of 1812, 95–96
war on terror: Abu Ghraib prison in,
16, 31, 50, 53, 58n42, 126; dehumanization in, 50, 54–55, 89–90, 126; Guantánamo Bay detainees in, 16, 54, 59n50,
110, 121, 126; human dignity vs. state
preservation in, 64; torture used in,
xviii*n*8, 33, 42–43, 121, 123. *See also*
"enhanced interrogation"; *and specific
groups*
wars: debates on use of torture in, 63,
89–92; international communities'
commitment to prevent, 176; morality
in fighting (*jus in bello*), 88, 91, 93–94;
prohibitions against causing undeserved and unnecessary pain in, 88,
92, 93, 95–96; UN report on sexual
violence in, 181–82, 183. *See also* rape/
torture-as-policy; *and specific wars*
Warsaw ghetto, 154
Weiss, Martin, 68, 69, 74–75, 76
Weiss, Thomas, 177
Weiter, Eduard, 68

West Bank, Purity of Arms doctrine questioned in, 90
Wiesel, Elie, 115–16, 143, 145
Wie war das in Dachau? (What was it like, Neuhäusler), 68–69, 72, 73–75
the will: blame for Holocaust and, 116–17; meaning of torture in context of, 104–5
Wistrich, Robert, 158
witnessing, 48–52. *See also* responsible witnessing
Women under Siege, xviin3, 185n2
Woodcock, Jeremy, 138
World Congress of the Commission of Catholic Prison Pastoral Care (2007), 100
World Medical Association (WMA), xvi–xviin2, 136, 186–87n10

World Organisation against Torture, xviin3, 21n38, 132
World Psychiatric Association, 136
Write to Life project, 140

Yassin, Ahmed, 158
Young Egypt movement, 157
Young Israel Synagogue (Atlanta, GA), 91
Yugoslavia, former: criminal tribunal on, 172; rape/torture in, 178, 181–82. *See also* Bosnia; Bosnia-Herzegovina

Zámečnik, Stanislav, 75, 82n54
Zero Dark Thirty (film), 53
Zevnik, Andreja, 58n41
Zimmermann, Karl, 75, 76, 82n58
Žižek, Slavoj, 62